THE DIARY OF A DEAD MAN

The Diary

of a

Dead Man

Letters and diary of Private Ira S. Pettit,
Wilson, Niagara County, New York,
who served
Company B, 2nd Battalion, and
Company F, 1st Battalion,
11th Regiment,
2nd Brigade, 2nd Division, 5th Army Corps,
United States Army,
during
The War Between the States

Compiled by JEAN P. RAY

Eastern Acorn Press 1981

this time for LAR

FOREWORD

Two decades ago I chanced to read the letters and diary of Private Ira S. Pettit. Although the continuity was broken by some missing parts, they were the most nearly complete narrative of an ordinary soldier of the Civil War which I had ever happened upon.

Years later I re-read those letters and diary and concluded that they, when put into a chronological sequence, would tell a story worthy of record.

In 1969 after compiling the diary and letters in rough draft form and putting together about forty-three copies for dissemination and discussion among acquaintances and history buffs, I applied for copyright while trying to determine what, if anything else, would be done with this material.

Having searched out partial records of a few of the soldiers mentioned by Private Pettit, the decision was made in 1972 to publish this compilation in hardbound edition for general distribution. At the time of publication I was torn between more definitive research and the urging by family members to publish the diary and letters with minimal additional (although salient) information.

The book became available in hardbound copy in a limited quantity by the end of December, 1972, but academically I was very unhappy with what had or had not been determined in relation to those people whom I had discussed. Too many questions went unanswered, and much wonder nagged my intellect as to whether the conclusions I had drawn from limited and under-developed information were sound.

Particularly, I was bothered by the information concerning Private Frederick M. Phelps, and facts subsequently uncovered justified my anxiety about this man's military career. Out of fairness to the Federal government, as well as Private Phelps, it became imperative that I provide a complete and accurate record of Private Phelps' military history based upon additional documents which had come to my knowledge. This additional information made it evident that the Federal government had reached a proper decision in denying this man a pension, even though it is doubtful that the pension bureau ever became aware of all his nefarious activities.

Besides the need to fully understand (for my own peace of mind) the complete account of Private Phelps, there was an unappeased desire to look more closely at some of the other soldiers whose lives I had touched upon. Especially there was a restive longing to learn more about Private John McMann, whose history, almost entirely, still eludes me.

Recently while reading the trial of Henry Wirz I noted the testimony of Private John A. Cain, which is included here in its totality. Re-researching Private Cain's life also provided much that had been missed at first glance.

As I have become more aware of the comprehensive records available at the National Archives I have sought to answer many of the questions which had arisen in my mind when first I read Private Pettit's notes and letters, and which continued to arise as I mused upon the plight of man in his eternal and inescapable struggle with man.

These remnants of Private Pettit's life are here set forth just as they were written by that young man, who found himself tramping the expanses of Virginia, Maryland, and Pennsylvania, chasing the illusive ideals embraced by a nation engaged in war. The grammar is his, the spelling is his, but more than that, the story he had to tell is a legacy of our culture.

But then, who was Private Pettit? Each reader will answer that in his or her own way.

J.P.R.

CONTENTS

APPENDICES

EIGHTEEN HUNDRED SIXTY-TWO

DIARY

and

MEMORANDUM BOOK

for

1862

Published Annually

FOR THE TRADE

1862

During the last twenty-nine months of his life, Ira S. Pettit, a young farmer from Western New York State, became a seasoned veteran of three major battles of the Civil War. Yet nothing he saw diminished his dedication to his country. He became a captive of the Rebels and a casualty of the Andersonville Stockade, Camp Sumter, near Americus, in the State of Georgia.

At the beginning of the year 1862, Ira Pettit lived with his family on Slash Road, now called Maple, just east of Wilson, New York, in the home which had been built about 1835 for his father, Clinton Pettit.

His family consisted of his father, stepmother, a sister (Lucina), and three cousins, Clinton, Lucina (also), and Georgie Pangborn. Another sister Mary Jane, had married G. H. Whitman.

He lived as neighbor and peer of Tip Wright, William Holmes, and Harvey Pease. No doubt he was acquainted with many others from Wilson and the surrounding communities who shared the Civil War with him.

The first five months of 1862 were, for the most part, filled with the events consistent with farm life. He cut wood, butchered, helped clear the roads during snowstorms, shelled corn, drew stone, plowed and prepared the fields with oxen, planted spring wheat and corn, and looked forward to fishing in Lake Ontario. His winter evenings were spent writing to Holmes, Pease, Wright and other friends who were already a military part of that war. He also devoted a great deal of his leisure time to reading the Bible and in the spring united with the Baptist Church.

On May 12, 1862, Ira became twenty-one. Although his father could probably have afforded the three hundred dollars commutation fee or the cost of a substitute, Ira decided to enlist. On May 29, 1862, he was enrolled by

Captain Thomas Oliver Barri, at Lockport, New York, for a period of three years in the Eleventh Regiment of the Regular United States Army.

Private Pettit came home but once after his enlistment, and he left the Wilson-Lockport area forever on June 20, 1862.

And this is the way it was . . . .

Ira S. Pettit
Slash Road, Wilson N.Y.

IF IT SHOULD BE MY LOT TO DIE, OR ANY ACCIDENT HAPPEN ME: IT IS MY
REQUEST THAT WHO EVER MAY OBSERVE THIS, WILL INFORM MY FATHER
OF THE SAME; AND ALSO SEND HIM THIS DIARY BY MAIL.

Ira S. Pettit

My father's name and postoffice adress is as follows:

Clinton Pettit,
Wilson, Niagara Co. N.Y.

JANUARY, 1862

Wednesday 1: Happy New Year! The boys and I drew wood with the oxen. Tremenduous windy, and thaws.

Thursday 2: Grown cold and frozen hard. Drew wood (sled lengths): having a grand time during dad's absence.

Friday 3: I drew a load of wood with the oxen, made a fine pair of bars to go in the woods, and trimed, and cut up a fallen maple &c.

Saturday 4: I went to Lockport after them: had bad luck with the waggon. They arrived all right. Ed came up at night after uncle Lawton & aunt.

Sunday 5: They started for home about noon. Aunt Marguerate cut my hair which was long enough to braid.

Monday 6: Snows. Father and I fixed for buchering tomorrow.

Tuesday 7: We killed 5 hogs, and uncle Stephen killed four. Favorable day for it.

Wednesday 8: Both went to Lockport with their pork, which sold for $3,50 per hundred even in this age of brass. Warm.

Thursday 9: Making preparations to kill again tomorrow. Warm.

Friday 10: Uncle Stephen and Em. drove over their's, and we done it all up under one. We killed nine. I stuck four for the first. Growing cold.

Saturday 11: Cold. Cut up and salted the pork. Uncle Lawton called here awhile; he had nine hogs weighing over 4,200! we bought a pig for 2½ live weight.

Sunday 12: I wrote a letter to cousin Dudley. Snowed last night; but it rains now. Toward night begins to freeze.

21

Monday 13: Made a finish of buchering; Corning hams &c. Severely cold.

Tuesday 14: I drew wood. Father helped mother straighten up. Very pleasant/last night it snowed. Received a letter from uncle Peter.

Wednesday 15: Stormed before noon, after noon we both hauled wood with both teams. Answered uncle Peter's letter. Cut sausage meet last night.

Thursday 16: Drew wood with both teams: Very windy, and good sleighing.

Friday 17: Drew wood before noon. Snowed a considerable. This evening I atended an evening exercise at the seminary. Mr. Walton Cornall my cousin, also arrived from Illinois.

Saturday 18: A considerable snow feel this fore noon. We drew sled lengths after noon. Good sleighing.

Sunday 19: Snowed more to day. I went to uncle Stephen's and spent the day. Cousin William, uncle Peters son; died friday, and was buried to day.

Monday 20: Snowed more: quite deep now. I took Lucina to school, visited with cousin Walton and went after the school children &c. Father is tapping our boots.

Tuesday 21: Father took a load of wood to uncle William; and we drew some from the woods.

Wednesday 22: Still, warm, and favorable to thrash. We helped Mr. Chapin thrash his clover seed before noon, and he helped us after noon, and finished. Foldier's & Griffin's machine.

Thursday 23: Received news of cousin Williams death! We had six acres of ground nearly, which turned 12 bush. of seed. We set the horsepower and machine for sawing wood. Mild.

Friday 24: Father Mother and little Lucina went to Lockport. No school to day nor tomorrow in this district. The boys and I done a good job cutting wood.

Saturday 25: Drew cord-wood from the woods and took the day somewhat easy.

Sunday 26: The wind blew violently last night and all day very cold; but the sun shone notwithstanding. Read the Testament.

Monday 27: The snow is drifted in large banks obstructing the roads somwhat. We commenced to saw with the machine.

Tuesday 28: Sawed with the machine. Windy & cold; and an icy rain towards night.

Wednesday 29: Quite crusty this morning; very mild all day. Sawed wood with the machine, Father and I alone.

Thursday 30: We sawed wood again, taking it moderately. Very agreeable weather.

Friday 31: Sunshiny and pleasant. Helped father saw before noon then went to sevral district school's programme at the M.E. Church. In the evening the Teachers association at the seminary.

FEBRUARY, 1862

Saturday 1: Cousin Walton and I started this morning for Somersett with horse and cutter. Agreeable.

Sunday 2: Joel started with us for uncle Clark's from James Whitlock's at one P.M. on unawares; and arrived at uncle Clark's (Medina) at dusk.

Monday 3: Somewhat stormy. Henry and Earl took us to Medina, where we enjoyed ourselves much and spent most of the day.

Tuesday 4: Got home this evening all right from uncle Clark's; with the exception of Joel leaving his halter, and I had an umbarella stole at Medina.

Wednesday 5: Went to the Auction at the residence of the late Simon Shelden. A favorable day and as large a turnout as townmeeting days.

Thursday 6: Sawed as much wood as the weather would alow; but it rained most of the time.

Friday 7: Sawed wood: got a pile of 100 cords: good day. Father and mother, Mr. Chapin & wife went to Curtis Pettit's this evening.

Saturday 8: Kept the saw runing.

Sunday 9: All went to church but me. I devote most of my leasure time to reading the Testament.

Monday 10: Kept the machine runing. Moderate weather.

Tuesday 11: Sawed wood. I went to uncle William's this evening and stayed all night with cousin Walton, who is going to start for the east tomorrow.

Wednesday 12: Finished sawing at noon. Got nearly 200 cords of stovewood. Father and mother are paying an evening visit to Deacon Robinson's.

Thursday 13: Father and mother went to Lockport. Snowed; which added much to the sleighing.

Friday 14: We cut sled lengths into stovewood &c: Mild winter weather. I attended an evening exercise at the Seminary; a rich one.

Saturday 15: We sorted potatoes: out of a hhd. full we got less than a bushall of good ones. Cut some wood. Full moon.

Sunday 16: I went to uncle Stephen's and stayed the day and evening. Very pleasant both day and night.

Monday 17: We are straightening around. Father and mother are making preparations to start tomorrow on a visit to Fairport, Rochester and Medina;

Tuesday 18: We got in Lockport this morn at an early hour. They took the ½ past 8 train for Roch. Thaws last night and all day. Sleighing about whiped.

Wednesday 19: Miss Louisa Pettit and I run this institution while the're gone. Georgie is very sick. I got Dr. Mc.Chesney to come and see him.

Thursday 20: A dreadful storm of snow and blow last night blockaded the road; so we were called out this morning to raise the blockade. Dr. called again: He is a very sick boy. Aunt Lucy is here to help take care of him. A great many call in. The sleighing is renewed!

Friday 21: George is no better. The Dr. called again. We have set up with him two nights. I devote what time I can to bucking wood but choreing and waiting on the women absorbs nearly all my time.

Saturday 22: I done a good job sawing wood to day, but had to hich up the team again nevertheless, and drive six miles. The Dr. came again. Georgie's symtoms are better.

Sunday 23: Louisa and I set up all night last night alone. I took her and the two Lucinas to church then drove home and planked off to bed. Rains and thaws. The Dr. called again. George is improving fast.

Monday 24: Emory and Lucina set up last night. Blows and snows tremenduously but is warm, and thaws notwithstanding. The hardest day we have had this winter!!

Tuesday 25: Louisa and I set up last night. The Dr. stayed here all night. Amazing change! Still; and the sun shone all day!! The road is drifted well with snow; and again we were summoned to raise the blockade!

Wednesday 26: I started for Lockport this morn at seven o'clock. Father and mother arrived on the 2,10 o'clock train. It thaws as we come home.

Thursday 27: Louisa and I set up again last night and wrote John O'Mar a long letter both of us. Worked at the wood. I took Louisa home.

Friday 28: The wind howled all night; and today it snows and the wind blows with all its besom; but had a lot of visitors tonight nevertheless.

MARCH, 1862

Saturday 1: Had to shovel the road again, shelled some corn &c. I finished writing a letter to Clark and Tip* this evening.

Sunday 2: I read the testament.

Monday 3: I wrote a letter to Mary Jane. Rather a stormy day. This evening the rain fell in torrents; but before morn. it snowed and drifted badly!

Tuesday 4: Quite a wintry day. We oiled our harness.

Wednesday 5: A pleasant day. I split wood and chored around. Father and mother are off. I wrote a letter to Ed Rumry to night.

Thursday 6: Father and mother went with uncle Stephen to the Fort. I took a load of wood to the villiage; sawed wood and done chores. Pleasant.

Friday 7: Father went to mill. I bucked wood. Pleasant, and the snow is rapidly vanishing away.

Saturday 8: We worked at the wood. Afternoon father and mother went to Thomas Pettit's. Thaws.

Sunday 9: All went to Church but Georgie and I. The funeral of Mrs. Hackett is this after noon, who died on friday. Warm.

Monday 10: Rained this morning. I finished bucksawing wood 10 cords nearly. Rained all day at intervals. Sleighing is whiped! Such floods of water I never saw!!

Tuesday 11: Loomis and Ward had a knock down last night. I split wood. Father, mother and Mrs. Susan Pettit went to Mr. Pangburn's on a visit with the waggon. Roads are overflowed badly! Thaws.

---

*See page 342.

Wednesday 12: We split wood. Thaws. Snow drifts obstruct the passage of the water and it covers many acres; but is going down some.

Thursday 13: Split wood before noon, then we helped Chapin set the sawing machine. Cold, raw, chilling air.

Friday 14: Rainy and lowry. I attended the examination this afternoon at the seminary which is the last day of this term!! I did not go to the exhibition this evening for certain reasons. It rained.

Saturday 15: Still continues to rain! all day it poured unceasingly and freezes as it comes. The trees are loaded to breaking!!! Lightning rods are bent &c, &c; T'will show for years! I wrote a long letter to Harvey Pease.*

Sunday 16: The ice still clings, the winds blow, and we can constantly hear the falling of tree limbs &c. Old men never saw such a time!!! I read the testament. Have got to Hebrews.

Monday 17: Objects wear a fine appearance. A day of sunshine. Thaws fast; but not sufficient to relieve the limbs of ice. A time to be remembered!! Father is helping Chapin saw.

Tuesday 18: Father helped Chapin finish sawing by noon. I split wood. After noon we helped open the creek so the water would not overflow the road: pleasant.

Wednesday 19: We split wood at leisure. Very pleasant weather. Father went to John Pettits to see his new machine work. Storm Brewing.

Thursday 20: Pretty cold all day: northeast wind, and clouds gathering; feels like snow. Split wood. After noon visited with Dr. Morley and Ed who happened to come.

Friday 21: Snowed all night and all day. Quite deep; but thaws fast. We just stayed in the house to day; gave our attention to literary matters and visited with Ed.

Saturday 22: I attended the last day of school at our district schoolhouse. Spoke a piece and preached a sermon. Had a fine exercise. Disagreeable going.

*See page 326.

28

Sunday 23: I went to Uncle Stephen's; read the testament.

Monday 24: Ed started for Somersett this morning afoot: rather splashy. We cleaned wheat all day for seed.

Tuesday 25: Finished cleaning wheat then we went to splitting wood and I cut my foot which laid me up. Mrs. Wright and Mrs. Pettit are here.

Wednesday 26: I finished reading the Testament through today. By reason of my cut foot, I have leisure to peruse reading matter and &c: much to my satisfaction.

Thursday 27: Read newspapers &c. The soreness has got out, so that I can get on a rubber. I walked or limped up to Mr. Whitneys. Pleasant; but very muddy!

Friday 28: I split wood all day notwithstanding my cut foot. Not cold.

Saturday 29: I split wood: the boys went on a visit: the roads are rather tuff: warm.

Sunday 30: I read some religious documents.

Monday 31: We all worked splitting wood. High wind. Thaws.

APRIL, 1862

Tuesday 1: "April Fool." Father went with uncle Stephen to Lockport. I slabed blocks all day. The snow is rapidly disapearing.

Wednesday 2: We made quite a hole in the wood. Cloudy and windy. This evening we had the first thunder shower of the season.

Thursday 3: We went to Mr. Millards and got two shoats (pigs); and visited with Aunt Lucy and Emory who spent the day with us. I rec'd a letter of reply from John O'Mar of Washington; a soldier; and a paper from Cousin Dud. Thaws rapidly.

Friday 4: We've got the largest wood pile we have ever had. Finished splitting wood! After noon I took a horseback ride on sevral errands to the Harbor and elsewhere. Wind blows up cold from the N.E.

Saturday 5: It rained by spells until noon: the mud renders it bad to get around. We did nothing to amount to much.

Sunday 6: Is a pleasant but rather chilly day. I read a few religeous documents. Emory is here.

Monday 7: I corked and painted my boat, so as to be ready for action in good season. Cold east wind: storm brewing. Killed an other sheep to save its life.

Tuesday 8: Townmeeting day. I went to the seminary and stayed all day. It seemed as it used to of old. Windy and cold: it freezes.

Wednesday 9: Drew a few rails and picked up around &c. A cold east wind prevails.

Thursday 10: Pleasant. Father helped uncle Stephen move. I painted my boat. The boys and I shelled corn 50 bush. of ears. Went on a visit to Louisa's this evening.

Friday 11: Shelled corn before noon, then cut off the broken limbs through the orchard which the ice storm done. 7th Cav. arrived this evening.

Saturday 12: Last evening Mr. Wright rec'd A Dispatch from Harrison and this morning he started! I greeted the boys of the 7th Cav. this evening who arrived last night.

Sunday 13: Miss Jane Wright was married this afternoon!!! I read Remingtons defense of "Restricted Communion."

Monday 14: Shelled some corn &c. and scraped the road. Snow has nearly disapear'd, grass has started, and little birds begin to sing. Bids fair for good spring weather.

Tuesday 15: Father went to mill. I helped mother fix the flower beds. Pleasant.

Wednesday 16: Father sowed his clover seed this fore noon. We again worked in the flower yard awhile. After noon father and mother went to the nursery got some evergreens, mountains ash &c.

Thursday 17: Hauled stone all day off the orchard and garden.

Friday 18: Done a variety of things: hauled manure, made tree defences &c. Rained a goodly shower. Got a letter from uncle Elisha.

Saturday 19: Father and mother went to Thomas Pettit's. We chored around and shelled corn.

Sunday 20: Easter. Pleasant sabbath. I read some war news and some scriptures.

Monday 21: Rained most of the day. Drew stone and shelled corn.

Tuesday 22: Shelled corn before noon then went fishing but got none.

Wednesday 23: A cold western wind arose and howled all night and day: froze. Shelled corn.

Thursday 24: Froze last night. Chilly but pleasant. Clear'd the stalk stack rubbish.

Friday 25: Uncle William's farm sold today. Father and mother went to Lockport. The boys and I built a boathouse and shellt the last of the old corn.

Saturday 26: Commenced plowing some. I took a load of stove wood to shoemaker Miller.

Sunday 27: I went to uncle Stephens and stayed all day.

Monday 28: We rooled meadow and plowed all day with both teams. Rained a little.

Tuesday 29: Father went to Lockport to get a deed of his new farm. The boys and I carted stone off the corn stubble.

Wednesday 30: We commenced to plow the corn stubble for spring wheat: ground works well.

MAY, 1862

Thursday 1: Plowed with both teams.

Friday 2: Finished plowing that field.

Saturday 3: Got the spring wheat sowed and harrowed in. Six acres only, and sowed ten bush. and one half. I mailed a letter to Wm. Holmes* which I have had written a long time not knowing where to direct.

Sunday 4: Perused reading matter. Nice warm shower this evening.

Monday 5: Furrowed out the spring wheat, plowed and draged the young orchard. Pleasant.

Tuesday 6: Commenced to plow six acres of sod for corn.

Wednesday 7: Plowed with both teams on one plow: the ground is dry and works well.

Thursday 8: We plowed: fine weather. I sowed my blackseed for onions.

Friday 9: Mr. Pangburn has moved on uncle Williams old place and Merrit and the rest are hustleing away as fast as possible. Plowed.

Saturday 10: Plowed before noon, then helped Mr. Pangburn drag in his wheat. Trees are leaveing out fast and look quite green. Getting dry.

Sunday 11: Harrison Wright arrived home today. Had a talk with him.

Monday 12: 21. 21. 21. Drew stone and got in some peas. I finished a letter to Mr. William Saulsbury.** I'M ONE-AND-TWENTY. Where will I be an other year?

---

*See page 323.
**See page 338.

Tuesday 13: The off ox is unwell. Father harrowed; I planted pop corn, sweet corn and June potatoes: went to the villiage this evening.

Wednesday 14: Commenced to plow again: fine weather to work.

Thursday 15: The trees are rapidly leaving out, cattle can now live on grass, trees are blooming and things wear a fine appearance. We plowed.

Friday 16: Finished plowing. Sultry and dry.

Saturday 17: Rooled and draged cornground. Warm and dry. Joel and Ed are up.

Sunday 18: I united with the Baptist Church for which I have long been preparing. Hot and windy.

Monday 19: Fitted the cornground nearly for marking. Quite a sudden change: Cold.

Tuesday 20: Somwhat cool to-day too. Marked out one way.

Wednesday 21: Commenced to plant! Rained some last night. We had two spells at planting but welcome showers drove us out the field each time.

Thursday 22: Planted Corn. The warm brisk south wind after the refreshing shower, rustling the newborn leaves brings new music to the ear.

Friday 23: We finished planting before noon, then helped uncle Stephen. I'VE CONCLUDED TO ENLIST!

Saturday 24: I helped uncle Stephen most of the day. Father is fitting the potatoe ground.

Sunday 25: I devoted my time to various reading matter of a religious character. Very cool! Frosts prevail every night.

Monday 26: We planted potatoes.

Tuesday 27: Finished planting potatoes and helped uncle plant corn.

Wednesday 28: I helped him plant before noon then we carted stone.

Thursday 29: Father, mother, and I went to Lockport. I enlisted in the regular service for three years!!! Sergt. Hale recruiting officer

Friday 30: I remain in Lockport with Sergent Hale. We stop at the Pavillion. I went with the engine co's, and watered Duginets extensive gardens.

Saturday 31: I got nearly all my regimentals this evening.

JUNE, 1862

Sunday 1: I attended the Baptist Church in Lockport and communed with them.

Monday 2: Lockport life is a bully life.

Tuesday 3: On the wings of love I fly, From grocer-ee to grocer-i!

Wednesday 4: I attended court and listened to interesting Suits on rape&c.

Thursday 5: The trial of Lloyd* for murder is now in court.

Friday 6: I heard something of the trial to-day. I rode home with Mr. John Sheldon.

Saturday 7: Had a small shower which was quite welcome the first in a long, long, time. I carried a crib of corn in the cornhouse.

Sunday 8: I attended church: listened to the morning sermon.

Monday 9: I am looking around for recruits and making preparation to start for Lockport tomorrow.

Tuesday 10: Mother took me to Lockport with horse and carriage. Tremenduous dry: drouth prevails over a large portion of the state.

Wednesday 11: The dryest time I have ever saw for the time of year! Dust flies shamefully. I now devote my time to rewriting my compositions.

Thursday 12: Recruits come in at the rate of nearly one per

---

*Claudius B. Lloyd, whose colorful trial was held in June, 1862, was found guilty and sentenced to death for the murder of Thomas C. Thody, according to the Niagara County, New York, Historian's Files. His sentence was later commuted to four years imprisonment. Lloyd went west upon his release on June 6, 1866, and is reported to have died in Michigan about 1874.

day. A welcome shower now prevails which lays the dust finely, and that's about all. We need almost a deluge to satisfy the thirsty vegetation.

Friday 13: The breeze is refreshing in consequence of the small shower of yesterday. Dust does not fly so now. Got three letters.

Saturday 14: I saw the eclipse of the moon last wednesday night. Quite a turnout today and some runaways.

Sunday 15: Rained some last night, enough to lay the dust for a short time.

Monday 16: Much more agreeable now in consequence of the dust being laid. A friend soldier and myself went to the mineral springs yesterday.

Tuesday 17: The dust is again stirred up. O horrible! and the heavy wind drifts it in clouds.

Wednesday 18: A heavy shower prevailed for a short time last eve. The thirsty mountain side, Drank gladly of the gushing tide. Windy and refreshing.

Thursday 19: Rained last night and drizzling all day. But bids fair for a good day tomorrow. We're off tomorrow morning!

Lockport, N.Y. June 20th/62

Dear Father: The time of my departure is at hand! A dispach was received yesterday from the Captain that our presence was needed at at Canandagua. We shall accordingly leave on the 5,25 train this morning. We have had a few refreshing showers here of late which were quite welcome. I received those letters which were forwarded to me: they were from Messrs William Holmes and Harvey Pease of Cothrans Battery and Nigger Jim of Seneca Falls. If you get any more letters for me, tell Holmes to forward them to Canandagua until otherwise ordered. I regret that I could not see you all face to face and bid you farewell I intended to come home next saturday, but this is not to be. I might get a ride home any time. People are here from our neighborhood every day. I should have come home last saturday had I known of this. Aunt Susan says that Uncle Lawton and Aunt Marguerite were up. I have not seen any of them out here since I enlisted. Tell them all I bid them an affectionate farewell. Now father do not work too hard. We draw our pay in about ten days which I shall send to you: take it and hire a hand to help you. I wish you all manner of prosperity: give yourself no uneasiness about me.

But the shrill wihistle of the cars gives warning that I must be up and away.

Adieu.

From your dutiful boy.

Ira.

Friday 20: Started this morn. on the 5,25 train, and reached Canandaigua at a quarter to ten A.M. The first I ever rode on the cars, and I am now the fartherest from home that I ever remember of being!

Saturday 21: Canandaigua is a delightful place. The sergeant paraded us some to-day. Yesterday after noon we took a bathe and a boat-ride in and on Canandaigua Lake.

Sunday 22: I attended the Baptist Church both morning and evening. Warm and pleasant.

Monday 23: Drilled some again this fore noon; and it rained the remainder of the day. There are now fourteen of us at this rendesvous. We all sleep in the office under our blankets, and have a time!

Tuesday 24: Rained all day without ceasation. We (sevral of us soldiers) visited the Jail, conversed with the prisnors, &c. I was never in a jail before.

Wednesday 25: Very warm and pleasant. I visited the printing offices, the reading rooms and other places.

Thursday 26: The Sergeant went to Lockport tuesday: so we have nothing to do now. The boys have all gone up the lake to a pic nic but two of us. Windy.

Friday 27: Another pic-nic up the lake which some of the boys went to. Hot.

Saturday 28: The Sergeant returned from Lockport this morning with an other recruit.

Sunday 29: I attended the Presbyterian church this morning. Sevral of the boys and myself are pretty well floored to day.

Monday 30: I attended court and listened to the lawyer's eloquent pleas on the Knapp Case.

Note:

Mr. Clyde M. Maffin, Ontario County Historian, Canandaigua, New York, provides a copy of an item contained in the Ontario County Journal for July 1862, to wit:

"The suit against Leonard Knapp of Manchester for habitual drunkeness, the object of which was to show him incompetent to handle his own affairs and place his property under control of a committee, has just been tried before Judge Dusinberre and a jury in this village. It was a tedious trial, occupying the whole of last week and a part of this. This case was given to the jury on Monday afternoon last. One of the jurors dissented and it looks like it would be necessary to have another trial.

"His children instituted the action because they felt he was under undue influence of his second wife who married him with the view of obtaining possession of his property which is valued at $25,000."

JULY, 1862

Tuesday 1: The Sergant gave us quite a drill.

Wednesday 2: Circus here:—I did not attend. No drill to-day.

Thursday 3: Very hot:—we were drilled a little this afternoon under the shade of some trees.

Friday 4: Glorious Fourth! Had a fine celebration and fireworks. In the procession we were marched behind the music, in advance of the firemen. No accidents.

Saturday 5: Sevral of us went to the lake and took a plunge; and washed some of our garments. Did not drill. Exceedingly hot.

Sunday 6: Did not attend church to-day. A hotter time I think I never saw.

Monday 7: The Sergeant has gone to Lockport again. About all we do is to lay around. Hot.

Tuesday 8: A lot of us went in swimming twice today. We now go where and do just what we choose. I wrote with a deaf mute down at the wharf.

Wednesday 9: Quite a refreshing shower. I wrote a long letter to father and Lucina, and sent two papers home.

My Dear Sister Lucina.

It seems rather strange to sit down to write to you, as we have never before held any correspondence. I shall not though write much to you this time. How are all the folks &c. I am in as good health and spirits as when I left home, I have not been to uncle Warham Williams' yet; the only reason is because I hate to be seen by my relatives with this bobtail coat on. I have sent them word that I am here;

40

they tell me that one of the twins is very sick; they live only 12 miles from here. I am at liberty to go where I choose, I could come home if I am inclined to. Three of the Lockport boys went home and two have just arrived the other deserted. Oh, how homesick they got, but I am proof against it. I have sometimes most made up my mind to go to Rochester and see the folks, and I think I shall yet. I must, if time will permit, go to uncle Warham's. I am not out of money. It was pay day on the first of July, and we expected it; but we are informed that we get neither money, coats nor guns, until we get to the fort. I have carried my housewife in my pocket ever since you gave it to me; It is invaluable. I often have occasion to use it. I have sown on lots of buttons. The Sergeant often asks favors of me which I have to open it to get to, and he often remarked that it is very handy, and asks who made it? I tell him you did. Tell aunt Susan that a fellow named Reuben Tenny who used to work for Shirtliff is in this squad and a very fine fellow. Lucina, a young man or boy rather of about 18 or 19 years, was sent on from Lockport, with another recruit, to this place, and from hence with a squad to boston. Soon after his arrival there, he was taken with the diptheria, and died in a very few days; but I did not hear of it until I arrived here. I do not now know many particulars of his death. I just inquired of the Captain, and he says that he must have died near the 12th or 15th of June: was buried with the usual honors of a soldier by firing salutes &c. Capt. Barri says he shall try to ascertain more particularly. No one knows where to direct a letter to his parents. But his name was Emmet Levan, a cousin to Clarrence. Please let Mrs. Levan at the Villiage know it as soon as possible. We will write farther particulars as soon as we learn them. I have written but one letter before this since I started from Lockport. And that was in reply to Wm. Holmes. I cannot tell how much longer we shall stay here, but I pre-sume that the next letter you get from me will be dated from some other quarters. I will not wait long. I understand that Harrison and the rest of those returned boys, have been recalled. How is it. Lucina, I have rewritten all my compositions and some other pieces in that new spatted blank book of mine, I just went to the office to send it to you, that you might take care of it. But just because it was written they would not send it any less than though it had been a letter just so heavy, so I will have to get it home some other way. I will soon have a lot of money when I get to the fort, then I will send you some. I suppose Mr. Carter has got his house most ready to go into. When did you hear from Mary Jane last? What does she say about my late movements. I shall soon subscribe for the Intelligencer* for her one year. I suppose they live in Henry yet. I have forgotten her baby's name. My post-office adress is is Canandaigua N.Y. Care of Capt. Barri. Who helps father now-a-days? Lucina, when we go to dinner we have to march regular in a line; and back again to the office also. We atract a considerable atention as we go marching on. We have most of the time to ourselves and go just where we please. I can almost wade across the lake in some places. It is not much like old Ontario. Tell Mother I will write to her some time, and all the rest. Tell Em. I will write to him and all the rest of the folks. Uncle Stephen, aunt Lucy, and Maria. Clinty, Georgie, and good little girly, My respects and best wishes to you all. How does those onions get along. I spose they show up some now. Does my poplar tree grow? How does the door yard look? full of flowers I suppose; send me a leaf of the most beautiful one in your next letter. next letter did I say? I believe I have had none yet. Line, I try to be a good boy yet, I am going to prayer meeting to night. Well this is quite a change in my ocupation; lounging around doing nothing, amid the bustle and noise of a buisy town; the cars go dinging past every half hour. But I have got

---

*The Intelligencer was published in Lockport, New York, during the Civil War years.

used to it now. But I had almost forgotten to make mention of uncle William how do he and aunt Susan get along? Tell him I often think of him. And wish I could do something for him. Now Lucina, forward all letters which you get for me at this place, unless it be a newspaper or something of that sort not worth the sending, and be particular when you write to state all that you have received from me. I have forgot to speak of the fourth but wait until next time. You may expect a newspaper.

Ira S. Pettit

Direct to this place if I go away from here they will follow me.

Canandaigua, N.Y.   July the 8th/62

Dear Father: I immagine that you are getting somewhat anxious to know something of my whereabout &c.! I have been anxious to hear from home, or to receive letters which had been directed to me at Wilson, written by some friends who did not know my present P.O. adress. But I have watched the office in vain. I wrote to you just before leaving Lockport, requesting that if any letters for me made their appearance; to forward them to this office as it would cost you no extra postage. I have not received a single letter nor paper since I have been here. While in Lockport I sent you, I think, three daily papers; one weekly, and an extra, containing Lloyd's trial in full. The last paper was mailed on the morning of our departure from Lockport. I wrote a short script on a piece of paper and done it up in the last paper that I sent, stating that we were off. After I had been here a number of days I sent you another paper printed in this place; and I believe that is all. I will go into the office again today and if they will give me another paper I will mail it to you. Now when any of you write (if you ever do,) please to be particular to state whether you have received all that I have sent.

I enlisted on the 29th day of May. I was in Lockport just three weeks which was as long as I cared about lounging around there; I therefore prefered to leave with this squad. The sergeant came with us and is here yet; we left a cunnuck in the recruiting office, and I'll bet he has a lonesome time. I have, since I enlisted, spent my time with much profit. I used to, while in Lockport, frequently visit those mineral springs and take good hearty draughts of the curious water. I delighted to go to the glass-house and see them blow glass into all shapes. It takes sevral hands to blow bottles for the gargling oil company. I also visited that Laboratory which is just back of McGraths store. I tell you father they make it on the big scale. I fell into conversation with one of the hands who was packing it for transportation, and he gave me a fifty-cent bottle, which I have now with me. If you ever have occasion to get any more It would be econemy to purchase the dollar bottles as they contain more than as much again as a half dollar bottle. I went to the gasworks too, I had a boat ride upon the lake the first day we arrived There are here great car sheds where engines are run under to be cleaned and repaired. Court has been in session here too, and I have been up to hear a few cases. They can whip Niagara by a considerable on court houses; it is much larger, and of the most exquisite style and finish: the _____* is kept in this one, and I have yet never seen a building that would aproach it. I must now tell you of a fine joke which was played on me the other day. Sevral of us went to visit the jail and gained admittance on conditions that we would not stay long. As I was around out of sight of the door talking with a prisoner; the rest of the boys were ushered out and the door locked, and there I was detained for the short term of an hour. It looked blue, and answered to the description which I heard you, father, give of the jail in our county. There are two features of this place however

---

*Undeciphered cipher.

worthy of note. Those are the extensive flouring business, and wool-trade. There is one gristmill which is connected with a still that has two small run of stone!! I have seen four loads of wool in market during my nearly three weeks stay in Canandaigua!!! I sometimes take a walk out into the country to see the beauties of nature. We can rather whip them on canada-thistles in our section: but of all the mustard, buttercup, and white daisey, that I have ever before seen, this caps the climax! Meadows and pastures at a distance look like fields of blossomed buckwheat. I have met a few men whom I recognized since I have been in this place. Mr. Gallup, the lightning rod agent, is now here with sevral teams and hands doing business in this county. He boards at the same hotel where we take our meals. I knew him as soon as I saw him. I introduced myself to him, told him who I was and where from, and he remembered me. He often speaks of you, asking how you get along, how I came to enlist &c. That fellow that you paid, is with him; he said he knew he had seen me before but could not think where. I see them most every day. Bob Merwin's brother Orlando, now lives in East Bloomfield not far from here: he was here to the celebration on the fourth and we were right glad to see one an other. McDonald that fellow at Lockport, sent word to me by a recruit that you was there inquiring for that law book. I left that and the new york reader, with Lorinda and Jane Brewer. That is all I left behind at Lockport. Father, I imagine that you are now hoeing and haying. I often think how hard you have to work and wish that I could help you. Happy times to you father.

From your dutiful boy. Ira.

Thursday 10: We drilled none to day.
Friday 11: Were paraded around some by the Sergeant. Two runaways to-day. Cool and comfortable.
Saturday 12: Have orders to leave next monday. Another

45

runaway!!! Had my likeness taken for the first time in my life and sent it home. I weigh 132 pounds.

Sunday 13: Sevral of us went to church, both morning and evening.

Monday 14: We all arose early, packed our knapsacks, and with one days rations in our canteens and haversacks, started at 9,50 for Fort Independence. Arrived at Albany at 8 P.M. and took lodgeings.

Tuesday 15: Left Albany on the 6 o'clock train and after a long and tedious ride among the hills of Massachusetts, arrived at Boston at a little past 2 o'clock P.M. and were ferried across to the Fort at 6 o'clock P.M.

Wednesday 16: We now live on soldiers fare and drill five hours per day. It goes bully.

Thursday 17: About thirty of us were striped and examined by the doctor, all that were accepted of received this residue of clothing.

Friday 18: Maj. Gordon Commands here. I received a letter from home. Us new recruits went on dress parade tonight with our nice clothes on.

Saturday 19: No drilling Saturdays; but we put on our dress suits and had a knapsack inspection. I wrote a letter home.

> Fort Independence, Boston Massachusetts,
> July the 19th, 1862.

Father, I received your letter yesterday, and was right glad to hear from home. About the time you were writing your letter, we were packing our napsacks to make ready for a start the next morning. We were furnished with canteens and haversacks, which contained one days rations, and last monday the 14th of July, at half past nine, A.M. Capt Barri at the head of twenty recruits marched us to the depot and took cars for the east; the Capt. going with us, and returned again to Canandaigua after seeing us safely at the fort. At starting a slight shower prevailed which laid the dust and made the air refreshing. For a while it seemed delightful to once more get aboard the cars and ride through the country, and see what the farmers were about. It looked natural to see the fields of waving grain: wheat was ripening; a great deal of clover had been, and was being cut: corn looked fine, but I rather think that yours will almost challenge any thing that I saw. I took my seat on the south side of the cars, and with pencil and paper in hand took down notes by the way, and set down the name of every station until we got out of the state of N.Y. But if I should write full particulars of everything which fell under my observation I could send you a fifty-cent letter this time instead of a sixpeny. The train which we were on stoped at every station, and sometimes where there was no signs of a city or villiage. We changed cars for the first at Syracuse and there I beheld those extensive salt works which I have heard you often speak of. At Amsterdam we made quite a halt; I steped off the cars and turned my eyes toward old Galway where you spent your boyhood, and wondered how all the relatives were, whom I was so near but could not be permited to go and see. Thought I, father has been to this place many a time. I looked among the croud of people standing at the depot, and thought it would be a fine thing if I could see Grandfather or uncle Peter there. Soon the cars moved on we were all on the hind car by ourselves; and I sood on the hind platform looking back to get something of an idea of the place, but could not see it fully from the cars. I rode on the hind platform from Amsterdam to Schenectady, making only one stop which was at Hoffman's Ferry. The railroad followed the Mohawk many miles among the mighty hills which were astonishing. At Schenectady, many of us got off to stir around a little, and wherever we showed ourselves we atracted no little attention. Where is this squad from? inquired a rather portly man of me. I told him, and asked him if he knew the Sitterleys. O yes says he I know sevral families of them. I told him what one I was acquainted with, he said he was not much acquainted with John, but knew his wife; a large fat woman aint she? he asked; and he said she was in market most every day. He took my name and said he would tell her about me. The next station was Albany, which we reached about dusk, and took lodgeings at a boarding house: we were conducted into a large room, spread our blankets and with our clothes all on, reclined our heads on our napsacks and snoar'd away the night. The rain poured in torrents until we started the next morning, when it cleared off fine: we were ferried across the Hudson, and again took the cars at six o'clock and were off. Again I took my stand upon the platform of the hind car, and as the sun shone brilliantly over against the capital of our native State I could behold a large portion of the great city until the cars had rooled on sevral miles, when Albany was lost to my view. Soon after we passed the state line and were in Massachusetts. Well I have heard people say, and when I used to study geography it described the state as being hilly I found it to be a reality as I traveled through it. Rocky, O gehu! I remember at one time we passed through a tunnel cut in unde a rocky ledge more than 40 rods, and as far again for what I know; it seemed as though we were plunged into the gloom of eternal night! Worcester and Springfield were the largest places we passed between Albany and Boston. A person may study geography, but when he comes to travel will find it much different than what he expected. I had an Idea that the railroad went over all the hills and could see all the surrounding country, but it follows the rivers of the lowest valleys; and on our whole journey nearly, we were shut up between hills and mountains, the tops of some of which I could not see by looking twice. But at last the journey was tedious and fatiguing and we were dirty, in consequence of keeping the windows up to see out, and standing on the platform. We arrived at the great city of Boston at a little past two P.M. and were marshalled through sevral streets as crooked as cow paths to a recruiting office where we brushed up. As we were in an uper story could see a considerable to satisfy the curiosity: The streets are much rougher than the main street in Lockport: but in the centre of each street a railroad is laid and cars drawn by horses are continually on the go; indeed, it is quite a novelty: we were again ordered to strap on our napsacks and were marched to the ferry, where we got aboard the boat Huron, and after a ride of three miles reached Fort Independence, which is situated on a small island, in Massachusetts Bay. We were conducted to comfortable quarters in the fort where we placed our lugage and went to supper, and for the first time partook of soldiers rations, which was a small loaf of the best quality of bread, and a large bowl nearly full of coffee; which was enough to satisfy the hunger of a very hearty man: sometimes we get in adition to this, beef and different kinds of soup, but no cake nor pie. There is now a garrison of nearly 200 at these headquarters. Maj. Gordon commands. Co. A first Batallion is now full and led by Capt. Cooley and Lieut' Greely: We are in Co. B. and when full Capt. Barri will undoubtedly take command. There is a fine brass band here and we have splendid music. There are eight snare drummers, some of which I can beat: but there is one who leads, no man I ever heard play can aproach. I presume that I could get in as a drummer if I should insist upon it and it would be much easier if I can. On thursday we were all taken into the Doctor's room and examined; three were rejected; one from Lockport whose name is Reuben Tenny was not accepted, and they will not pay his fare back: After examination, we were marched to the clothing room and fully equiped. I got an other pair of pants, blue like the overcoat, a nice dress coat, and a pair of shoes. When we drill a while longer we shall be suplied with guns, cartridge boxes and a pair of white gloves. We drill five hours each day (Saturdays and Sundays excepted) in the fatigue suit: after supper at seven o'clock, every man puts on his blue pants and dress coat, buttons are to be kept bright and the shoes well polished, and ready to "fall in" at the command for dress parade. Then you may believe we show up. Uncle Sam takes as good care of his boys as any parents can of their children; we dress up every day in much better style, than most of people do when they go to church. There is perfect order here; every man is to keep himself clean and take good care of his clothes; if he makes his appearance in the ranks without his buttons well brightened and shoes well polished, he gets severely chastised; no spitting even, is allowed upon the floor nor upon the stone walks within the fort: the squad rooms are to be swept sevral times per day. The Fort is well constructed, and there are good acomodations for soldiers. I have not slept in as good a place since I left home: within the walls there is no more space than in Fort Niagara: ball proof walls extend all around, and mounts four times the number of cannon; and outside batteries are planted at different points. Cannon and Mortar firing is practiced on most every day. This indeed, is a delightful place: we can see part of Boston, and the briny waters of Massachusetts Bay are spread before us; hundreds of ships, and and all kind of crafts are constantly in view. The tide rises here about twelve feet which is quite a novelty: when the tide is out you can see bare ground where in a few hours after the largest boats can glide: we go in swiming every day; and, father, it is like plunging into the brine of your pork beryl. I can swim twice as well and as far again as I can in the fresh waters of Ontario. Yesterday a fisherman came over and no sooner than his hook droped a fish would take it (mostly perch) which were the first salt water fish I ever saw. Father, for one reason you would like to be here I know; clams are to be found in great abundance on the shores of this island. It is rather a bad time of the year to eat them and we are forbid of it but it dont do much good. They are not the kind we get in Lockport but taste the same. They are much smaller the shell is long and black:

50

by going to the main land we could get the other kind, but that is not often allowed. I find many oyster shells but no oysters; we have to dig to get to the clams: crabs and lobsters too are plenty. The stars and stripes float from the flagstaff every day. In adition to drilling we have to work some: the steamer brings us a load of wood or something every day and we are detailed to shoulder a stick or two at a time and carry it some fifteen rods or more and pile it. Uncle Sam provides a horse and cart, and also a cow but I dont get any of the milk. Some are haying now and have got together sevral tons. The day after my arrival, I was chosen with five others to row a boat with three of the officers to an island, but a short distance off, on which was an old fort and some batteries of revolutionary fame. I did not go to William's nor Rochester. On Saturday I riged up to go to Bristol the Capt. gave his consent and I got a chance to ride: but the Capt. got orders to start monday and he thought I had not better go as I might get detained by storm or something and left: but had I insisted he would have let me went I think. I got my picture taken and sent it to mother before leaveing Canandaigua. It did not suit me no better than it did any of you. I had a half a mind to have it taken over again and take a different position. I for got to state that I saw Auburn State Prison and had a fine view of it and saw prisoners at work for crime. I saw thousands of acres of broomcorn before reaching Albany. I was glad the whole journey was performed in the daytime. We were not terrified to see the conductor for we owed him nothing. We rode on one car from Albany clear to Boston. Your letter was promptly forwarded from Canandaigua. It cost me nothing for that. You stated that three papers were received and eight cents postage charged. While in Lockport I sent you three or four papers and on the margin of each one I wrote I R A, and not another letter except the last one which I sent on the morning of our departure and sent a letter in it: that was very wrong I know. When I got to Canandaigua I sent an other and just before starting a few days, I sent three or four all at one time nearly. One was a Rochester Democrat one Repository and Messenger, and a copy of the Ontario Republican Times. One was directed to Clinton, another to George, and the other to little Lucina Box 121 and in your care. I may have written I R A, on some of them but that is every word. I noticed *that* one Repository and Messenger had had a name written on it, but the printer tore it off before he gave it to me. I done it up and sent it home. But Major General Holmes never sent a paper back to me nor wrote to me on the subject. He knew too well that I help take care of Uncle Sam now-a-days and Uncle Samuel takes care of me. I will some time, send box 121 chock full of papers and tell you how they were done up and if he breaks the wrapers let me know it. Perhaps Dudley or someone may have written on papers: but I have never written more than my first name on any paper except the one I sent the letter in. I am sure I wrote that on Lloyds trial which Lucina says you received. I sent a half dozen of the trial to friends and I never sent a paper any where without simply writing upon the margin my first name. Indeed! You must have had a high time over papers. But I find it is cheaper to write a letter than to write even my name on a newspaper. We have not received our pay yet; I have got money enough, if I don't get paid off in two months. I am glad to hear your crops look well. I expected that the dry weather would injure them badly. I imagin that you will be at the winter wheat when you get this letter. I was sorry to leave you alone to do so much work. I am now far away from home: the sun sets in that direction and I love to watch it as it goes down. It is sunday afternoon and is raining fast for the first since I have been here. Tell mother I have just put on a fine shirt which was done up at home, and have an other clean one left. heretofore we have done our own washing. Tell aunt Lucy I never once thought of that Peter Vanauken until you spoke of it in your letter but now it does occur to me that I did see his sign and wondered what Van Auken it was but my head was so unaccountable thick that even then I did not think of what aunt Lucy said about Peter's being there. I am provoked at myself. There are two law offices at every door in Canadaigua. But I must now close.

From Ira.

Sunday 20: Rained hard most of the day. (Ira has here drawn a small diagram of the fort.)

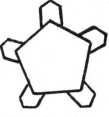

Fort Independence

Monday 21: Cool and refreshing: a fine time to drill. We drill about four hours per day, and have a dress parade after supper at 7 o'clock.

Tuesday 22: I had a chance to tap the drum for the first since I have been here.

Wednesday 23: We had a lot of luging to do in adition to the drill, removing the covers of cannon. Had no dress parade in consequence of a slight shower.

Thursday 24: A squad of 23 recruits arrived, quite late last night from Iowa, Illinois, and Indiana.

Friday 25: Two soldiers attempted to desert, last night, but were detected and arrested. The rejected recruits were sent home.

Saturday 26: In the fore noon we were set to removing a wall. After noon had a knapsack inspection and dress parade.

Sunday 27: Had a feast of clams. Received our new muskets (Springfield rifled.) cartridge-boxes, belts &c. Read my bible.

Monday 28: Drilled with our new Springfield rifled muskets.

53

Tuesday 29: We each purchased of the sutler brushes, and other cleaning material to keep ourselves shining. The new guns encourage us.

Wednesday 30: Rained. 'Twas a violent thunder shower too, so that we had only a dress parade after sunset.

Thursday 31: Dressed up in our best this morning, and had an inspection of arms, a monthly inspection. Rec'd a letter from home.

Note:

In 1634 the Colonists selected Castle Island as a suitable site for a fortress to 'defend' the Boston Harbor community. Improvements developed over the years as destruction by fire and other occurrences were experienced.

By the time of the Colonists' revolt accommodations had become fine enough to house the Crown's governing officials and to garrison two regiments. These were blown up by eighty-seven mines when the British vacated, March 26, 1776.

The Fort was sufficiently repaired to confine British prisoners of war under Paul Revere's custody, and by 1785 the island was established as a confinement center for convicts sentenced to hard labor.

In 1799 President John Adams renamed Castle Island, Fort Independence. Massachusetts had ceded it to the United States of America in 1798.

A pentagonal fort mounting fifty guns was completed in 1809 as the Federal government invested in a number of defenses for major harbors. A new Fort Independence replaced this in 1842.*

Castle Island is now connected to the mainland, South Boston, and bus service from Columbia Circle to the fort is available from May through September each year.

Fort Independence is presently undergoing restoration.

*The information in this brief summary of the evolution of Fort Independence is extracted from a *"Chronological Listing of Events Concerning Fort Independence,"* by Captain Albert A. Swanson, Historian, Metropolitan District Commission, Boston, Massachusetts.

AUGUST, 1862

Friday 1: Chislem,* a private of our Company, struck the sergeant with the but of his gun cutting his head somwhat badly, for previous abuse. He is now under arrest. Several others are also under arrest for expressing opinions in regard to it.

Saturday 2: We have an abundance of leisure saturdays. A battalion drill this after noon.

Sunday 3: Read the scriptures, and wrote a letter for another soldier which make three. Dress parad every sabbath when the weather admits.

Monday 4: I am at leisure writing to a newsboy of the Lockport Journal.

Tuesday 5: Walked as sentinel for the first time. My hours were from 1 to 3 P.M., 7 to 9, 1 to three; Post No two.

Wednesday 6: I walked as sentinel this morning from 7 to 9, when we were relieved and a new guard mounted. Salute of 75 guns in honor of ex-President Van Buren who recently died. The officers wear the acostomary mourning badge.

Thursday 7: I rec'd a letter from Tenny a rejected soldier; and mailed one to a newsboy of the Lockport Journal. Co A rec'd pay.

Friday 8: It is not so hot here as it is in western New York. A violent thunder shower both night and day. Drilled in the barracks before noon.

Saturday 9: Sevral of us were detailed to clean and scrub the quarters; and others to lug off a stone wall. I rec'd two letters.

*See page 362.

Sunday 10: I finished reading the book of John. A warm and pleasant day. Sold a shirt for one dollar in cash.

Monday 11: I paid the sergeant for a months washing.

Tuesday 12: Twenty-one prisoners (chiefly deserters from other regiments) are now here and kept at work, which saves us much fatiguing.

Wednesday 13: I am a member of the guard again. I prefer it to drilling. Francis, a recruit from Indianapolis, Ind. is misteriously missing.

Thursday 14: It makes one's eyes feel heavy after up and on guard all night.

Friday 15: A battalion drill this afternoon. Francis, who disapeared last wednesday, was found under the new cook-house in a fit!

Saturday 16: A knapsack inspection this afternoon. About 60 prisoners (chiefly deserters from other regiments) were brought here this evening. Quite an addition to company Q.* (as it is called.)

Sunday 17: We (Co. B.) moved in the new barracks. The prisoners are to take our place.

Monday 18: We used to have to do much fatiguing, but all such duty the prisoners are now compelled to perform. I am again detailed for guard tomorrow.

Tuesday 19: A larger guard is now mounted, to keep the prisoners from escaping: we (the guard) also have our guns loaded and two rounds of cartridges in our boxes. A dozen more prisoners or recruits for Company "Q" were brought here to night.

Wednesday 20: Sent a letter to David Berry of Lockport. Company "Q" is the largest, numbering 113! A hard and

---

*Companys "Q" were made up primarily of soldiers who had in one way or another offended the propriety of the military code. A novel entitled, "Company Q," written by Richard O'Connor and published in 1957 by Doubleday and Company, Inc., depicts a fictional Company Q. It is made up of deserters, drunkards and other renegades (as well as scapegoats who were victims of corruption in high places), who, by serving in it, are given a chance to regain their previous military status. The movie, "Advance to the Rear," also deals with the Company Q phenomenon.

sorry looking set!! We discharged our guns at a mark when we came off guard this morning. I hit it.

Thursday 21: They are very strict here; sevral are now posted, at different points, upon beryls for very simple crimes. The members of Co. "Q" are buisy slicking up about the island.

Friday 22: Had a battalion drill yesterday afternoon, and each fired sevral rounds of blank cartridges. Sergt. Hale arrived with 7 recruits.

Saturday 23: Done our scrubing and police duty early. Afternoon had a knapsack inspection, and the usual dress parade at sunset.

Sunday 24: Quite cool. I am again detailed for guard.

Monday 25: I am on post No. two third relief. I devote my leisure to writing a letter to Emory Pangburn.

Tuesday 26: We discharged our pieces at a mark. I hit it. We then had the fun of taking our guns apart and cleaning.

Wednesday 27: A Major and a Brigadier General visited this post to-day. Twenty more prisoners!!!

Thursday 28: Quite cool: we now wear our great coats mornings and evenings.

Friday 29: I succeed very well in learning the drill. Mailed a letter to Mr. Emory Pangburn.

Saturday 30: No knapsack inspection; nothing but dress-parade. An insane prisoner is misteriously missing from his cell striped of *every garment!* Cannot be accounted for.

Sunday 31: Monthly inspection. We were assigned to the Co. and regiment, and mustered for pay. We were called out on the parade ground in our uniforms, also with our guns for the purpose. An unusual performance. A knapsack inspection in the barracks also.

SEPTEMBER, 1862

Monday 1: I am on guard today. Heavy showers and very high winds.

Tuesday 2: Rained most of the forenoon. The wind blows with great force. Very cold! We shiver!

Wednesday 3: Orders were read this evening to the effect that the hours for drill were to be changed.

Thursday 4: Drill hours changed to ½ past 9 until 11 A.M. and from 3 until ½ past 4 P.M.

Friday 5: Another attempt was made about noon, by a prisoner, to escape by swimming, but was picked up by a boat and brought back.

Saturday 6: No inspection until to-morrow. Eighteen prisoners were released. I am detailed for guard again to-morrow.

Sunday 7: I am on post No. one; 2nd. relief. The insane prisoner who was missing from his cell nine days ago was found dead floating upon the surface of the water! He was taken out and buried.

Monday 8: Over 200 prisoners were taken from here to camp Day;* and were they not pleased eh, to get off from this island!!!

Tuesday 9: The Band, accompain by Lieut. Bentzoni, left this after noon with three days rations, for the regiment in, or near, Washington. Eighteen more prisoners arrived only about 30 here now.

Wednesday 10: Received a letter from Lucina, my sister.

Thursday 11: Am engaged, at Leisure, writing a letter to

---

*Camp Day was located at Cambridge, Massachusetts.

send home. Heretofore I have not kept memorandum of who was officer of the day; but will observe it henceforth.

Headquarters of the 11th Infantry,
U.S. Army, Fort Independence,
Boston Harbor Mass.
Sept. 10th 62.

Dear Father:—

Some time has now elapsed since I have written directly home, and I thought perhaps that you would like to know as to my whereabouts, and how I am getting along &c. We still remain at the above place, and are nearly all in exelent health; no deaths have occurred from sickness since I have been here. It is a very healthy place in consequence of the fresh sea breezes; and the frequent ebb and flow of the tide washes away all filth. I am in as good health as I was when I left home. It is quite a change in my business to leave home and the quietness of a farm life, and become a soldier. This does not appear to me like other summers which I have always spent at home; and I can say that I have enjoyed no more happiness than when I was at home laboring with you, although I have much less to do now, and see a great many wonderful things; am well provided and cared for, and get good wages. The thoughts of home often makes my heart throb with emotions of pleasure. I have received three letters from home since I have been here: the one which was forwarded from Canandaigua, to which I replied, and an answer to my letter; then Lucina wrote again very soon after, and also inclosed the one which Mr. William Holmes wrote to me and sent to Wilson. I suppose you saw the picture in it of Gen. Beauregard watering his horse. And there father, just as I finished that last sentence the Sergeant handed me another mailed at Wilson! Now let me see what it says. It is from Lucina! Oh how I wish I could see Grandfather! I am pleased to hear that Emory got my letter: and as I suppose they told you a great many things that I wrote, it will be unnecessary for me to repeat it. Day before yesterday, over 200 of those prisoners which I spoke of in my letter to uncle Stephen's folks, were removed from here to camp Day where most of them belong: and were they not glad though to get off from this island eh! They all got aboard of the government boat "Huron," and as she swung from her moorings, it would have done you good to hear the vociferous cheering from the mouth of every prisoner: 19 arrived here last night, and there are but about 30 here now. I tell you they have slicked this island up pretty nice. Oh! What a time they had removing a stone wall which was built with the refuse stone of the fort. There were some huge blocks of stone, some more than twice as large as the big platform of your front door. A large pair of wheels just like Dan Haner used to haul logs on, and a car such as is used to draw logs up into a saw mill, were used: and about 60 would get hold of a rope which was attached to each, and when loaded, would start off on the run, hollering and yelling, making an abundance of fun for us all! but we are not sorry that the most of them have left, for they were a lousy set. Two were insane: one became rational: the other was one morning misteriously missing or removed from his cell, and every garment remaining in the cell. He was either murdered it is thought, by an officer whom he pounced upon the day before, or, escaped through a loop hole, which is thought impossible for any man to squeeze through. Nine days afterwards, which was last Sunday, a body was seen floating upon the surface of the water; It was hauled out and recognized to be the missing man. His head was badly bruised, either from strokes, or by falling upon the rocks. No inquest was held, nor ceremonies; but immediately buried without any honors of war. Strange it is how he escaped even in the night, without notice, as so many sentinels are posted around about the island. In digging his grave, the bones of another man were struck upon at the depth of four feet, and there were no signs of a grave. There are not so many graves visible here as there are at fort Niagara. Fort Independence is built upon the ruins of Castle William; which was, in olden times, garrisoned and held by the British. O! father how we could whittle a fleet if it should try to come in on Boston! One hundred cannon are, or can be, mounted upon the top, and 34 port holes to fire cannon through from the inside; and 66 loop holes for musketry. A loop hole is about 5 feet long, and measures 5¾ inches wide outside. So that the contents of sevral guns can be dischged through one of them at one time: they stand perpendicular thus and widen as they extend inside so fashion.

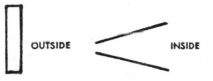

OUTSIDE   INSIDE

There are two outside batteries; one mounts 16 cannon, and the other 10. Hundreds of new cannon and mortars of the largest kind, are brought here from Boston, tried by the artillerists by firing, and then shiped away. I do remember me, when I was quite young, and listened with pleasure to hear you sing Old Kentucky Boys, and other war songs; and thought how I would like to become a soldier: that childish wish has now come to pass. I can perform the facings and flankings, and understand the manual of arms very well. I have got a neat gun and bayonet, also the other accoutrements. We had sport not long ago on a battallion drill: the two companies united, and each soldier had 12 rounds of blank cartridges in his box; we would load and fire by battallion, fire by company, fire by rank, by platoon and by file; also at will. We would charge upon the enemy and retreat, loading and firing on the run; practice skirmishing, and many other manavers. It was the sound of battle, but no dead were carried off the field. I know not how long it will be before we will come to the stern realities. The band started for the regiment last night, which is near Washington: each man taking with him three days rations: Dress parade went off rather dull to night without the band music. I tell you they are accomplished, and have splendid instruments. What are you doing now-a-days father? cutting corn? Who helped you this summer? Do you change work with uncle Stephen? Have you thrashed yet? I want you to write and tell me all about things; the summer fallow the turnips (was there much of a call for turnip seed)? Your hogs look well I'll bet. Are the squirrels plenty this summer, did they trim the wheat and are they now at the corn? If so, how I'de like to be there with my rifled musket and "charge bayonets" on them! Do you keep the oxen yet? How are old billy and johny? I expect you have had so much to do that you did not have time to put up the wall. How is uncle William, do you keep his cow for him yet? Father, do all for him you can afford to. What did Grandfather think of his predickament! I suppose he was sorry to have Grandfather find find him in such a condition. Co. B. have not received any pay yet but we expect it every day: that is the reason why I delayed writing so long so that I could send home some money when I did write. I will not risk it all in one letter but send $10 at a time. I see Lucina is getting over-anxious to hear from me, so if I am not paid before I finish my letter, I guess I will not wait for it. Two dollars per. month is kept back of every private soldier's wages until the expiration of their term of service. Now on the next sheet you will find particulars concerning other things which you may keep private if you choose to do so.

(hence, it was kept private, i.e., it does not comprise a part of what remains. Ed.)

Friday 12: Capt. Cooley* officer of the day. Both companies drilled togather.

---

*Captain Francis Morgan Cooley served from May 4, 1861, until April 14, 1869, in the Eleventh Infantry; was commissioned brevet major for

Saturday 13: Heavy rain last night. Second Lieut. Farnesworth officer of the day. I am again detailed for guard tomorrow.

Sunday 14: I am on post No. four which leads through the sally-port. I am also 2nd relief. First Lieut. Greely, Officer of the day. Countersign is Jones.

Monday 15: I sent a letter home. We (the old guard) each fired two shots at the target. Capt. Lattimer Officer of the day.

Tuesday 16: Fine weather to drill. Capt. Cooley officer of the day.

My Dear Sister Lucina;

Was you getting anxious to hear from me? as I think about it, I must come to the conclusion that I have done you an injustice to neglect so long to write to you, when you have been so kind and sisterly to write to me so often. I had commenced a letter to father, intending to have it ready, so that when we were paid off I could send part of my wages home immediately: but before I got the first page finished, your letter was handed to me; and as I observed that you was very anxious to hear from me, I therefore concluded to finish it as soon as convenient and send it off. I made a bad mistake in telling Maria that the last letter was all I had received from you; I thought of it when it was too late, and knew that you would take it as it read. What I meant to have stated is this: that it was the last I had received from you and not all. I have received all that you stated you had sent. They now all lay spread in order before me on the table. The first, inclosed in a large white envelope and forwarded from Canandaigua to which I replied. Next is in a small white envelope, and has on it one of those red things which says: For Particulars inquire within. and I did so, and found that Ella Johnson

gallant service at Spottsylvania, Virginia, and lieutenant colonel for gallant service at Petersburg. Was discharged upon his own request on September 1, 1870.

was married! The next is the large yellow one in which was inclosed an exelent letter from Mr. Wm. Holmes, upon which was the picture of Gen. Beauregard letting his horse quench his thirst, and demons flying after him. I was not offended at you for reading it. The other is the one I received from you last. I got most every one in two days, and always in less or within three days after they were mailed. The postmarks are plain, and they were mailed and received as follows. Mailed July 15th and 29th Aug. 7th and Sept. 8th Rec'd July 18th and 31st Aug. 9th Sept. 10th which make four letters from home. I have got those flowers yet: they put me in mind of the front yard. Your letters were directed correctly, but it would be more appropriate to put the Co. B. on first; thus: Co. B 11th Infantry. I made a mistake if I ever taught you otherwise. I am pleased to hear that uncle Stephen's folks got my letter, and I expect to hear from them soon. You ask if I have forgotten you; why no! do you give yourself so much uneasiness about me? I have not been sick nor in suffering as you immagined. but when I am, I will let you know if I am not too far gone. Lucina! you had better lay those dreams aside. The seal upon which was inscribed The hope of return takes the sting from Adieu was on the letter you sent to Canandaigua. You think I would have enjoyed myself well if I could have sat down to the table yesterday, and partook of the many delicious eatables which you named. Well, I would you know, Siner! but above all, I would like to have seen Grandfather. Why did you not tell me who brought him there. You read my letter to Him eh? Tell him I'll try and write to Him sometime. But He will be gone though most likely, before you get this letter. A slew of soldiers left Lockport did'nt they. It is sad that Thomas Hill is killed but it cannot be expected otherwise than that many will be left behind! I wonder if Harvey Pease is *dangerously* ill? If Tip has gone to His Company he will not be likely to cut around with Kate Starkey any more at present. I would have been highly pleased if C. B. Lowell would called over to the Fort. Excitement must run high indeed, thereabouts, if they have come to having war meetings on the Sabbath. Then Albert has enlisted eh? What Braman going to try it again! Will his wife go too? Ike and Ambrose will make make good soldiers. Tell father I am glad to hear that he is drumming up recruits. Are you sorry that I enlisted? It was indeed very unfortunat for Timothy Pettit to loose his exelent wife. It is strange that Henry Pattengill lingers so long. Poor fellow, what a sad accident he met with. You speak of my picture in your last letter also in a previous one. It cost 50 cents; and the postage was 24 more. It appears as I would at a distance; and that is the reason perhaps it suits you so well because you like to see me a good ways off. The eyes look queer, the features are not plain and the visor of the cap shades the forehead badly; but, thought I let it slide. Did you see the bulge the housewife made on one side. I knew that it would please mother to send it to Her. I cannot get my likeness taken at present. I have not written to Mary Jane since I enlisted. Perhaps she thinks it very strange, but I have been waiting and waiting for my pay, so that I could send her my likeness and make her a present of the Niag. Co Intelligencer for one year. I shall commence a letter to her as soon as I finish this, and then write to Fanny and Merrit. Now I want an accurate explanation in your next, about that small red book that aunt Marguerate gave me, and the one containing my eloquent productions. I sealed the large book carefully and wrote fathers name and P.O. adress on the wrapper in large caracters. I tried to send them by mail but as it was written, instead of printed matter, they charged me letter postage. I then went to the Express office and there they charged me 25 c. I then told Sergt. Hale to take them to Lockport when he went, and leave them at the Pavilion hotel, where we boarded; and he promised to do so. I then wrote a letter to Lorinda Brewer, requesting her to get them from the Hotel and give them to some of my folks when she had an oppertunity, and gave the letter to the sergeant and told him not to mail it until he took the books to Lockport, and then, mail it there; so that Lorinda might take them in her care immediately. But when He got here he told me that he had sent them by express (and I think he said to Lorinda at Lockport). Now who were the books directed to? What hotel did father get them to: was it in Wilson or in Lockport? Were they broken open or not? What was the express charges. Who paid it? whoever did pay it, pay them promptly. I am very glad you got them. Did you look it through? Has Samuel given up the *Idea* of enlisting entirely, or has he gone? Indeed, Wilson must now be very short on for boys. Tell mother I will try to be a good boy after this and keep out of jail. I have not had to stand on a beryl yet nor go to the guard house. The Sutler keeps all the fruit and delicacies which we want to eat if we are a mind to take it and let him have a draw on our wages. No beer nor whisky is kept here for sale. We always go to the table with our caps on, and when we let fall a piece of bread there is no danger of its striking butter side down. When all those prisoners were here the bakers had a buisy time. The bread is first quality and all baked here. Large squads of prisoners now arrive every day and will soon be as many as before. They are always searched and often large dirks and bowie knives are found on their person. A grand reception of Col. Corcoran took place in Boston some time ago, and many flags were floating. I keep Diary yet. I will state the particulars of the death of Levan in my next. Remember me particularly, to uncle Wm. Aunt Susan, and Clarissa. Once more I bid you Adieu.

Ira.

(A drawing such as follows, accompanied with comments and explanation, was placed at the end of the preceding letter.)

Fort Independence,
Sept. 14th. 1862.

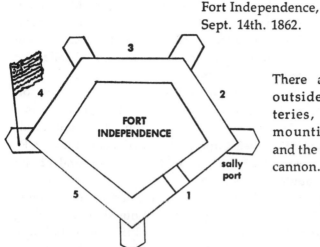

There are two outside batteries, one mounting 16 and the other 10 cannon.

There are four flight of stone steps to ascend from the inside and a road to haul up ordinance. The sally port doors are exactly like that at Fort Niagara. The Fort is built of large blocks of stone. The walls are 35 feet high and it is 12 long paces from the outside of the walls to the inside of the fort. It is 12 paces through the sally-port. There are three pair of doors in the sally-port and a huge slide can also be let down from above in case of necesitty. The outside walls are six feet thick or more and inside about four, and arched strongly from wall to wall; which makes a place to fire cannon out of the port-holes &c; and also squad rooms for soldiers, store rooms, bakery, cook and eating houses, Officers Quarters &c. &c. and an abundance of room for all purposes. Co. A. takes up their quarters within the walls; but we are in the new barracks outside the fort. 100 cannon can be placed upon top of the fort. The port and loop holes are distributed as follows: Side No. One; 4 portholes 38 loopholes: no. 2, 10 p, 2 L: No 3, 12 p, 6L: no 4, 4 p, 3 L: No. 5, 4 p, 11L.

Tuesday 16: Fine weather to drill. Capt. Cooley officer of the day.

67

Wednesday 17: I began a letter to my sister Mary Jane. Delightful weather. Lieut. Farnesworth officer of the day.

Thursday 18: Purchased $1 worth of sutler tickets. We were aroused last night by a false alarm! I am again detailed for guard tomorrow. Lieut. Greely officer of the day.

Friday 19: Private Bloss of co. A was found sleeping on post last night. He is confined in the guard house. Paymaster Gen. is dead, saluted 9 guns. I am on guard: post no. two, 3ᵈ relief. Capt. Lattimer officer of the day. R. Powers Sergeant of the guard, Isenbal Corporal of the guard. Countersign is Miles.

Saturday 20: I hit the target as we discharged the contents of our pieces this morning. Devoted our time to cleaning up for inspection tomorrow. A patrol fired 4 shots into a boat last night. Lieut. Farnesworth officer of the day.

Sunday 21: Weekly inspection of guns knapsacks bunks &c. We all signed the pay-roll. Officer of the day the same as yesterday. Pleasant.

Monday 22: Capt. Cooley of co. A. pushed one of his men accidentally down upon a stone who came over from Boston drunk, which cut his head badly, and knocked him senseless. Officer of the day same as yesterday.

Tuesday 23: Sent a letter to Mary Jane. Beautiful weather. Orders were read on dress parade that co. A. were to leave Thursday next. Capt. Lattimer officer of the day.

Wednesday 24: Got 2 letters & 2 papers from home. Both companies were paid up. I rec'd $33,71 cts. Co. A is making rapid preparations to leave to morrow. No dress parade to night. Capt. Cooley officer of the day.

> Fort Independence Mass.
> Wednesday evening
> Sept. 24ᵗʰ 62.

I had the pleasure to receive your letter this morning, and also one from Emory. I was highly pleased to hear so much of what was going on in Wilson. I read the letters over and over and intend to peruse them more still. The reason why I hasten to reply is because we have at length received our long looked for pay. Before I had fairly finished reading your welcome letters, we had orders to "fall in for pay." Our hearts then swelled high in our bosoms, and we were not slow to obey orders. We were paid up to the 1st of Sept. I have now on hand quite a stack of money. I was paid $33,71 cents. There is two dollars per. month deducted from every privates wages and is not to be paid until the expiration of our term of service. It is for this reason: If we draw more clothing than we are allowed, it is to be taken out of it: and also that we will have enough to convey ourselves home if we squander what has been paid us: and one shilling per. month is also deducted which goes to the Soldier's Home. The money with which we were paid has never been handled. I have three $10 notes; one 50, and two 10 cent postage stamp notes, of the late issue, and one cent in coin. I expect to send you the three tens at three different times. As soon as you receive each send me a newspaper that I may be assured of its safety and make a pencil mark upon each side of the paper. I owe the children some: please divide $1 among them as follows: to Clinty 50 cts. Georgie 25 cts, and Little Lucina 25 cents. I have not now sufficient leisure to write a fitting reply to your excelent letters as I am anxious for this to go out with the 11 oclock mail to-morrow so that they may get this Saturday evening. I will write again as soon as I am assured that you get this. I have written a long letter to Mary Jane. There is quite a stir among us now. Orders were read on dress parade last night that Co. A. was to take their departure tomorrow for the regiment near Washington. To day, they have been packing and gearing up all sorts. Three days rations have been prepared and to-morrow at half past 3 P.M. will leave the island. They are highly pleased with the idea. I can buy almost new shoes and clothing of them for ¼ price. I know a pair of government shoes would suit you well they are all sowed and are very easy to wear. I now wear them and save my boots for winter. The prisoners have again accumulated to the number of 102 and it will be a nice little job for us to guard them: each of us will now be on every other day; only one night in bed out of two: nineteen are detailed out of our Co. for guard tomorrow and I am among that number so I will have to bring this letter to a close; shine up my gun, polish my cartridge box, black my belts &c. In consequence of a slight shower this evening we had no dress parade. It will make a great difference with us to loose Co. A. Friday morning: This promises to be a fine day. I am well and in good spirits. Remember me to Grandfather and the rest.

Yours truly
Ira S. Pettit
Co. B. 11th Infantry
U.S.A.

I had forgotten to state that I got all thre papers. They were highly appreciated.

Thursday 25: Sent $10 home in a letter. Subscribed for the Intelligencer for Mary Jane—$1. I am on guard again: post No 4, 3[d] relief. Co. A took their departure at 3 o'clock this P.M. Seems lonesome now. Lieut. Farnesworth officer of the day. Countersign is Cooley.

Friday 26: Rather a small business carried on here now. 1st Lieut. Bentzoni is officer of the day. Brilliant northern lights and great fire in Boston last night.

Saturday 27: The number of guard posts has been diminished so we will not have so much guard duty. Capt. Lattimer officer of the day.

Sunday 28: I am on guard: post No. 2, 2nd relief. Rained most all day and night. Dense fog. 1st Lieut. Hartwell officer of the day.

Monday 29: Three prisoners made their escape last night, taking two boats. Lieut. Farnesworth officer of the day.

Ford sergeant of the guard. Creighton, corporal of the guard.

Tuesday 30: Monthly inspection. No drill this fore-noon. Sent a letter to cousin Mrs. Fanny Brown. Lieut. Bentzoni officer of the day.*

Note:

The following excerpt from the *"Bicentennial Daybook, October 1975,"* compiled by the Mid-Atlantic Region of the National Park Service, U.S. Department of the Interior, may be an explanation for the already occupied grave at Fort Independence which Ira mentioned in the letter to his father, dated September 10, 1862:

"October 23, 1775—The Royal Army in Boston, a British deserter says, is ill with scurvy and buries eight or ten of its numbers every day who died from the sickness."

---

*Charles Bentzoni was from Prussia, and had been a private, corporal, sergeant, and first sergeant in general service. He became a second lieutenant in the Eleventh Infantry on November 20, 1861, a first lieutenant on March 17, 1862, and was transferred from the Eleventh to the Twenty-ninth Regiment on September 21, 1866. *And the recruits at Fort Independence knew him as their DS.*

OCTOBER, 1862

Wednesday 1: Stormy. Capt. Lattimer officer of the day.

Thursday 2: On guard; post no. 1 third relief: very stormy. Lieut. Hartwell officer of the day. Two prisoners attempted to escape on a raft this evening but we pursued and captured them.

Friday 3: Lieut. Farnesworth officer of the day. Got a letter from Mr. Reuben Tenny. I did not drill at all being detailed as one of a boats crew to row over to South Boston.

Saturday 4: I rec'd a paper from home marked, showing that the letter I sent with $10 enclosed was received. Bentzoni officer of the day.

Sunday 5: A squad of 16 recruits of Indianapolis, arrived last night. Good for co. B. Very high winds. Full moon; night clear and cold. On guard to-day.

Monday 6: Capt. Lattimer officer of the day yesterday; to day Lieut. Hartwell. Cold.

Tuesday 7: Lieut. Farnesworth officer of the day. Delightful weather for the time of year.

Wednesday 8: On guard post 2. 3ᵈ relief. Bentzoni officer of the day. Sent another $10 note home in a letter. Seven more prisoners. 128 in all. Hot!

> Fort Independence Mass.
> Oct. 8ᵗʰ '62

Father: I was right glad when I got that Tribune; for I was then assured that you had received my letter in which was inclosed the $10 note as soon as my eye caught the pencil marks. I had been looking for some time for something to show that you had got it. I will now send another ten. I hoped to send you $30 but I leant $2 to a responsible fellow, and my sutler bill is $1/50: so the other $10 note is broken. I have put in for a pass to go over to the City next Saturday. I want my boots taped, shall get a few pictures taken, and make a purchase of sevral articles that I need; so I cannot tell how much I will have left. The last letters which I have received from you was mailed on the 22 of Sept. I am always well pleased to hear from you. I am sorry that you have so much work to do alone. I feel that I ought to be at home to help you. I hesitated much about enlisting on that account. I was fully aware of the importance of my position and good home; but I could not see so many of the boys go, and me stay at home. I did not leave from malice. Soldering is good constant employment and we are punctually and well paid: if we have only a mind to save our pay, there is a chance to accumulate quite a sum of money. You are welcome to all I send you, use it as your own, hire a plenty of help and not do so much alone. I was glad to hear that things looked so well as they do. You will not be apt to get your wall laid very soon as Pat Nash is dead. I supose you have the corn cut by this time. Did you and Grandfather have a good time at the falls? Where did uncle William move, or hes not he left the 10 acres yet? Will Grandfather go any farther West. It is very fine weather here for the time of year; and the full moon makes it delightful in the night to be on guard. No heavy rains have yet fallen. Our co. lacks about ten of being full. One hundred and twenty-eight prisoners are now here. I have not so much leisure to write now as usual, so, I will close.

From your dutiful boy.   Ira.

Sister Lucina:—
I was glad to get those papers which you sent me. I tell you it looked old fashioned to see those Rurals. I have perused them, and am going to more yet. I read the pieces which you marked over and over. I put that piece of cloth into my housewife. The money which I send home has been kept

in it ever since I was paid. When I finish this letter, I will take out another ten and carefully inclose it. I have done a considerable at sewing on buttons and closeing up rips. All the needles are in it, and many other articles as when I left home. It will save me many dollars in three years time providing I live so long. I have written to Fanny and Mary Jane; but have had no reply. I will now write to Ruth. It seems that all who dont enlist are dieing in that section. Sorrowful times! How did the county and town fairs go off? I can not get my picture taken with my gun and belts on; unless a picture taker comes over here. We are not allowed to take our accoutrements from the post. If I succeed in geting a pass I will send you some papers. I hope that this letter will get home by Saturday if it does tell me. Tell mother I shall be looking for that letter that she is going to send. But I must close.

Your's truly.
Ira S. Pettit.
U.S.A. Fort Independence
Mass.

Thursday 9: Very pleasant weather for the season. Capt. Latimer officer of the day.

Friday 10: Capt. Latimer is at present commanding officer of the post; Major Gordon being absent. Lieut. Farnesworth officer of the day.

Saturday 11: On guard. Post 2, 3^d relief. Had no dress parade in two weeks or more. Lieut. Bentzoni officer of the day.

Sunday 12: Inspection day i.e.: weekly inspection. I escaped it by coming off guard after it was over. Very windy and chilly. 2nd Lieut. Huntington officer of the day.

Monday 13: Rained all day: windy & chilly. I wrote a long letter to Mr. Reuben Tenny. Capt. Latimer officer of the day.

Tuesday 14: On guard, Post no. one; 3^d relief. Lieut.

Farnesworth officer of the day. About the right temperature to walk post.

Wednesday 15: 1st Lieut. Bentzoni officer of the day. Got two stoves up now in my quarters which will make it more comfortable. Three months since we came here.

Thursday 16: On extra guard for not shaving when on before! Post no. 2, 2nd relief. Countersign Pulaski. Lieut. Huntington officer of the day.

Friday 17: Got a pass to go over to the city of Boston from 11 A.M. until 5 P.M. The first I have had liberty to be absent since I came here. Capt. Latimer officer of the day.

Saturday 18: We drew clothing. I drew a cap and pair of shoes. Signed the clothing receit rools. Got a dollar worth of sutler tickets. Rec'd a paper from home. Lieut. Farnesworth officer of the day.

Sunday 19: On as a prisoner guard only to night. Weekly inspection. Lieut. Bentzoni officer of the day.

Monday 20: Clear sky but heavy chilling wind. Capt. Latimer officer of the day.

Tuesday 21: Sevral members of yesterday's guard are confined into cells on suspicion of being concerned in stealing a pair of boots from a prisoner. Lieut. Farnesworth officer of the day.

Wednesday 22: Lieut. Bentzoni officer of the day. Six prisoners escaped from their cells last night and in attempting to get off in a skift two were drowned and we saved the rest. We found the two bodies when the tide went out. Heavy wind.

Thursday 23: The bodies of the two drowned prisoners were buried today. I helped carry them to the hospital last night. Capt. Lattimer officer of the day. I'm on guard Post 3, 1st relief, countersign Newport.

Friday 24: Our boys were released from the cell except Smith, and French a prisoner is confined with him on suspicion. Got my pictures. Sent one in a letter to Aunt Marguerite. Lieut. Bentzoni officer of the day.

Saturday 25: I mounted guard but was chosen for the

commanding Officer's orderly. Capt. Latimer officer of the day. Windy & cold.

Sunday 26: Owens succeeded me as orderly. Detailed twice to help row the barge over to South Boston windy & rough! Lieut. Bentzoni officer of the day. *Cooper* took my washing.

Monday 27: Rained all night heavily and tis a very stormy day. Bad time for the guard. No drill. Capt. Latimer officer of the day. Got $1 worth of sutler tickets and sold all to Titus.

Tuesday 28: Sent a letter to Emory. On guard. Post No. 1. 1st relief. Lieut. Bentzoni officer of the day. Prisoners engaged at unlading a boat of wood & coal. Very pleasant after the heavy storm.

Wednesday 29: Purchased another dollar's worth of tickets of the sutler. Smith, the last of our boys in the cell was released. Capt. Latimer officer of the day.

Thursday 30: On guard: post 3, 1st relief. A boat load of coal and also of wood has landed and the prisoners are buisily engaged unlading and taking it on wheel barrows to its propper place. Lieut. Bentzoni officer of the day.

Friday 31: There are now here 165 prisoners. Pleasant weather for the time of year. Monthly inspection this morn. before guard mount. Mustered also for pay. Escaped the inspection by being on guard. Capt. Latimer officer of the day.

NOVEMBER, 1862

Saturday 1: A very pleasant day. We done our scrubing and cleaning up and fixed for inspection tomorrow. Received two papers from Aunt Marguerate. Lieut. Bentzoni officer of the day. Six more prisoners came.

Sunday 2: Weekly inspection before guard mount. On guard. Post no. 4. 3ᵈ relief. Fine weather; pleasant nights. Capt. Latimer officer of the day.

Monday 3: Windy & cold. Got two letters to-night: one from Sister Mary Jane & one from Cousin Fanny Brown. Lieut. Bentzoni officer of the day.

Tuesday 4: Still & cold last night. General Election in the states. Capt. Latimer officer of the day.

Wednesday 5: On guard: post No. 3, 1ˢᵗ relief. Sent a letter to Sister Lucina. Very windy. Countersign: "Fairfax." Lieut. Bentzoni officer of the day.

> Headquarters 11ᵗʰ Infantry, U.S.A.
> Fort Independence Boston Harbor Mass.
> Nov. 6ᵗʰ 1862.

Sister Lucina:—

I received yours of Nov. 21ˢᵗ* on the morning of the 23. and was glad to hear from you and that those two $10 notes reached home safely. I have sevral dollars left yet but will send no more home until we are again paid.

I have been over to the City but did not send you papers as I promised, as I did not take along enough money to

---

*This, apparently, is an inadvertent error on Ira's part; he must have meant October 21ˢᵗ.

buy any after footing other expenses. You say Grandfather was to uncle Seth's before he came to Wilson. How was Dudley? I have not written to him since I left home. Is that old mill capable of making cider yet? I'de like to have a draft. I frequently read that piece of marked poetry in the Rural: it is very appropriate. That lint society *was* a smasher. I suppose those 32 who attended were mostly femenines, as the majority of the boys have departed. I am glad you gave the names of those who have died, and was sorry to hear that so many had died. I had not before heard of cousin Fanny William's death. I can hardly forgive myself for not going to see her when I could! I suppose there was a large turnout to Mrs. Dearborns funeral. I rec'd that paper which you sent announcing uncle Wm. Pangburn's death! It caused me to sit a long time buried in deep meditation! I was about to write him a stirring letter. I wish to know the particulars of the case as soon as possible. Has Tip recovered from his sickness yet? I hope his Court Martial may go well with him. Did Caroline come back with uncle John Young? How long did he stay there, and what did he think of matters in general? 'Tis strange that none of my friends who come to Boston do not know that I am here. How many bushalls of onions did that pach yield? It must have been much trouble to take care of them while growing. I did not really think that they would grow so large. I'de like to see them. That was a large one you sent me the measurement of! I hope the boys will have many a good corn-poping frolic next winter. That was a heavy loss for Mr. Bigfords! Has Ezra got home with Sally yet!

I am well and have been in good health ever since I arrived here. It is very pleasant weather here for the time of year: last night was the coldest we have yet experienced: but I have seen no frost, nor snow here. I have written a long letter to aunt Marguerate (as I was not certain that Joel was at home) and requested her to send me a paper when she got it: She kindly sent two, and I observed that snow had fell even this early! Last night I rec'd two letters, one from Mary Jane and one from Fanny, which gave me much satisfaction and pleasure. Fanny speaks of a snow-storm in that section, and says that aunt Susan and Clarrissa are there. Where is uncle William and Caroline? It is the first letters I have had from either of them since I left home. They report themselves in good health. Fanny says the children all go to school but George: the school-house is but about 60 rods distant. Mary Jane begins by giving me a good *combing* for not writing to her before. But she says mine of Sept. 23 is before her and is an old buster! she wishes next time I would write ten sheets. She inquired who my sweetheart was that I left behind to mourn for me! Nary one. "Now, she says "my little brother, the first cent you get do you please to send me your likeness with your uniform, gun, sword, pistol, knapsack, blanket and all on." I wonder if she did'nt think that infantry carried cannons too? She says she has about as much of an idea of war as a goose. They have not heard from Perry and Aaddie in a long time: they were in a battle but none of the company were killed. That was a neat picture on your letter. Where did you get it? I seen you giving me a drink of water! I have written to Emory recently. I suppose he has got it. The number of prisoners has increased to 170. They do not send any more away. I expect we will all be quartered here this winter. A mountain of coal has been shiped here and two boatload of wood; and another boatload of wood has just arrived and being unloaded. Upwards of 50 of the prisoners were engaged with wheelbarrows moving the coal, also with a large cart and about 20 to draw it. A great many are sawing and spliting; some are diging and fixing the batteries: those who are carpenters are repairing things; painters are at their trade, the masons are walling under our barracks which sets up sevral feet from the ground: a shop has been built expressly for two or three blacksmiths: we sometimes get a little job done by them on the sly and generally give them soap, candles, tobacco, or something, which they highly appreciate. Most of the new recruits have now learned the guard duty so that we now always get two nights in bed and sometimes three. Did you read any of my compositions? I felt green to think of your paying so much to get those books when I expected to send them home without cost. I might as well burned them as far as their value is concerned! Are Lorinda and Jane in Lockport yet? Who were those visitors you said was comeing to see us next winter? Do people inquire of me? Has anyone joined the church since I left? I want you to have that row of quince trees extended from end to end of the garden by the time I get home If I ever do. I have rec'd pay to the amount of $32,71. I have sent home $20: when I was at Boston I spent $4,56 for the following articles. Razor, strap, box, soap & brush $1,41: four photographs $1,00 Knife & Fork combined for the pocket $1,00: gloves & mittens 70 cts: funnel to fill canteens 10 c white thread 04c: to the barber for haircuting shaving and having my head shampooned 31cts. I paid the Sutler $1,50 subscribed for the Intelligencer for Mary Jane $1,00, leant $2,00 until next pay-day, and the rest I have yet. Mary Jane did not write any thing about geting that paper and I guess that dollar is a gonner. Now as soon as you get this send me 12 new postage stamps: those we get here have been passed so much they are soiled up badly and it is not safe to send a valuable letter with one on, as was the case with that. I wrote to the Editor to send me a paper if he got it but none came. Do you know that I gave Jason Pettit that coat? tell what was said about it. I have left in my housewife, that I brought from home, the needles, yarn, comb and most of the buttons. I suppose there was a good turnout to election day before yesterday. If I was at home I could voted "ye see" Tell Father perhaps I can get him a two berrel gun sometime, but furloughs to go so far these times are but few: though A boy got one for 15 days to go to Buffalo and deserted. In times of peace a soldier is granted 30 days a year for furloughs and I think more. But I will close for I have not space to write much more.

Direct your letters 11th U.S. Infantry
or 'twill be thought I'm a volunteer.,

> Your's truly,
> Ira S. Pettit.
> Co. B. 2nd Batt[n]
> 11th U.S. Infantry.

Thursday 6: A steady rain last night made it bad for us to walk post. Heavy wind & bitter cold. It made our fingers sing to to hold the guns while drilling this afternoon. Capt. Latimer officer of the day.

Friday 7: Windy stormy & cold. No drill. First fall of snow!!! Worst day yet. Slopy. Bentzoni officer of the day.

Saturday 8: Stormy again this morning. I mounted guard as supernumerary. Capt. Latimer officer of the day.

Sunday 9: Rained and blowed severely all day. Cold. Chislem* deserted his post last night and with three prisoners escaped in a boat! left his gun only. I being supernumerary was called up to walk the rest of his time, only 2 hours. Picket, 2nd relief. Lieut. Bentzoni officer of the day. Countersign Fort Monroe.

Monday 10: Detailed with two others for the cooks police. Froze last night: came off clear. Pleasant day. Capt. Latimer officer of the day.

Tuesday 11: On guard, post no: 3, 3[d] relief. Got of the sutler $2 worth tickets last sunday. Brilliant Meteor this evening. Countersign;—Forwart. Rec'd a paper from sister Lucina. Cool but pleasant. Lieut. Bentzoni officer of the day.

Wednesday 12: The boat which Sentinel Chislem and the three prisoners deserted in last saturday night was found and brought here to day. Nothing has been heard from the deserters. Capt. Thomas is now here trying to form a co. from the prisoners! It is to be company C.

---

*See diary entry August 1, 1862, and page 362.

Thursday 13: Warm and pleasant again. Rec'd a letter from Mr. R. Tenny. Over 30 of the prisoners have enlisted in Co. C! Capt. Thomas officer of the day.

Friday 14: On guard; post No. 1; 3^d relief. Co. C. is now equiped and being drilled. Pleasant weather. Lieut. Bentzoni officer of the day.

Saturday 15: Cleaning up for inspection tomorrow. Cool. Capt. Latimer officer of the day.

Sunday 16: Inspection early before guard mount. Froze last night. Lieut. Bentzoni officer of the day.

Monday 17: On guard; post no. 3, 3^d relief. Rained all day, but good to-night. Countersign: Texas. Capt. Latimer officer of the day.

Tuesday 18: Company C. is progressing finely. Fine day. Lieut. Bentzoni officer of the day.

Wednesday 19: Rained all day. No drill. Nothing else special. Capt. Latimer officer of the day.

Thursday 20: On guard:—post No. 3; 3^d relief. Rainy day & night. Capt. Thomas officer of the day.

Friday 21: All had to shift and take bunks alphabetically. I now bunk with Corp'l Hickey instead of private Dunkelberg.*

Rainy day: no drill. Got a letter from sister Lucina & little Lucina. Went to South Boston as one of the boats crew: we got aground, had to wait for the tide and got drenched with rain.

Saturday 22: Stormy all day. Done the usual scrubing.

Sunday 23: Came off clear and cold this morning. On guard post No. 4; 2nd relief. Sent a letter to Little Lucina. Countersign; Watertown. Capt. Thomas officer of the day.

Monday 24: The coldest night yet: we felt it keenly while on post. To day is clear but cold: it makes our fingers sing while on drill. Bentzoni officer of the day.

Tuesday 25: Went to South Boston as one of the boats crew twice this fore noon. A number of prisoners were sent off and we brought over 7 recruits.

*See page 315.

82

Wednesday 26: On guard: post No. 4, 3^d relief. Rained all day and nearly all night: we stood in the sentry-boxes while on post. A number of prisoners arrived and about 120 volunteers of the 8th Mass. who will stay here a few days.

Thursday 27: Thanksgiving Day. No drill nor any other duty. Came off clear and pleasant this moring. Had a rusty lot of guns to clean after coming off guard this morning. Pleasant.

Friday 28: Sent a letter to cousin Daniel Sitterly; and also one of my photographs. Fine day. The volunteers drilled. Capt. Thomas officer of the day.

Saturday 29: On guard; post No. 1: 1st relief. got rid of the scrubing. Fine day. Capt. Latimer officer of the day.

Sunday 30: Monthly Inspection got rid of it before guard mount. Rained last night. Sent a letter to Sister Mary Jane.

DECEMBER, 1862

Monday 1: Heavy shower of rain. No drill. Dress Parade tonight! First we've had in a long time.

Tuesday 2: On guard: post No. 1; 3^d relief. Good weather. Dress parade. to be held every night now again. Prendergast sergt. of the guard. Lieut. Pratt officer of the day.

Wednesday 3: Capt. Latimer officer of the day. Froze quite hard last night Clear; and pleasant moonlight. One-hundred-and-eleven prisoners to leave here tomorrow! Ten of co. B are detailed for detatched service to escort them to Washington.

Thursday 4: Lieut. Bentzoni officer of the day. One-hundred-and-seven prisoners left this after-noon for Washington. An escort of 11 of co. B. went with them. Still and pleasant.

Friday 5: Fifty-seven recruits arrived this night from Indianapolis. Rained and snowed tremenduously! Fourteen more prisoners came! The boys had much dificulty geting through Boston with the prisoners yesterday. Some of the prisoners were shot and bayoneted!!!

Saturday 6: Capt. Latimer officer of the day. On guard post no. 1; 1st relief. Ground covered with snow. The 20 volunteers who arrived here Nov. 26th left at 11, o'clock A.M. Bright moonlight nights.

Sunday 7: From 3, o'clock until guard mount this morning, it was so windy and cold we had to be relieved every hour. Got rid of the weekly inspection again being on guard. Capt. Thomas officer of the day.

Monday 8: We feel the cold keenly. No drill. Sweeny (a prisoner) died yesterday or saturday.

Tuesday 9: Not so cold. We drilled. The recruits are being put through. All of co. B. signed the pay roll!

Wednesday 10: Sergeant Boyce, with the prisoners escort, arrived this fore noon from Washington. They succeeded in getting there 91 out of the 111. They shot a number !!! We received pay! I got $23,75.

Thursday 11: On guard yesterday; post No. 1, 3^d relief and got a letter from cousin Dudley of P.A. First dress-parade this evening in some time. Corp's Keely and Blair are reduced to the ranks for drunkenness.

Friday 12: One of the 57 recruits, who arrived last friday night, died last evening. Thaws fast. Went as one of a boat's crew with the Capt. to see the new "Monitor." Lieut Pratt officer of the day.

Saturday 13: Military funeral at 3, o'clock P.M. The first I ever witnessed! Lieut. Bentzoni officer of the day.

Sunday 14: On guard. Post No. 1, 2nd relief. Capt. Thomas officer of the day.

Monday 15: No drill for co. B. Another of the recruits died last night. Lieut Wright officer of the day.

Tuesday 16: Another Military Funeral. I am one of the firing party! The snow has all disappeared. Lieut Pratt officer of the day.

Wednesday 17: Co. B. did not drill this A.M. A number have lately deserted from this co. when on pass; namely:—Miller, Youst, Mc.Donnell, Clevland, Wood, Pewett, Kelly, Finton, Cook and Chislem* from Post on night of Nov. 8th. Lieut Bentzoni officer of the day.

Thursday 18: Sent a letter to Sewell Miller. On guard: post No. 1; 3^d relief. Froze last night. So cold this morning that tis very uncomfortable to drill. Capt. Thomas officer of the day.

Friday 19: We had a skermish drill this P.M. *Finished the new Testament and commenced the old.* Lieut. Wright officer of the day.

---

*See page 362.

85

Saturday 20: Very cold last night, and to-day it cuts keenly; rather cold scrubing out the quarters this P.M. Lieut. Pratt officer of the day.

Sunday 21: On guard:—Post No. 2, 2nd relief. Lieut. Bentzoni officer of the day.

Monday 22: Got a pass to go to the City and be absent until 10.30 tomorrow. Got three dollars worth of pictures taken. Stayed over night at Wrights N. 14 Portland Street. Another of the prisoners died this morning which makes the third one in a short time.

Tuesday 23: Took boat at 10 A.M. for the Fort. Got my boots taped, bought a few necessary vittles &c and kept sober. Leant five dollars to Beals co. C. and took a watch worth 10 for security. Lieut. Wright officer of the day.

Wednesday 24: Another funeral yesterday P.M. which makes the third one since the 13th of the present month!!! Preparations are being made to observe Christmas! Turkeys, pies, beer &c. is on hand for the dinner!

Thursday 25: "Christmas." On guard:—Post No. 4; 2nd relief. All but the guard had a merry time. Had a good dinner of fowl: two barrels of ale was furnished, had a plenty of pie.

Friday 26: A fine ball went off here last evening, the boys got a lot of girls from Boston to dance. The cook house was fixed up finely in military style. Capt. Thomas officer of the day. Bentzoni yesterday.

Saturday 27: All the snow has disappeared. Very warm and pleasant again. Saw the new floating battery "Monitor" steam out on her trial trip. Lieut. Wright officer of the day. Mrs. Sergt. Boyce died.

Sunday 28: Weekly Inspection. On guard: post No. 1; 3d relief. Still and pleasant. A large number are on the sick list and in the hospital so we get but two nights rest to being on guard one.

Monday 29: Pleasant day. I have been in the service just seven months. 48 prisoners left or taken away last saturday. Officer of the day yesterday, Lieut. Pratt, to-day Lieut Bentzoni.

Tuesday 30: No drill, as we had to clean up for monthly inspection which is to be to-morrow. Capt. Thomas officer of the day.

Wednesday 31: Quite a snow storm last night. The inspection came off this A.M. and we were again mustered for pay. I got a letter from aunt Marguerate and finished one to cousin Dudley. I weigh 145 lbs. Gained. Farewell to 1862. Lieut. Wright officer of the day.

MEMORANDA
(page 1)

In a different hand, there is written:

> Henry Fessenden
> Naples
> Ontario, Co
> *N.Y.*

and in Ira's hand: "The above P. O. adress was written by a deaf mute." Perhaps this is the person to whom he refers on Tuesday, July 8, 1862.

(page 2)

My fathers name and Postoffice adress are as follows:

> Clinton Pettit,
> Wilson, Niag. Co.
> N.Y.
> Ira S. Pettit
> Company B.
> 11th regt. infantry
> U.S.A.

EIGHTEEN HUNDRED SIXTY-THREE

as we march through
the valleys and shadows
our muskets comfort us

Private Pettit's boot training at Fort Independence was drawing to a fast close as the year 1862 ended.

With three days' rations in their canteens and haversacks, the men of the Eleventh Regiment of the U.S. Regulars set out on January 6, 1863, for the South and their appointment with Johnny Reb.

Enroute to camp at Falmouth, Virginia, the train was held over in Baltimore, Maryland, and it was there that Ira visited for a few hours with other soldiers from Wilson and Lockport who were stationed at Lafayette Barracks.

On January 9, 1863, Ira was in his nation's capitol, which he evidently enjoyed seeing.

At the time of Ira's arrival at the camp at Falmouth, General Burnside was still smarting from the faux pas which had been Fredericksburg. Most of Ira's January diary has been torn out, but we know from other sources and from one of his letters home that he had accompanied General Burnside on his 'Mud March' the latter part of that month.

History tells us that on January 20, Burnside led his army up the Rappahannock, intending to cross it and strike the Rebels a devastating blow. An unwanted and drenching rain turned the roads to mud, and this Yankee army could not navigate in the foreign mire of Virginia terrain. Burnside eventually got his army back to camp and his resignation to the President, and General Joe Hooker promptly succeeded him.

The rest of the winter and the early spring of 1863 was spent in camp near Falmouth with guard duty and picket duty consuming most of Private Pettit's time.

91

It was during this season that Ira became ill and was off duty for a short period. His medicine consisted of quinine and whiskey. By now, the soldiers were sleeping in wedge and shelter tents—on the ground. The dampness no doubt contributed greatly to the many cases of tuberculosis among the Union soldiers, and the dry cough which Ira mentioned makes one surmise that he may have been one of those who contracted it.

In early April Abe Lincoln reviewed the troops. Ira's regiment marched about five miles to the parade grounds for this display, just across the river from and in view of Fredericksburg. The Battle of Chancellorsville was soon to erupt nearby, and Lincoln's visit was perhaps intended to inspire a patriotic fervor that would carry many of these newly-made soldiers into battle.

As May 1863 approached, the Army of the Potomac numbered about one hundred, thirty-four thousand well equipped troops, while Lee's Army of Northern Virginia totalled approximately sixty thousand troops, not so well supplied or equipped.

On April 27, 1863, General Hooker sent three of his seven corps (the Fifth, in which was Ira, the Eleventh and the Twelfth, in which were Marvin Pettit, William Holmes, and others of Ira's friends and relatives) marching across the Rappahannock and Rapidan rivers toward Fredericksburg, bent upon entrapping Lee's army.

On the night of April 30, Ira writes of General Hooker's ultimatum to Robert E. Lee for surrender, retreat, or immediate destruction. And with such assurances from their general, the men of the Army of the Potomac slept peacefully.

As the first day of May dawned upon him Robert E. Lee did not consider surrender or retreat, and he did not anticipate destruction. Generals Lee and Jackson *attacked*. And on May 2 Jackson marched around Hooker and *attacked*. On May 3 Jeb Stuart, leading Jackson's saddened, weary men, *attacked again*, and Ira was among those who

92

fled the battlefield. His letter home, dated May 18, 1863, tells about a small segment of this retreat of the Army of the Potomac during the Battle of Chancellorsville.

The imminent peril of battle may have contributed to the decision of Private John McMann, Company B, Eleventh Regiment, U.S. Infantry, to suspend his connections with the Army of the Potomac, as he took leave at Aquia Creek on May 15, 1863. But his leave was by no means the end of his association with the Eleventh U.S. Regulars.

Shortly after his introduction to war at Chancellorsville, Ira's regiment began its movement northward toward Gettysburg—his duties being that of guarding post while encamped and guarding supplies and Sesech and other prisoners while in transit. They covered many hard miles in the northeastern part of Virginia, crossing the Potomac River into Maryland at Edward's Ferry near Leesburg, as they hunted Lee on his second attempt to invade the North. They passed near Frederick, Maryland, going toward Hanover, Pennsylvania.

It was shortly after crossing the Potomac, and before they came to Frederick, that Ira saw Battery M, of the Twelfth Corps, which was made up of many Wilson men. He saw the One Hundred Eleventh Pennsylvania Volunteers, also of the Twelfth Corps, in which was his cousin Marvin Pettit.

On July 1, 1863, the Eleventh Regiment passed near Hanover, Pennsylvania, not far behind a force of Rebels.

The Fifth Corps arrived on the battlefield on the morning of July 2, and Barnes' and Ayres' Divisions (Ira was in Ayres' Division) were dispatched barely in time to save Little Round Top from capture. Although the struggle was agonizingly horrendous and prolonged, they had successfully assisted in maintaining a part of Cemetery Ridge. At the end of that day many of the march-worn and battle-weary men of Sykes' Fifth Corps were at ease in death.

It was at Gettysburg that Captain Thomas Oliver Barri, Ira's recruiting officer, received the wounds that took his life before July 2, 1863, had ended. And it was on that day at Gettysburg, also, that First Lieutenant Irvin B. Wright was breveted captain.

After the battle ended, the Army of the Potomac pursued Lee southward from Pennsylvania. Ira's regiment again crossed South Mountain in Maryland and camped at the foot of it. It was here that Ira and Willie Holmes of Battery M had a chance to chat briefly. This, in all likelihood, was their last visit with each other.

On its return to Virginia, the Eleventh Regiment camped briefly near Beverly Ford, and from there it was ordered from the field. The men of the Eleventh Regiment were sent in mid-August to Alexandria and then by ship to New York City for rest and recreation, returning to Virginia in mid-September.

The Twelfth Corps, of which Willie Holmes, Harvey Pease, and Marvin Pettit were a part, was dispatched to the Army of the Cumberland, and theirs became another and different story.

—DIARY—

Ira S. Pettit
Wilson, Niagara Co. N.Y.
Co. B. 2nd Battalion
11th Infantry. U.S.A.

JANUARY, 1863

Headquarters 11th U.S. Infantry,
Fort Independence Boston Harbor Mass.
Jan. 4th 1863

Dear Sister Lucina:—

The last I received from you reached here Dec. 4th just one month ago. I presume you have been anxious to hear from me before but as I wrote to one of our north neighbors I concluded that you would hear something of my welfare. But now as the time of our departure is near at hand I of course will let you know. I wrote a letter to Clinty and sent it today inclosing a $5 treasury note for him to give to father. I will also send $5 more in this letter and also pay you up for those stamps which you were so kind to send me: hereafter when you write me a letter always inclose a stamp as I cannot tell whether they are easily obtained where we are going or not. It is candlelight. I wrote to Clinton that were destined for Fredricksburg, but orders were read to-night on dress-parade that we would leave for Falmouth V.A. on tuesday Dec. 6th* instead of monday as I wrote to Clinton. I wrote to him some particulars which I will not take take time now to state. There are not quite 100 prisoners here now as 10 armed

*He must have meant to write January.

95

soldiers of our co. escorted 111 to Washington near the 1st of Dec. 48 were sent for not long ago and the rest or most all, we will take to Washington with us. Co. C. is full and will stay here at headquarters yet awhile. We will go to join our regiment and will again see co. A and the splendid regimental band "which are away down South in Dixie." Half of co. C are those who were once prisoners but prefered to enlist in the regulars than to be sent to their regiments. Monday, Dec. 5th* It is pleasant today and we are packing our knapsacks to be in readiness to start. I have just bought a rubber blanket for $1,50. I have my other also. We were paid some time ago for Sept. and Oct. and we have again been mustered for our pay for Nov. and Dec. Would get it in a short time if we were to remain here, but cant tell when we will get it now. I rec'd 23,75 cts. only $1 was kept back from each month's wages this time and the shilling per. month which goes to the soldiers Home. I will send home my pay by $5 at a time as I write. I was to Boston and stayed over night before Christmas, which cost me five dollars. I had $3 worth of pictures taken. Paid 62 cts. for supper, lodgeings and breakfast at Wrights No. 14 Portland St. gave 75 cts for getting my boots taped! The eight photographs have not come yet and if they do not come with to-morrow's mail I will have to go without them: but presume all mail coming here for us when gone will be forwarded to us. They may have sent them and got miscarried for it is time they were here long ago. You know it takes sevral days to finish them. I guess I will write to-morrow and have them send them all to you in two letters. Lucina I went to old Faneuill Hall which Daniel Webster used to rock with His eloquence. I did not have quite time to go to Bunker Hill. I sent that letter back in Clintons letter. When I get to the field I will write again immediately so you will know my P. O. Adress. I rec'd a long and good letter from aunt

---

*This, also, must be an inadvertent reference to December rather than January.

Marguerate Dec. 31st in reply to one which I wrote to her some time ago. She gave me Joels P. O. adress and I wrote him a long letter the next day. I have rec'd a letter from Dudley and sent a reply newyears. I have not had a reply from my letter which I wrote to Emory but tell them I will write again soon when I get in V.A. I can then tell you about the big fights with the Rebs. May be Ill get killed but no matter: Uncle Sam has used me tiptop since Ive been with Him and I'll fight like jehu for him. He pays me good wages clothes me well and takes me "all over" for nothing. Perhaps you think Im speaking lightly, Siny, but I feel good. God in his mercy has given me good health thus far for which I am truly thankful. I've gained a number of lbs on bread and coffee since I have been on this little Isle. My Bible must find a place in my knapsack somewhere. It is whole yet and makes me think of you. I finished the testament again and got a good ways in the Old and will soon make a finish of that. I do not nor will not yield to the many evil influences which surround us; for trying to do right has cost me too much self denial to ever turn back. I'de write a different letter than this if I had time but I will have to cut it short now. I will write a little more tomorrow just before we start off.

Yours truly
Ira S. Pettit
Co. B 2nd Battalion
11th Infantry U.S.A.

None of our boys are on guard to day in consequence of going of tomorrow.   Ira.

P.S. Tuesday morning Dec. 6th* We are now ready Lucina we will start at 2 o'clock P.M. The weather is agreeable we will not wear our great coats. We are in shining order. The prisoners are being got readdy to go with us: we have each

---

*Here, again, he must have meant January rather than December.

ten rounds of amunition and three days rations. in our canteens and harversacks. But Adieu.

Now for the field!

Ira.

Washington D.C., Jan. 10th 1863.

My Dear Father:—

It has now been some time since I have written directly to you. I am now in the City which is the Capitol of *our* Country. Before starting from Fort Independence I wrote two letters, one to Sister Lucina and the other to Clinton Pangburn with $5 inclosed in each for them to give to you. I suppose therefore that you are aware of my starting. From Boston we went to New London C.T. and Took the steamer "City of New York" and after a night of riding the length of Long Island Sound on rough waters we arrived at Jersey City just before sunrise which is oposite of New York. We took cars for Philadelphia from thence to Baltimore and had a smash-up on the road which delayed us a long time. It was in the night and most of us were asleep but were awakened by a sudden halt which pitched some who were standing "endways"! No one was badly hurt in our cars. On arriving at Baltimore I had the extreme of talking a long time with Capt. Lurin Wilson, Enoch Pettit, Azor Shearor and his brother Wm.* and other boys from Wilson of the 151st regt. N.Y. V. Little did I expect to see anyone whom I knew there. We then started on the 8 evening train and after a safe and the fastest ride I ever had, we arrived in Washington at 11 in the night and slept on our blankets upon the floor until dawn. The next day which was yesterday friday the 9th. I went up to the Capitol building and went most all over it. It was an interesting time to me. I wish you could have been here too. I also got my picture taken out doors which I will send you. I stand at "Shoulder Arms." The sun shone so that I could not look natural. It made me scoul. Those buildings

---

*See pages 329 and 340.

which you see behind me are barracks for soldiers the nearest is where we are quartered. I put an extra bayonet in my scabbard which you can see. The cap box is in view but the cartrige box hangs well behind. We did not take any prisoners with us as we calculated at first. We will start for the regiment which is at Falmouth V.A. perhaps to morrow and maybe not in sevral days. but I will write as soon as I get there. I am in good health, never better.

> But I must close.
> I am thoughtful of all.
> From Your Boy
> Ira

(The following notes referencing the Capitol were enclosed with the preceding letter.)

Dimentions of the U.S. Capitol

Whole extent of Building

751 ft. 21 in. Length of wings, including steps, 324 ft. Width of Wings, 142 ft. 8 in.

Width of old Capitol   352,   41

Area of ground actually covered 153,112 sq. ft. or more than 3½ acres.

Height of Dome above basement floor 264 feet.

Lucina, as I write this I stand in the National Capitol.

Saturday, JANUARY 31, 1863: On guard; post No. 2, 2nd relief. Monthly inspection according to custom on the last day of every month. Pleasant.

(Pages covering the first 30 days of January, 1863, have been torn from the diary. Historically, it would seem that the most significant military happening during that period for Ira's 11th Regiment was Burnside's "Mud March" which took place January 20-24, 1863.)

FEBRUARY, 1863

Sunday 1: Read my bible. Our company drew shelter tents.
Monday 2: Drying off so that it is some better to get about. The whole regiment is to go out on picket tomorrow.
Tuesday 3: Started out early with three days rations and all of our accoutrements; Distance to the line three miles.
Wednesday 4: We are on the second relief. This is our first experience in picket duty.
Thursday 5: Rain and snow. Rec'd two letters one from Mary Jane and one from cousin Dudley.
Friday 6: Continues to rain: we keep tolerably dry in our shelter tents. We are in the forrest and keep big fires.
Saturday 7: Froze up last night. We were relieved this morning in good season and returned to camp. I think it the best kind of duty. Done my washing. Pleasant.
Sunday 8: Read my Bible. Finished Deuteronomy.

                       Wilson   Feb 8th 1863

Dear Brother

Is it possible that you have not received my letter, I have waited long and anxiously to hear from you; as I am now living in the village and attending school. I watch the office Daily, but night after night I am oblige to return to my room with no tidings from you, and that you say you have written 2 or 3 letters to us but received no answer: we received yours safely money pictures & all, and I replied as soon as we received your directions which you sent to Emory. Clarrissa and I wrote together 2 weeks ago to-day, and I enclosed a postage stamp for you to send one back as you requested me to in your last letter. I wrote quite a long letter and hope you may get it yet, for fear you will not, I will simply state a few particulars in this; I wrote in that of my journey to Rochester, and the Death of Milton Whitneys little boy; also the sudden death of the widdow Pettit, she arose in the morning and was building a fire she fell dead in a fit of the apoplex (ap o plex). Harriet Mix is also dead and buried; there has been a great many deaths here lately, I only write of those with whom you were acquainted, as we were going to church to day the tolling bell again sounded upon our ears, it was for a young man 19 years of age, his name is Borum. it is a sad thing to walk through our cemetery and see the newly made graves there. Mr. King said he dug 7 *graves* in 2 weeks. Oh Ira I tremble at the thought of your being away from home, we may never see each other again, but may we be prepared for death so that we may meet in Heaven to part no more. I am aware that life is short, and that our days are all numbered, I hope you will not be neglectful in Prayer, and while *you* pray remember our Father who *never* prays, for he must die as well as we, and what will be his condition without a Savior. Mother says I must write for her while she is getting dinner and tell you she wishes you were here to eat. Father has a very lame back, Tip Wright has got home again, he has his discharge he is so glad he says he does not want to hear from war any more nor any one that is there. Ira you must write as often as you can we always get your letters and always answer them when I know where to direct them if you do not get a letter from me every time you write one you may they have been mislaid for I shall be prompt in answering and so must you. Father says so.

I received a letter from Mary Jane a week or 2 ago she is well she says her baby is the smartest one this side the rocky mountains. Uncle Green went south after Perry (he was sick) while he was gone one of his twin (Loren) boys died, and was buried be fore he got home. Ed has sold his place to Erv Brewer, he and the girls lives together. I can

think of nothing to write at present and I want to write to
mary jane so I will close So Good bye for to-night

> From your affectionate
> Sister
> Lucina Pettit

Monday 9: Funeral of private Mullen co. A. 2ⁿᵈ Battalion, at
retreat. Agreeable weather again.
Tuesday 10: Drew more rations of loaf bread! quite a rarity.
Drying off finely.
Wednesday 11: Detailed for guard. Rainy this P.M.
Received a letter from Sister Lucina.
Thursday 12: On guard; post Nº 4, 2ⁿᵈ relief. Pleasant
again.
Friday 13: We have scarcely any duty; not even to drill, but
every man has to do his own cooking in our company, as
most of the utensils are lost.
Saturday 14: Wrote a letter to Georgie. Received one from
Lucina last evening. Three days rations were issued to go
out on picket to-morrow.
Sunday 15: Started out on picket this morning in the rain
which continued until noon: then it cleared up and we
made ourselves comfortable.
Monday 16: Weather to-day is pleasant and agreeable.
Devoted my leisure to writing a letter to Sister Lucina. We
are kept on reserve. None of us went on post.

Monday Feb. 16
Dear Sister   I wrote to George last Saturday and hoped to
have it mailed to-day so it would be sure to reach you this
week certain for I am aware that you are uneasy not having
rec'd a letter from me in so long a time. Saturday night we
were issued three days rations each and ordered to be
prepared to start out on picket early in the morning—our
whole regiment and sevral others also. I had about all I
could do to pack up and get ready for we most always take
along everything we have for it is not safe to leave

anything behind. I therefore brought the letter with me and thought I would write a a few lines to you. It rained steadily from the time we left our camp early Sunday morning until we reached the place where we were to be posted but my rubber blanket and haverlock kept me and my knapsack quite dry. However it came off clear; we stacked our arms pitched our shelter tents built fires and made ourselves as comfortable as we could wish for. We are about 5 miles from camp and there are two lines of pickets beyond us still. As we are the third relief we will not have to go on post until wednesday. I would rather be out here than in camp. We find any quantity of sassafras and make lots of tea. Our rations consist of four hard crackers for each meal a lot of pork and a good ammount of coffee and sugar which we make in our cups: you ought to see us cook. You had a fine time while on your visit to Rochester I suppose. Has Fanny been back to Wilson? You say she told you that she wrote to me. I received the letter in due time and was highly pleased to hear from her. I have not yet answered it. Mrs. Pettit died very suddenly indeed! I was very sad news. I wrote to that photographer in Boston to send you those 8 photographs if he had them to inclose them in two separate envelopes and also to write me a letter concealing them. I sent 25 cts for his trouble but have not heard a word from him; have you? His name is J. D. Heywood 145 Hanover St. No matter. What for a school do you run at the seminary and who goes? Where do you live? I hope you have a good time. To day is very warm and pleasant and I am enjoying myself finely leaning with my back against a stump writing in the sunshine. I feel well and strong to-day and hope to enjoy good health so as to be able to do my duty while we are in the field. Tell Clarrissa she must write again. In this letter I will send you a list of every letter I have written or received since I came to the fort until now. Those soldiers who were garrisoned at fort Niagara a year ago have been exchanged or something and are here close by us. It was

Co. G 7th regulars. I have talked with them a number of times. Lucina, you spoke of having my body sent home if I should die or get killed; but what better am I than 10,000s of of others who have died and are buried here? Better give yourself no uneasiness about that. Mr. Whitneys folks must feel quite bad as they have lost their only child. I also rec'd a letter from Mary Jane not long ago. she spoke of Perry's being discharged and the death of one of the twins while uncle Alonzo was gone after him. O she says how bad he felt. She brags big of her little girl. Harriet Mix is dead too then! I had been anxious to hear from him for sometime. So he has succeeded in getting his discharge at last? How is he now broken down in health? Did Sewell Miller ever get my letter as you know of? You need'nt ask him. You say Mother asks you to write for her while she is getting dinner and wishes I was there to eat. I would like a good meal at home now right well. If I could but get into the cellar once I'll bet Ide have some apples and other things. There are plenty of Sutlers here who keep all the good things for sale but they have their own prices though and nearly all the soldiers as soon as they get pay spend it nearly all to get something good to eat. I will not deal a bit with them as such prices. I can live on my rations. Apples are 5 & 6 cents apiece and other things accordingly. I went to him to get a common bottle of ink and he charged 20 cts! I let him keep it. Paper and envelopes are sold for like prices. My supply which I brought along is not yet gone. when you write send me all the paper and envelopes you can for the 3 cts. I will pay you well for it. All the small currency that I send home I mean for you to have and you have not so much as mentioned it to me. I have also asked what was said about that coat I gave Jason Pettit.* You seem particular not to make any reply about anything I ask you. Mary Jane too after a scolding has made out to let me know that she gets the Intelligencer I subscribed for her

*See Pages 80 and 333.

104

months ago. I saw Miss Scott's alias Griswold and Mat's wedding in an Intelligencer sent to one of our boys who lived in Lockport. I suppose Mat. now thinks himself all O.K. Do you ever go to visit Lorinda and Jane in their new habitation up yonder on the Lake road? I hope they will be able to buy it and have a good home. But I must close for the present. Well Lucina, we have got back into camp; and O what a time we have had! It commenced to snow monday night and continued all day Tuesday thawing partly as it fell. Wednesday we were relieved and tramped back again into camp through the mud and mist a long five miles. We were on no relief at all only held back as a reserve. There were 2 or 3 lines of pickets beyond us. It comes our turn to go out about every 10 days. You would think just to see the picket go out that a large army was on the move. To-day is Thursday the 19th. Last night the rain poured in torrents and and a heavy mist prevailed until noon to-day: but I think the storm will now cease. Even if we have fine weather it will take a long—long time for the roads to become good. No movement is possible now. I have just rec'd an Intelligencer from a friend and in it I notice the account of our getting stuck in the mud the time we undertook to make an advance on Fredricksburg. I also noticed the death of one of the Davis boys of the town-line. It was Samuel Davis I think I never knew him he belonged to Co. G 2nd Ill. Artillery at La-Grange, Tenn. his case was Typhoid Pneumonia aged 31 yrs. Do you often hear from Jane Reeves and Eliza? How do they prosper? You hardly ever mention uncle Stephen's folks when you write. I dont believe you are on good terms with one another. Emory owes me two letters. Now Lucina if read this letter to anyone exercise your judgement and not mention every little stingy sounding thing and what I intended that none but you should know about. What are you studies? Tell Clarra I am glad to learn that she goes to the seminary. But I must stop writing. This letter will not get off until to-morrow. I am all right now and if I am not so then I will mention it. Now for a big draught of good sweetened coffee.

From your Brother Ira S. Pettit Co. B. 2nd Battalion. 11th Regulars.

(The preceding letter was superimposed crosswise upon the letter his sister Lucina had written to Ira, dated February 8, 1863.)

Tuesday 17: Commenced snowing last night and continued all day; making it disagreeable in the extreme. It partly thaws as it falls or it would make easily eight inches.

Wednesday 18: We were relieved this morning and returned to camp through deep mud and in a sleety storm which continued all day. Got $1,00 worth of articles at our sutlers on credit.

Thursday 19: Rained nearly all night. A heavy mist now prevails. Received a paper from Mr. Tenny.

Friday 20: I was sent out with a large detail to throw up fortifications near the Rail road bridge crossing Potomac Creek. I used the pick-ax. Pleasant.

Saturday 21: Twenty more were detailed out of our company for the same duty as yesterday. Sergeant Ricketts is being court martialed.

Sunday 22: Washington's Birthday. Salutes were fired by the Batteries. Heavy snow-storm last night. The cold embraces us snugly.

Monday 23: On guard; post N° 5, 3d relief. Pleasant overhead. Snow is about eight inches deep. Received a letter from uncle William's family.

Tuesday 24: Another detail of twenty were sent out to work on the forts at Potomac Creek R. R. Bridge.

Wednesday 25: The same 20 who were on fatigue yesterday went out again to-day. Very sloppy. Pleasant overhead.

Thursday 26: On Brigade guard; post N° 2, at the commisary, 2nd relief. Rained: had rather a wet time on guard. Snow most gone. Got a dollars worth of rasins of the sutler on credit. 2 lbs.

Friday 27: On fatigue duty at the commisary. Saw a Reb. cavalryman brought in by our pickets. Some of our pickets have been driven in and we are ordered to be prepared for an attack. One of our band died.

Saturday 28: I set up last night in the hospital. Funeral of a member of the Band. I am one of the firing escort. Capt. Barri arrived to-night. Monthly Inspection. Mustered for four months pay. Rec'd letter from Mr. Tenny.

Note:

Perhaps the following excerpt is responsible for the diary entry of February, Friday 27, 1863:

"On the 9th of February Fitz Lee's brigade broke up camp in Caroline County, where it had been stationed since the battle of Fredericksburg, and moved to Culpeper Court House, where, on the 12th, it relieved Hampton's brigade, and assumed the duty of picketing the upper Rappahannock. On the 24th General Fitz Lee crossed the Rappahannock at Kelly's Ford with 400 men from the 1st, 2d, and 3d regiments, to make a reconnoissance on the Falmouth road, under orders from General Stuart. It will be sufficient to say, that in executing his orders General Lee advanced to Hartwood Church, where he encountered the enemy's cavalry, which he attacked and drove before him until he came within sight of the camps of the 5th corps. He captured 150 prisoners, representing seven regiments, with their horses, arms, and equipments. Among the prisoners were five commissioned officers. He returned to his camp on the 26th, having sustained a loss of 14 in killed, wounded, and missing."*

From Ira's statement it would appear that at least one of the fourteen men General Fitz Lee lost was captured by the pickets of the Second Battalion of the Second Brigade, 2nd Division, Fifth Corps, U.S. Army.

*H. B. McClellan. *I Rode with Jeb Stuart (Life and Campaigns of Major-General J. E. B. Stuart).* With an introduction and notes by Burke Davis. Bloomington: Indiana University Press, Civil War Centennial Series, 1958. p. 204.

MARCH, 1863

Sunday 1: Rained last night and until nearly noon to-day; but has again came off fine and a warm and heavy wind dries the soil rapidly. We get rations of loaf bread quite often now.

Monday 2: On the fatigue detail to work on the forts at Potomac Creek R'¹R'ᵈ bridge. Hundreds of soldiers are employed. Pleasant but rather cool.

Tuesday 3: We went to the woods and brought timber to make us a fireplace, but on returning found that the company was to be split up and sent into the 1ˢᵗ Battalion. Squally this P.M.

Wednesday 4: Another fatigue party sent out. Geting dry again.

Thursday 5: On Brigade guard: post N° (3) 2ⁿᵈ relief. The sun shines pleasant but the air is cold. Our regiment started out on picket. I being on guard did not have to go.

Friday 6: On fatigue, loading and unloading fresh beef and burying the entrails. Rec'd a letter from Emory.

Saturday 7: Wrote a letter to Lucina but did not quite finish it. Detailed for guard to-night. We who are left in camp have it all to do while the regiment is out on picket.

Camp near Falmouth V.A. March the 7ᵗʰ 1863
Dear Sister:

Your's and Emory's of Feb. 22ⁿᵈ was gladly received last evening. Tell Emory he wrote me a good letter and it was highly appreciated. I sent a letter to you and George Feb. 20ᵗʰ Directed to Geo- and presume you have got it before now. I also rec'd those other two letters you said you sent. I am glad you rec'd those pictures. Did they come in two separate envelopes as I told him to send them? did he write anything? are the pictures inferior? my eyes never take well. Give Carroline and Clarrissa each one and if they are good ones send one to Mary Jane they are of two kinds, haint they? I got Clarrissa's letter Feb. 23ᵈ tell her it was an old smasher. I read it over lots of times. You wrote about the death of one of uncle Alonzos twins during his absence after Perry and M. Jane gave me the particulars of the case. As for myself I am not in full strength but I do all my duty. I have fell away much since I came here. I have not got a cold but a dry heavy cough lurks about me: coughing is a very common thing with us all, caused perhaps by a damp sleeping place. Tents are of various kinds. Wall tents are what

officers use they are about as comfortable and have about as high living as though they were at home. Our co.

have wedge tents 5 to each tent. One whole regiment have Sibley or bell tents shaped like a bell they are very high and large around at the bottom and are best of any, will accommodate 15 and 20 a hole is in the top and a fire is made right on the ground in the centre the smoke rises and escapes through the opening at the top. All lay at night with their feet toward the fire. Then there is the shelter tent for three, there are many of those; each man carries a piece in his knapsack each piece is about 6 feet sqr or more 3 pieces buttoned togather make a tent, but hae to stoop down and crawl in: but generally wide slabs are hewn placed up edgewise and the tent raised on them, then by diging down some it affords a considerable room all tents are well ditched around outside. We gather pine boughs and spread them all over the bottom of the tent which keeps our knapsacks and blankets out of the dirt and makes it softer to lie on. All of our co. have been issued shelter tents and we always tak them with us when we go out on picket. we also at night each one lays down his piece and spread a blanket over them and cover ourselves with the rest of the blankets and overcoats we never fail to sleep warm. Our tents can be made very tight. Lucina, I have not the most of time to write now-a-days. They are building sevral small forts and diging rifle pits along a railroad bridge 2 miles from here to prevent it from being destroyed by the Rebs again. about 400 are at work on them every favorable day. We are sometimes sent out day after day. 'Tis easy diging here, by the way we can haul out heaps of sasasfras. It has snowed and rained much here lately which makes it very nasty but as soon as a storm ceases it very soon becomes dry. On Sunday, Feb. 22nd was the birthday of Washington. Each battery fired a salute. It sounded like a heavy connonading.

I did not intend to write home again until I rec'd pay but that may not be in a month yet. We were again mustered for pay the last of Feb. They now owe us 4 months pay. I can send it all home. Our fare is much better than it has been. Instead of those hard crackers constantly which I loathe we now get good loaf bread two days per. week: we often get onions, potatoes and all the fresh beef we can lay to. We get plenty of rice which I like cooked thick and sweetened or made into soup. Coffee and sugar a plenty the quality of the sugar is better than you ever get or seldom. The bakery is a great git up there are 5 ovens 60 loaves are baked at a time in each oven 2400 loaves are run out every 24 hours. It takes a lot of wood and we are often detailed to cut for it which we are willing to do for the sake of having the loaf bread. There are no prevalant diseases here now but the burial place is growing fast. I have been on two funeral escorts here the last one was one of our band. I fear we will drop off fast by sickness when warm weather comes. We have to wash and boil our clothes often to keep free from lice. I have none yet. But I will now close it has been quite fine for a number of days past but begins to get squally again.

Your's as ever.

Ira.

Capt. Barri arrived here last week. I am sorry to say that the 2nd Battalion is to be broken up to fill the 1st consequently our co. will be divided into sevral parts and what company I will now belong to comes to be seen. It causes much dissatisfaction. Some say they will stop soldering as soon as the thing is brought about. The rebs have advanced on our pickets lately but met a warm reception. I saw a captured reb cav'man as they brought him in the other night.

(The preceding letter was written, in part, on the back of a school program of Essay and Declamations in which, under DECLAMATIONS Speakers, was listed "The Sacrifice" ____ I. S. Pettit. It indicated at the bottom of the program that "Spring Term Opens Wednesday, April 3rd., 1861." Part of the letter was also written on a sheet of narrow tablet paper and finally, part of it was written on the other side of a letter from Lucina which follows.)

Ira, what has become of you, why don't you write, I have written 2 letters since you have been to Falmouth and cannot find out if you have received them or not. Mr. Heywood from Boston kindly sent me your photographs, 8 in number, which I received last Monday. have you any particular friends which you would like to have us give one of your pictures to, if so let us know. Again I will state that your money and pictures which you sent from Boston, also the one from Washington, reached us safely. Caroline and Clarissa have answered your letter. No more this time. Write often.

From Lucina

PS I have forgotten whether I told you in my last letter that one of Uncle Greens twins were dead.

Sunday 8: On Brigade guard; post N° 2, 3^d relief. Rained hard last night; had a good fire. The guard got very wet. I

111

was well protected by rubber blanket and havelock. The rest came in off picket.

Monday 9: On fatigue to cut wood for the new guard. Sent home my diary for 1862. Pleasant sunshine: cool air.

Monday, March 9th   To-day is pleasant and the sun shines warm and genial: roads are rather muddy. Our regt. has been out on picket and returned in the Rebs. are very troublesome to the outer lines of *picketts.* I happened to be on guard when they went out so I did not go this time. I have found I am to belong to Co. F. 1st Battalion but direct your mail as usual as exchanges and transfers may yet be made. This is the 5th army corps 2nd division (Brigadier Gen. Sykes division) and 2nd Brigade. I have that same blanket, overcoat, blouse, pants, knapsack, 3 shirts, and boots, I started with from home; the binding and I P are on the blanket yet, and it would have been stolen at the fort for good had it not been for the binding. With this or these I will send my old diary (1862). If I put on too much postage tell Holmes to pay you back. Tell Tip to remember me. Is he and Clark so so disable they cannot work? Tell him that Elias A. Dunkelberg of Lockport who got his discharge from Cothran's Batterry belongs to our co. We were always bunkmates. Tell Clarrissa she need not mind about that map and go to any trouble I knew that maps used to sometimes appear in the papers and I wanted one sent me of the operations on the Potomac and hereabouts so that I might get an idea of the surrounding place, situation of places &c. But I will again close and try to get this parcel seal'd in time for this mail.

My love to all
Ira.

(On a small piece of paper which may have accompanied this package there was written: "Should this get miscaried please forward on to its destination." And the reverse side reads: "Should this get miscarried and any one chance to observe this please take their 25 cts and forward it as follows: Miss Lucina Pettit, Wilson Niagara Co. NY")

Tuesday 10: Wrote a letter cousin Fanny. Rainy. The 1st and 2nd Battalions 11th U.S. Inf. are now consolidated. I now belong to co. "F." 1st Batt^n. We now go to our respective companies for our rations.

Wednesday 11: Heavy shower of rain. A severe cough and the diarrhoea has ailed me for sometime. I am very poor and weak. Had my name entered on the sick report. I am excused from duty and under medical treatment.

Thursday 12: The regimental camp group is being newly laid out and tents removed. Took up our quarters in the companies to which we were assigned.

Friday 13: Squally. Cold and chilling air. We are now in small shelter tents. I feel mserable and uncomfortable. I am still taking med^{cn} Ramsey is our Surgeon's name.

Saturday 14: Cold and unpleasant out. Received a letter from Sister Lucina and wrote one to cousin Joel.

Sunday 15: Very cool yet. Rained and snowed this afternoon and evening: frequent and heavy peals of thunder accompained the storm.

Monday 16: Had I only comfortable quarters, I might have a pleasant time. Being on the sick list affords quite a respite from duty. I now tent with Conway an old member of co. F.

Tuesday 17: St Patrick's day. A great time was held by some of the regiments. A severe accident happened by which two officers and their horses were all killed by collission!

Wednesday 18: Quite warm and pleasant. Washed a shirt, pair of pants and stockings. My medicine consists of three doses of quenine and whiskey per. day.

Thursday 19: Cold. I keep my quarters pretty close. Cough hard yet: my medicine strengthens me and creates a sharp appetite.

Friday 20: A heavy snow storm, which nasties things up

113

badly again. Wrote a letter to John Snider Fort Independence.

Saturday 21: Stormy. Wrote to mother to send me a box of something good.

Sunday 22: Somewhat stormy. Read my bible: kept my quarters closely. The men drew rations to-night to go out on picket to-morrow.

Monday 23: The men started out on picket. I am not strong enough for duty yet.

Tuesday 24: Agreeable weather. Washed up and read my bible. Quiet times in camp while the men are on picket duty.

Wednesday 25: The picket came in through storm and mud. I am geting much better and stronger.

Thursday 26: Review of troops. Fine day for it. Received a letter from Sister Lucina which she wrote while on a visit to Somerset.

Friday 27: I am now about fit for duty again, but in consequence of the stormy weather just now I am still kept off.

Saturday 28: The weather looks promising again. I am on the gain in health and strength.

Sunday 29: Companies C. and D. of the 2nd Battalion arrived here from Fort Independence. Very windy.

Monday 30: Very fine weather indeed. Detailed for guard to-night.

Tuesday 31: Post Nº 7, 2nd relief. Began to snow and rain last night at (11) o'clock and continued without ceasation until (3) o'clock this P.M. A dubious time to us on guard. No kind of a guard house for shelter! Thus closes March.

APRIL, 1863

Wednesday 1: Begins with pleasant weather. Had the day mostly to myself. The men have much April Fooling. Drill and Dress-parade for the first in some time.

Thursday 2: On fatigue, loading gravel to fix bridges. Windy: drying off rapidly. Dress-parade again.

Friday 3: Drill both after and before noon and dress-parade in the evening. I have had the pleasure to ocupy the tent alone the past three days as my bunkmates are on picket.

Saturday 4: Went out with a fatigue party to chop wood. Windy and cold. Conway and Leighton, my tent partners, came in off picket. I was into a house for the first time since I came here.

Sunday 5: Pass or Easter Sunday
Rec'd two letters and a newspaper last night. A letter from cousin Joel and the rest from home. Heavy storm of snow, but cleared up again.

Monday 6: On guard; post N° 3, 1st relief. A cloudless day. A full moon beautified the night.

Tuesday 7: Abraham Lincoln, President of the U.S. Reviewed this brigade in person accompanied by escort and staff which was many and grand! Chilly.

Wednesday 8: Grand review of a portion of the Army of the Potomac by the President; we were marched nearly 5 miles to the review place in sight of Frederick'sburg and Reb. Camps. Have seen Old Abe two days in succession. Chilly.

Thursday 9: Brigade drill this A.M. Detailed for fatigue to go out with the wood chopers. Rec'd a box of good things from home this evening! and a letter from Snider with 50 cts inclosed! Lucky day.

115

Friday 10: A muster and inspection this morning. Dry and windy; hot; and dust flies. Drill this P.M. Have a good time feasting on what came in my box yesterday.

Saturday 11: No drill this P.M. Very hot. Devote my leisure to writing a letter home. The Paymaster is in camp—most of the co. have signed the rools.

Sunday 12: I signed the pay rools. Our brigade were inspected this A.M. knapsacks &c. And this P.M. by a General. Detailed for Guard. Hot.

Monday 13: On guard; Post 6, 1st relief. Rained last night. Cool and fine to-day. Got a letter from cousin Fanny last night.

Tuesday 14: Got pay for four months: we each received $47,50. I sent home $20,00. Drew five days rations and ordered to be prepared to march at a moments notice!

Wednesday 15: Rained hard and incessantly all day long which will delay our movement. Sent a letter to Mr. Tenny.

Thursday 16: Got my hair cut and shaved for the 1st time since I left Washington.

Friday 17: Drill both A.M. and P.M. Very pleasant weather. Devote my leisure to writing letters.

Saturday 18: Review of Sykes division we turned out at 11 A.M. It was quite an affair. Detailed for guard to-night. Hot day. Sent a letter to Cousin Dudley.

Sunday 19: On guard; post No. 3, 2nd relief. Wrote and sent a letter to Sister Lucina with $5,00 inclosed to father. An accident happened to the battery inguring two men badly by the blowing up of a cassion. Hot.

Army Of The Potomac Camp Near Falmouth V.A.
Sunday Apr. 19th 1863.

Dear Sister Lucina:

To-day is very pleasant; the weather at times is hot: I am on guard. As we are apt to break up camp and start off at short notice I feel that I would like to write to you again before we move. I sent two letters directed to father on the

14th acknowledging the receipt of that box of things and sent $10,00, in each as we got four months pay that same day, I presume you got the letters last evening. I intend to send home $25,00, more. I will send $5,00, in this letter. I have written so recently that I have not so much to write this time and I intend to write soon again so as to get my money home as soon as possible. I hardly think that you will be able to keep up correspondence with me for a while. Yesterday I sent a long letter to cousin Dudley. I have written to Mary Jane since I have been in camp but intend to soon. Make mention of me when you write to her and tell her I have not forgotten her: but perhaps I will have a letter prepared for her before you get this if I have time and do not have to go on a march. Yesterday this army corps was reviewed by its commander Maj. Gen. Meade its commander. It was an affair, but nothing to what it was when Old Abe reviewed us! To-day there is another review of this brigade and I guess that tomorrow we will start. We would have been on the tramp the next day after I wrote before but a heavy and long continued rain set in and delayed us. The balloon has been let up sevral times since the storm at Falmouth and when we see that we begin to understand that something is being studied upon. Tell father that if I become Major General it will be more profitable for me to hold on to the position than to resign; no, I still remain a "Brigadier Private" and shall be content to remain as such until the expiration of my term of service. I think sister that I have rec'd all the letters you have written to me, but I did not get the last paper you speak of sending containing the seminary programme. I rec'd the letter you wrote me from Somerset also the one you sent just before that. It is sad to hear of so many deaths of our friends and those who are dear to us. When I read of the death of Mr. Hayne's children your sabbath school schollars, It was so touching I could not help but cry. I often read your letters. Tell Emory I will try and reply to his letter soon. Give them my best respects:

tell them I thank them all much for their kindness. I have not opened the can of honey yet. I have used the sack of peaches and I did not know what the others contained until yesterday, when I put down nearly half those dried grapes without stewing! The honey and berries will soon come to it now. I have used over half the flour making flapjacks &c. It goes good with the sauce. I have left some butter, dried beef, flower, a few cake, all the honey, one and a half sacks dried fruit, a little butter &c. I fried that piece of raw ham and it went bully. Those gloves come good on guard chilly nights to hold the cold gun with. I wish you were here to see how neat we have got the camp fixed up. The tents are pitched so as to have streets which we sweep clean every day: pines are planted as regular and nice as village shade trees and it is delightful! more so than you can possibly immagine. I am sorry to learn that uncle Wm. and family are so destitute. Harm. and Jake too according to father's letter are pretty well striped of what they have. Tell Georgie that the paper he sent is under this letter to keep it clean. I love to read in it. You say you have a specimen of our hard crackers but I wish I could send you a box or two that you might have a fair trial of them, you would rather live on chips I think but I have now got so I like them: we have them now in abundance. I rec'd a letter from Joel not long since he appears to enjoy himself well and likes the school. You warn me against *getting* lousy and ask me to use my fine comb freely. I have the comb yet there is not a tooth gone. I used it but little we keep our hair bobed off close; but head lice are no plague. It is the large body lice darn em. I have lately had the fun of cracking a few on my shirt! I'll give em jessie. Did you not find some curious statements on record in my diary? how does the soldier's seem compared with the citizens life side by side? But I must close in order to get this off in to-night's mail. From your brother Ira S. Pettit. Co. F. 1st Battallion 11th U.S. Infantry 2nd Brigade, 2nd (Sykes) Division, 5th Army Corps.

Monday 20: Our regiment started out on picket this morning with three days rations. Rained on our march out and stormy all day nearly. Our squad was first relief.

Tuesday 21: Very favorable to-day: have good times in good weather. Grass begins to start, peach-trees are in bloom, and it is delightful.

Wednesday 22: Rained last night: we are well sheltered: our rations will hold out finely.

Thursday 23: Relieved at 10, o'clock A.M. The rain fell in torrents from early morn. nearly until night. Had a wet time marching in and rather an unpleasant picket throughout.

Friday 24: Rainy day again. Our blankets are still wet to-night the weather not being favorable enough since we came in from picket to dry them.

Saturday 25: Battalion drill this A.M. P.M. was detailed to dig a trench. Testaments were issued to the soldiers through the brigade and other religious documents distributed.

Sunday 26: Listened to a sermon by a chaplain. The first religious sentiments I have heard put forth since I left Canandaigua N.Y. Rec'd two letters one from home one from Willie Holmes.

Monday 27: The command ordered to be ready to march at 10 A.M. We have started—Made nearly 10 miles. Hot. Overcoats &c were disposed of by the hundreds. I let mine go.

Tuesday 28: Rained just enough to make it good marching, laying the dust and making it cool. It was rapid and tiresome: did not halt until sometime after sunset as we did not start until nearly 3 o'clock P.M.

Wednesday 29: Started in good season and continued it moderately until after day. Crossed the Rappahannock on pontoon bridges at Kelly's Ford and finished the tramp by wading the Rappa Dan by moonlight which was ass deep. Took off our pants and drawers. T'was cool.

Thursday 30: A shower of rain last night drenched us so

119

that much lugage was left and thrown away, also making it very slipery and tiresome to travel. Countermarched again & again to find the best point to attack the enemy for a large force of them is near. Did not march late.

MAY, 1863

Friday 1: I was detailed for one of the rear guard of our divison to pick up straglers, guard prisoners, the supply trains &c. The Army marched at 10, A.M. and engaged the enemy after proceeding two miles. Cannonading and musketry was kept up until after sunset! First I ever heard. We fell back a little. Fine day.

Saturday 2: We (the guard, supplies &c) fell back a mile or more before sunrise and remained all day: firing is heavy and constant in front. Warm and pleasant nights: full moon.

Field of Battle

May 2nd 1863.

To All.

Dear Parents &c:

I received your's of Apr. 18th also from William Homes on sunday evening Apr. 26th. It was with regret that I learned you had received no answer from me, for I had sent four letters since Apr. 14th (which was pay day) and money in each. On the 14th I sent two by one mail a $10,00, check in one and a $10,00, greenback in the other; both of which had time to get home when you mailed your letter which was on the 21st. The other two did not have time to reach you so perhaps you may get some of them. The two last contained a $5,00, treasury note each, making $30,00 I have sent you of my last pay. I rec'd $47,50, four months pay. I intend to send you $10,00, more at least when I hear how much you got of what I have sent i,e: if all is well and I come out of this alive. Our sutler established a military bank and I bought a $10,00 check which you can get the money on at any bank if you get it and if it is lost I can get another of him in a certain length of time so there are some hopes of that. The Army mail has been robed of thousands of money between Aquia Creek and Washington since pay day. So says the papers. I wrote to you and to mother at some length of the safe arrival of my box of good things and how *very* thankful I was for your kindness. It was opened and closed as usual but I dont think by the appearance that a cake even was taken out or overhauled as things were so completely packed. Others have lost half of what the box contained. "Thou Shalt not Steal" must have been the first thing which met their observation and they halted. The box kept whole and was useful to me as long as I remained in camp. The sutler would have sold what it contained for $20,00, I wrote of my good health since I was sick. I feel better than before, stand the long marches well which we are now making: but yesterday we met and engaged the enemy. I am all right thus far.

Ira.

Dear Sister Lucina:

I was happy to get a letter from you to know what was going on about home. I regret that I have not the leisure to answer it at length. I am on the field of battle but up to this time no accident has happened me for I am in the rear as a guard over prisoners and the supply trains; but have seen and heard the cannon roar and tremenduous ratling of musketry also mangled bodies of the wounded which are brought off in the ambulance waggons. I have not time to give lengthy details now but if it is well with me I will do so when I have Leisure. Cothran's Battery is in the field and I think the 111th P.V. but could not yet get to see the boys. I have to tend to my duty. It was indeed quite a loss for Douglas Pease to get burned out so. Is Mary Mix dead! Indeed! Oh, Lucina, what a fine box of things they did send me. Thank all concerned in it. That red handkerchief which father has so often used dried much sweat from my brow too during the march. I dont part with them things. The little sacks are the things *now* to carry my sugar, coffee &c in. I a little of the flower in my harver sack yet. Tell Little Lucina that mince pie and lemon pie were delicious, super-fine! I received your somerset letter and the paper stating Tip's marriage and the death of Kemp but I saw nothing of the one containing the seminary programme. Bully for George Wilson and Oliver's Ester! Also Fen. Ward! I may see Holmes before we are dismissed from battle. I got a letter from him at the same time I got your's it was written at the same time mailed the same time and received the same time and he only 10 miles from here. but it had to go via Washington.

Ira.

Well Georgie;

You cant think how glad I was to read your letter cause you told so much news. I did'nt know you could write any. I read all about what you wrote of Lucina's farmer's wreath. I did'nt know 'twas so nice! How does that concern work that father got to Lockport so new? and how does my gristmill work? You say you do some grinding with it. Mr. Furgason's hostler met with a very sad accident. Do you think he was murdered or whether he got drowned! A good many have died about home lately, havent they Georgie within the past year. But here this very monent ah, many are being shot to death It may be my fate before the action is over. It is after noon nearly five oclock. We are where we stoped this morning guarding the trains &c have got lots of rebs too. Our force's have driven the Rebels up to this time. The roar of cannon and ratling of musketry is tremenduous. But I must close.

Ira.

(The preceding three letters, as well as the postscript, which is dated May 7th and appears after that diary entry, were all written on one sheet of paper—back and front—and addressed to Miss Lucina Pettit.)

Sunday 3: Recrossed the Rappahannock where two pontoon bridges were put across and where extensive rifle pits had been dug by the Rebs. The battle is now raging hot. Recrossed at United States Ford.

Monday 4: At early dawn the enemy shelled our hospital killing a few helpless wounded: a few went over and came near us hurting only one man: they were soon repulsed and captured. Fell back with the trains a mile or so. Hot.

Tuesday 5: Started with the prisoners trains for the old camp at 3 P.M. but a heavy rain compelled us to halt for the night.

Wednesday 6: Came into camp at about noon or before and pitched our tents: the division came in toward night. Bad going; rainy and cold. This is called the battle of Chancellorsville. The battle is over.

Thursday 7: Rained much last night. I was on post. Cloudy cold and lowry: Very uncomfortable for the army. Many are without tents, blankets, overcoats &c. We signed for clothing.

Thursday May 7th

We came back into camp yesterday at noon with the supply trains. I am yet alive and all right. I will hurry this off without further particulars to quell your anxiety about my wellfare. Your's &c.

Ira. S. Pettit.
Co. F. 1st Battalion
11th U.S. Inf.

Friday 8: Received a letter from Sister Lucina. $20,00 of my pay which I sent home is lost. Sent another letter home.

Friday, May the 8th

Sister Lucina: The mail has just opened this morning, I also just rec'd your letter mailed at Lockport May 1st which was the 1st day of the battle. I was sorry to learn that the

$20,00 of my pay which I sent home was lost: but $10,00, was a check which I bought of Murray the Army and Navy banker so I will be apt to recover that when I see him. He is not in camp now or I would send it in this letter if he would give me another check. You can judge that my letter has been in some tuff place by its appearnce. Yesterday we were issued 11 days rations and I aprehend another immediate battle; for pontoon bridges are passing along and also large numbers of cavalry. Those verses you sent in your letter were beautiful; thank you for them. "Work while you are able work, work away and I'll be a true soldier and send you all the money I can if it does get lost by 20s. I am conscious that I tried to have you get it and not squander it by gambling and foolishness as many of my fellow soldier's do. I will send another ten. But I must close. I am now all right for another battle. Remember me to Father, Mother, and all. My two letters contain $10,00, each. I sent by one mail.

Your's Truly.
Ira.

Saturday 9: Very hot weather. We are constantly receiving prisoners sent us and return them to their proper reg'ts.
Sunday 10: On guard: post No. 2, 1st relief. Very hot.
Monday 11: Wrote a long letter to Mary Jane. We are to be a permanent Provost Guard so we hear. Our brigade are shifting and regulating their Camp. Pleasant.
Tuesday 12: Finished Mary Jane's letter and sent it quite early. On guard; post No. 1, 1st relief. My Birth Day. I am 22 yrs of age.
Wednesday 13: Moved and regulated our tents in good shape. Pines are being planted and the camp beautified as if we were to remain here a long time. Hot.
Thursday 14: I tent alone and have ever since we came in. Two recruits who came from Alexandria stayed with me last night. Hot and showry.
Friday 15: Done my washing early this morning. On guard

Post No. 2, 2nd relief. Guard mount at 10 A.M. Post 2 dispensed with in daytime. Went to the woods with team and prisoners for pines. Hot.

Saturday 16: After being dismissed from guard devoted my time to geting my tent righted rambling about, reading, sleeping &c.

Sunday 17: Read the Scriptures, eat, slept, and walked about. Lazy weather.

Monday 18: Wrote a long letter to Father. Weed's, 5th regular, Battery and the 1st Ohio are moving from here somewhere near the R.R. . . .

Army of the Potomac,
Camp Near Falmouth V.A.
May 18th 1863.

My Dear Father:

You have no doubt received my letter which I sent you immediately after having arrived into camp from the late engagement. I have delayed writing this letter much longer than I intended as my duty has demanded much of my attention. I have also written Mary Jane a very lengthy letter. You have read accounts of the late battle of Chancellorsville with more satisfaction than any I can give as I am a private in the ranks and have not the means of posting myself about the whole affair as those who give their whole attention to the matter; but I presume you would like to have me write of what fell under my observations from the time we decamped until our return to the place from whence we started. Eight days rations were issued to us some time before we took up our line of march but heavy rains prevented a move. So much rations was enormous, more than was convenient to carry: we knew not where we were going until we had proceeded a number of miles from camp. All expressed opinions in regrad to it but all differed. On Monday Apr. 27th the

Command was ordered to be in readiness to move at 10 o'clock A.M. We immediately began to pack our knapsacks, strike tents and get ourselves in readiness. We marched a little after noon: the day was favorable but the temperature rather hot: we packed into our knapsacks all we thought we could carry but found after a march of a few miles that we would have to get along with less. The road was lined with overcoats and blankets nearly all disposed of which they they thought would be of least use. I had the heaviest knapsack in the company but as it began to be a burden I bade farewell to mr. overcoat. We enjoyed the afternoon very much as they could not well overmarch us for often we had to wait a long time on coming to a crossroad for other troops to pass in advance of us. We also halted for the night in fair season. Tuesday: Did not march until 3 P.M. A light shower of rain fell sufficiently to lay the dust and make it good marching; it was however a rapid and tiresome pull and did not halt for the night until some time after sunset. Wednesday. Started early; I tore my blanket in two leaving nearly half of it to lighten my burden as we were notified that a long and rapid march was to be made almost every one left something of their burden. However it was not so teageous as we expected to find it; I actually stood it better than I did the day previous notwithstanding we were on the move until sometime after day: but the crossing a number of streams caused us to move slowly at times. It was a day which I shall long remember. We crossed the Rappahannock on a pontoon bridge at Kelley's Ford, and to top off with waded the Rappa Dan (I think it is spelled and pronounced) in the night by moonlight! I will give you a few of the particulars of that incident father. It is a wide and rapid stream. The pontoons had not yet got along so it was thought best to cross it by wading. Orders were given to take off our belts and hang them about our necks to keep the amunition dry and prepare ourselves otherwise as we choosed. So we pulled off our pants, drawers, and stockings, tucked up our shirtails and went in. It was cold, the night chilly, and you can well immagine how it felt. Of all the fun and yelling I ever heard that caped the climax! The water was very deep and so many going through kept the water continually damed up so that it streamed between us with dashing rapidity and almost wash us away! After crossing we stoped for the night. It had showered occasionally during the the day and the ground was wet to lie on; a heavy shower occured during the night making things wet and heavy to lug and slipery traveling: many threw away the last blanket, overcoat or half tent they had. So considering the whole we had rather a moist time of it just then. Thursday. Marched and countermarched back again time after time following roads leading through dense forrests the whole time: came upon places where the enemy were but recently encamped, earthworks thrown up but the night previous and a deserted house which bore appearances of being left in a hurry into which we went and stowed into our harversacks the two barrels of flour left, smashed valuable furniture and killed their poultry as we were halted for a while. We well understood by the looks of things that we were somewhere near our game. A mile farther and we halted, in good season, for the night. We were first drawn up in regular divisions and the Adjutant of our regt. read to us orders to the effect that "The Gen. Commanding, was gratified to inform his gallant troops that he had succeeded in so completely surrounding the enemy as to oblige them to surrender, ingloriously retreat, or come out of their stronghold and fight us where imediate destruction awaited them"!* (Vociferous Cheering!) We stacked arms, made fires, and steeped our coffee, fried meat and flapjacks and refreshed ourselves finely: pitched our tents planked ourselves down within them and enjoyed a night of peaceful, quiet

*Commanding General Hooker's wishful thinking was somewhat premature, as history well substantiates.

rest. Friday, May the 1st Hitherto, the 10th regulars had done the Division guard duty, Provost guard, to take charge of prisoners, arrest straglers and skedadlers, and guard the Division suply, and amunition trains &c, keeping them entirely in the rear to prevent their capture; falling back when the forces are driven and advancing as the army advances. This morning the 10th were relieved by the 11th Fifty seven were detailed for the guard; I am one of the number detailed: we have not been relieved to this day. I suppose we are to be a permanent Provost Guard of Sykes' Division. Our forces did not move until about 10 o'clock A.M. (we the guard) remained and after they had left we skirted the woods picking up a number who did not keep with their companies. After having proceeded one mile or less "the ball opened!" musket firing became general and soon batteries opened in thunder tone! The heavy notes grew more and more distant and squads of sesesh were occasionally brought back, disarmed and committed to our charge for a while. Rebel flags were also captured and borne back with the prisoners all which went to show that our men had the better of them but with the cost of lives and much spilling of blood. The ambulance trains laden with mangled bodies of the wounded came back and hospitals were established; one at the very house we ransacked the day before. Toward night the war sound grew nearer and it was evident that we were being driven or purposely falling back. Artillery which had been in action came back on a road leading through the forrest in a hurry and made a stand on a hill directly behind us. Infantry which were coming to the front halted and formed in line of battle along beside the woods. The firing was now very near and I expected to see a large body of the enemy come through the woods and capture all our trains: but as they drew near in large masses our guns opened and belched forth volleys of destruction into their midst which sent "Johney Rebs" kiting back on the four times double-quick! We then fell back with the supplies and prisoners nearly a mile met troops pouring in to the front by thousands. Firing was kept up until after sunset then all was tolerably quiet until morning when canonading and musketry opened in good season and we moved on towards U.S. Ford about two miles before sunrise; the firing was terrific during the day and night: the moon was full, the weather warm and pleasant and favorable for battle both night and day during the whole affair. On Sunday the 3^d the battle raged as fiercely as at any time previous. It was very hot day. We recrossed the Rappahannock at United States Ford where two pontoon bridges were put across. Extensive rifle pits and fortifications had been thrown up by the enemy but left them for fear of being surrounded and captured as they surely would have been. During the night a rebel battery riged in our style and costume and supported by some of Stewart's Cavalry succeeded in geting around and obtained a favorable position to shell one of our hospitals across the river near where we lay. Monday morning at early dawn they opened upon us firing a dozen or so shots. A shell burst directly over the hospital tent killing sevral wounded, a few came hobling along through the woods where we were panic stricken! A shell came whizing along striking in a hollow some 20 rods before reaching us another directly over us striking about as far beyond us and mortally wounded a man while packing a mule. That was the closest. The teamsters flew into excitement trying to hitch up and get off! we slung on our knapsacks and got in readiness in short order. The Rebels yelled tremenduously and all was confusion,we could not see how many there were for the extensive forrests. I supposed that they had by some cunning plan during the night got in our rear and that we were gone ers sure: but however we were soon pacified by the intelligence that a force of our cavalry made a dash on them and took every one prisoners; they have been or will probably will be all shot for thus coming out in disguise and commiting so cowardly an act which is contrary to all rules of civil warfare. We cooled down however and did not move again until after noon when we proceeded onward sevral miles and stoped over night again. The battle sound throughout the day was as usual. Tuesday: The war sound was distant: we started at 3 P.M. for the old camp. It rained heavy showers all during the march and night came on with no better prospects so we halted and had a wet time indeed. Started again in the morning early and arrived on the old camp ground at 10 A.M. The regiment and Divison came in towards night it was rainy and cold and the need of the articles which we were obliged to throw away was keenly felt. It was indeed a very uncomfortable time for the army; many were striped of every thing but the clothes they wore; being obliged to cast off every thing when hotly engaged with the enemy. I picked sevral pieces of tents which was thrown away just before we came in and I have a comfortable shelter now all to myself and put in good order. Clothing was issued as soon as possible after our arrival we could draw tents and as much clothing as we wished to make us comfortable: all I drew was a pair of stockings! It is now warm and I can get along with my rubber and other half blanket and the rest the clothing I have, comfortably this summer. Many drew a new full equipment to be thrown away again on the next march. I still keep those boots which I got plated; they are in wearing order yet and stood the march well. It is astonishing to see the valuable things cast away on such a march. I picked up a few neat pair of comfortable gloves and other small articles. could have picked up any discription of clothing and boots costing $12,00 were often thrown away on account of being painful to wear! but all such things look small in a man's eye when he is overcome by fatigue in marching. It is often severe no matter what a man's condition is he cant sit down and rest when he has a mind to; he must keep with his company. If he falls out without a written permission from his captain or the

131

doctor he will be forced along at the point of the bayonet and made prisoner kept in confinement by the Provost guard until court martialed!!! I can march well but they step off to fast sometimes: up hill it is always on the run. the advance assend slowly then walk off fast and the rest can gain the time going up the hill: just so when the path is so narrow that we have to go single file when those ahead get through they do not wait but move off rapidly and those in rear must run to close up and form sections of fours. We march without step and cary arms at will. Sixty rounds of amunition is issued to every soldier and he is supposed to keep that ammount on hand but forty rounds is all that the cartridge boxes will conveniently hold and it is quite a lump to carry: 'tis a sloven waste to issue any more for it is in most all cases destroyed save the caps. It is done up in papers of 10 rounds each and 12 caps the latter are waterproof so are the patent cartridges. Well we have made long marches to go a short distance fought severe and bloody battles and again returned without accomplishing what was expected. Our company regiment and division was engaged and did a good part without suffering severely. We have regulated the camp and again beautified it exceedingly. the bakeries are again established and every thing righted up as if we were to remain here for months. We (the guard) are stationed at the headquarters of our (the 2nd) brigade keeping the prisoners we brought in disposing of some occasionally and more are sometimes sent to us. We are detatched from our companies at present but how long we are to remain so I know not. It is said that the rebels buried all the dead: but we are allowed to cross the river and bring away our wounded from the hospitals which were established there during the action. Ambulance trains are buisy bringing the wounded away every-day. Load after load passes here as they are being conveighed to the railroad. Thus, Father, I have been to one engagement and came out with no injuries. I was not in the thickest of it to be sure but I did the duty required of me; I am willing to stand up to the mark and do it manfully the best I can any where. I feel greatly thankful for thus being spared. Many have fell heroically on the field far away from home and friends, but such is the consequences of war. I might enumerate many other incidents which I saw and experienced but this letter is already long enough. I will try and write often. I will send you $4,00 more in this letter; in my last I sent two. I wish I could have sent the whole $40,00, to you at once then it would have looked like something but $20,00, of my last pay is lost, ten sure. The banker has not been in camp since the battle. I will make him give me another check when he comes in for he promised to if it got lost and not returned in a certain length of time. Two months more of pay is now due us viz. March and April, I will not be discouraged at this loss and do as many would not send any more but spend it: no I will try and have you receive all my wages except a very little which is necessary for me to use. $20,00, *must* be sent every two months and more if I can. My labors are not so severe as yours but many privations have to be endured at times: You have most likely commenced active farm operations: Do not work too hard. Send me a paper immediately and when you write send a number of stamps. I will soon write again. I was 22 yr's of age on the 12th but a few days ago, and one year has elapsed to-day since I united with the church how short the time. On the 29th I shall have been in the service a year. What the next two years may bring fourth comes to be considered. I was never in better health than at present. Farewell.

From Your Boy.   Ira.

Co. F. 1st Battalion 11th U.S. Infanty.
2nd Brigade 2nd Division 5th Army Corps.

P.S. I saw none of my friends, relatives nor acquaintances during the march. I.

Tuesday 19: Finished and put the letter in this morning. On Guard: Post No. 4; 3^d relief. Got a big wood pile from where the battery moved.

Wednesday 20: Teamsters are buisy hauling boughs and pines and the camps of our division are now well fix't up, so that it is delightfully shaded.

Thursday 21: We have now completed our bough-house Set pines about our tents &c. so that we are well shaded.

Friday 22: On Guard; post No. 1; 1st relief. Every thing is generally very quiet in camp: no signs of commencing active operations very soon.

Saturday 23: Fitzgerald (corporal of the guard) with four file of the guard was sent on an escort with fourteen zouave prisoners to Gen. Meades headquarters 5th Army Corps. We had a hot tramp of it.

Sunday 24: Got a letter from Sister Lucina last evening. Only four prisoners left now so the number of guard posts is only two instead of four. Very hot spell of weather. Rec'd a Rural from home.

Monday 25: Wrote a letter to Wm. Holmes battery M. 1st N.Y. artillery; and one for Monroe as his fingers are shot.

Tuesday 26: Quite a change of weather; quite cool; cloudy. Wrote a letter to John Snider Ft Independence. We're having a good thing of it: easy times: an abundance of leisure.

Wednesday 27: On guard; post No. 1 2nd relief. Cloudy and cool. Durkee co. b. came to tent with me.

Thursday 28: The Pay-master is said to be in camp. The 21st P.A. Vols. who recently encamped near us have again moved and we are laying in for the wood &c which they leave.

Friday 29: I enlisted just one year ago to-day. I took a walk all through the division. A great deal of artillery is moving their camps. Signed the pay-rools.

Saturday 30: Received a letter and a paper from home stating that my last was safely received. Built our tent up high on slabs so it is quite roomy.

134

Sunday 31: On guard; post No. 1, 3^d relief. We have now four prisoners, three of whom are sentenced to be shot! We are cautioned to be strict. Received pay for March and April $23,75,

JUNE, 1863

Monday 1: Very windy both yesterday and now, raising the dust in clouds. The three prisoners sentenced to death are now handcuffed and shackled!

Tuesday 2: Not so windy nor so much dust flying. Washed and boiled my pants and shirt. Sent a letter home with $5,25, inclosed.

> Army Of The Potomac;
> Camp Near Falmouth V.A.
> June 2nd 1863

Sister Lucina: Your letters of May the 16th and 24th were duly received also those two papers, viz: the Rural and the State League. They were all perused with no small degree of pleasure. It gave me much satisfaction to know that you were all well and had received my last two letters safely. I observed in the papers those marked pieces and all you intended me to notice. "The soldiers letters." "Minnie Mintwood's" letter &c &c. Corp'l Adams you spoke of was killed but I know no soldier in the regt. by the name of Trecor did it mention private Arnolds death? I told Mary Jane in my last to send me a paper immediately on the receipt of my letter but no reply yet. When you write always mention the letters you have received from friends. We received pay for two months more $23,75, last sunday May 31st and you will be apt to hear from me briefly and frequently until I get it all sent home five dollars at a time. Did the burning of the Intelligencer office by the recent great fires cripple the Editors so that they had to discontinue the paper? I am in good health yet and on the provost guard. Three of our prisoners are now handcuffed and shackled as they are sentenced to be shot next friday between the hours of 12 and 4 P.M. Lots of youngsters getting spliced or married thereabouts aint they? let em drive. As Minnie advises I'll wait till I have a (free land.) So Jason has lost his wife! Gus is well enough to be married eh? Is it Fannie Elton? This will be a rambling letter I'll bet ye but no matter I'm going to send $5,00 in it. Perhaps Lawyer Onderdonk could have got me a commission on the start. The lieutenants of this regiment invariably show that they were appointed green from civil life by those who have authority. They don't understand the tactics so well as ¼ of the privates! although highly educated otherwise. The idea of many that none but graduates from West Point get commissions is a mistake. Few are promoted from the ranks as they should be. No, I will rise on my own merits if at all. I can say, and not boast, that I know more about the drill than half the lieutenants. In your last you wisely cautioned me about that flour against ever again eating any thing left by the enemy as it might be fixed and left to destroy us. We talked the very matter over but all seemed to regard that but slightly. It was remarked that such things had been done but was played out! We also drank their well dry; the 1st we seen in Dixie. I have written to Wm. Holmes. So Clarrence is dead. Tell me more about it. You speak of the return of the gallant 28th. I suppose they feel greatly relieved and think they have done their share. I know that mother's cares and labors are enough to prevent her from writing much: thank her for remembering me. Father too has enough to ocupy all his time. Tell Clarrissa and Louisia I am not unmindful of them. I expect the boys are into the onion business all sorts. But I wont write any more now or I wont have any thing to write next time. Send me a paper every time I send money for I' going to let it slide rite along now and make ye rich. Look at old lake Ontario once in a while for me and the boats that glide along but don't spend too much time at it but wash up them dishes and fly around! I have just washed my breeches and a shirt. I am a considerable of a cook and washerwoman. I have just cut off the buttons and threw away my blouse having worn it exactly a year. That extra pocket you made in it done good service. I miss it in my new one. All my late pay is in my housewife: I have got some neat money so I'll inclose $5,00 and away she goes! So go safe. Farewell. This is the same stamp and paper you sent me tis the only stamp I've got.

Yours Truly
Ira S. Pettit.
Co. F. 11th US Infantry

P.S. Our Captain's name is Layton; a very fine man.I.S.P.

Wednesday 3: On guard: post No. 1, 1st relief. Hot weather. Devoted my leisure to writing a letter to Cousin Emory.

Thursday 4: The bugles proclaimed rev- at 2 o'clock this morning and orders came for the Division to strike tents and make ready to move. At early twilight we were away. Marched 10 miles near U.S. Ford where we stuck in the mud last winter.

Friday 5: Three details, of 7 each, were chosen from the guard to shoot the three prisoners. I was one of the number detailed to perform the painful duty. Fortunately orders were received to suspend the execution. We are buisy slicking up the new camp.

Saturday 6: Finished and sent off the letter I commenced last wednesday, and inclosed $6,00. for father. Our camp is in a pine forrest and the shade is equal to that of the pleasant bowers we left behind. Heavy cannonading yesterday off towards Fredericksburg.

Sunday 7: Every man his own cook now, we did not have our camp kettles brought for us as the companies did. Guard mount changed from 10 A.M. to 4 P.M. On guard: post no 3, 3^d relief.

Monday 8: Wrote and sent a letter to Mother with $5,00,

Samples of Private Ira S. Pettit's Stationery

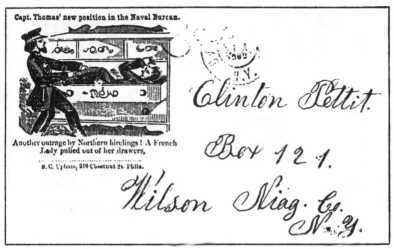

July, 1862, Canandaigua, New York, postmark. Letter to Clinton Pettit, dated July 8th, 1862.

October, 1862, Boston, Massachusetts, postmark. Letter to Mr. Clinton Pettit and Sister Lucina—dated October 8th, 1862.

inclosed. Quite cold last night. Borrowed $2,00 of Durkee my bunkmate.

Tuesday 9: Detailed for Guard. Twenty Sesesh. prisoners were brought in this morning which the old guard took to Gen. Meads headquarters.

April, 1864, Alexandria, Virginia, postmark. Letter to Clinton Pettit, dated April 12, 1864.

April, 1864, Alexandria, Virginia, postmark. Letter to Sister Lucina, dated April 22nd, 1864.

Wednesday 10: On guard; post No. 3, 3ᵈ relief very hot. A number of prisoners were brought in today. Some of whom were loyal citizens, taken on suspicion of shooting our pickets.

Thursday 11: The prisoners brought in to us yesterday were sent to their regiments or elsewhere. The three prisoners sentenced to be shot are yet in chains. Received a letter last evening from Sister Mary Jane; also a paper from her to-night.

Friday 12: Detailed for guard. Finished and sent off a long letter to Clinton Pangburn with $5,00 inclosed for father.

Camp Near U.S. Ford V.A.
June 12th 1863.

Cousin Clinton.

I think I have not yet replied to your last letter. I have such a large correspondence that it takes a long time to get around to them all. I got a good long letter from Mary Jane night before last and a newspaper from her last night. I was very glad to hear from her as it has been so long since she has written to me before. She received the letter I wrote to her a few weeks ago. It is now over a year since I left home to try living with "Uncle Samuel." I believe I left you picking stone in the extreme lower lot. Well do I remember the last work I done on the old farm. I expect you have not got that wall laid up yet. I often wonder what crops &c you have got in each lot. Now before you write your next letter to me (which I hope will be soon) take a pencil and paper and write down what you have got growing in each lot: begin first with the orchards, then call the next lot number one, and the next number two, and so on and take down what you have in each of them. Tell me the number of sheep, cattle, hogs, pigs &c. I expect that you will begin to think about washing sheep by the time you get this. I am in the best of health about these times and will weigh, I think, a number of pounds more than ever before. I am often asked if my face is swoolen. I wear a big moustache, have not shaved my upper lip since I left Washington and had not used the razor at all until just before our move on Chancellorsville! You may believe I was a fine looking bird when feathered out. Would you not have been glad to seen me? You enquired, in your last, more about the mules. Well they all look very slick just now after sheding their old coats and in fine order too.

Mules do not whinner like horses but make an unearthly queer noise and can be heard a great distance: when the teamsters come around with their grain they then set up an orful cry as if to say, hurry up there thats just what we like. They are used on the baggage, supply, and amunition waggons; the waggons are all iron axeltree, very heavy and substantial; and three spans of mules are used on each waggon and I never saw any teamster use but one line to drive them all: the heaviest span are on the tongue to hold back in going down hill: the nigh one is called saddle mule on which the teamster rides he has a line extended to the nigh mule's bit of the front span which is called the leader and a stick is fastened to the hamering of the leader and to the off mules bit so wherever the leader goes the other must: when the driver wishes to "file left" or haw, he pulls the line, and if he wishes to gee or file right he hits the leader a slap with the line which knows what it means and goes accordingly. Thus, you see that three teams are driven with less leather to guide them than we use at home to drive one span of horses. Every full company is entitled to a team of that sort, and a man detailed from each to drive it: but a waggon to two co. is all we generally have. The mule teams are kept buisy nearly every day hauling away rubbish, fetching in wood, commissary stores drawing dirt &c to fix roads and bridges and all such labor which requires team work. They used a great deal in the pack line, to carry loads on their backs where waggons cannot be got along. I have seen loads put upon them, that it seemed impossible for them to stand up under, and at the battle of Chancellorsville were not so much as unpacked to lie down and rest for days as it was necessary to be on hand for a skedaddle or advance at any moment. Many did lie down with their burdens, but had to be relieved of them to rise again, after being kicked and pounded by monsters of cruelty until it was found impossible to arise under them. In spite of such mistreatment of all I had a chanc to witness, I saw only one lie down to rise no more—before that I had almost come to the conclusion that they were proof against death by hardships. Horses are used by cavalrymen, artillery, or ambulance waggons and by officers entitled to ride on horseback. One span to each ambulance waggon, three span to each cannon and there is one waggon in each battery which requires four spans of horses. **U.S.** is burned indelably with a hot iron on one of the shoulders of every horse and mule belonging to the Government. We the infantry might properly be called pack animals, or you would think so to see us on the march under our knapsacks: but they look rather gaunt now-a-days as it don't require much clothing this weather. I have give you a decent mule story and now must strike on something else. You called to my mind in your last letter a number of incidents of the good times we used to have pleasant to think of, and which I remember well. Yes I often, with a smile, think of the time we were husking corn and Georgie (stark naked) broke your windmill to pay for hiding His cose (clothes)! I do not now-a-days get pie, cake, and all those delacacies only when I buy them at a very high price; in fact, I do not hanker after such now: nothing tastes better to me than a good meos of pork, beef, bacon, "hard tack," and coffee. We have an abundance of pork and bacon; droves of cattle are feched in in large herds and we sometimes get our fresh every day, always three rations a week. I have got so that I can stew up a tasty meal. Even on the field of battle we got a plenty of fresh meat. Droves were chased along by the herdsmen, and buchering was done for us every night, and big rations of fresh dealt out to us. It would have done you good to see the cattle with blankets rooled and tied around their necks and knapsacks and other light trash packed on them by the drovers and butchers. You might think it a fine thing to pick up a neat sword or gun at home but they were regarded as little as stone over at Chancellorsville: a man would hardly stoop for any thing scarcely, for each had

143

what burden he wanted. A neat revolver or a pile of greenbacks would not of course be overlooked or any thing light and valuable. Clint. Uncle Sam is a pretty good paymaster. He has almost always paid me up as he agreed to. I have received over $100,00 from him since I have been in his service: two months pay will again be due me the last of this month. I have in my pocket at the present time $18,00, $5,00 of which I will send in this letter. I sent a letter to mother last monday with $5,00 inclosed. I have heard nothing from home since Lucina and Clarrissa wrote which I received on the evening of May the 30th I have written a number of letters since with money inclosed, I do not request a letter of reply to each of them, but always send a paper with the ammount, in figures, which you found in each letter penciled on the margin for I am always anxious to know whether what money I send is going safe or astray. If you will but mail a paper before leaving the office on receiving my letters it will give me almost immediate satisfaction of its reception and a newspaper with home news gives me much pleasure. Who teaches Your school this summer and how many of you goes? I expect that you and George have got such a big bed of onions to tend that it will take all your spare time so that you will be able to attend school but little this summer. I believe I'de rather soldier than to pick stone, hoe corn, taters, beans, mow, rake, pitch and mow hay, rake and bind wheat, oats and Canada thistles combined, in the stifling heat of the summer. Then comes the dirty work of threshing; then cutting corn, husking and all that sort of arduous labor. But dont let these sayings ever induce you to enlist; if you do, you'l wish yourself back again. What pay you would receive would look small in your eye. Many would be willing to be drumed out of the service to get out. I have seen sevral drumed out for certain crimes. Their heads are first shaved all over; four men with their guns, and bayonets fixed, with a lot of drummers are his escort. Two men follow behind him at charge bayonets, ready to prick him if he is disorderly and two men in front of him with arms reversed so that their bayonets also point towards him: thus he is surrounded completely with pointed steel and drumed around the whole divison to which he belonged, at the tune of "Poor old soldier, poor old soldier, Tared and feathered and kicked about, Because he would not soldier"! How would you like that? I could mention many interesting things incident to a soldiers life, but this sheet could not give room to them. In one of my letters which my money was lost in, I gave a long account of Old Abe's visit our here and how we turned out by thousands and thousands to be reviewed. I had a fine look at the old man. I also wrote in one of the lost letters a great deal about receiving that box of good things you sent me. I wrote of every-thing it contained and the fine condition in which it reached me, so that you might all be well satisfied that I had got it sure. Its wholesome contents again put me on the way to health. I would almost as soon lost the money it contained as the letter. There has not been a death in some time about this place, last winter nearly every day one would be borne to yonder burial place beneath the old oak tree. I trust that no raging disease will prevail among us and that we may continue in the fine health we are in at the present time. Those three prisoners are yet in chains awaiting for what is to follow. We are yet where we were when I wrote to mother and Emory. We may remain 10 days longer before being relieved. A number of our pickets have lately been shot. The Provost guard does not have to do picket duty. A big lot of prisoners are brought in to us quite frequently, and we have a plenty of guard duty to do. Long black snakes and other big kinds are frequently found here: one of the boys, not long ago killed and brought in a large and poisoinous copperhead snake. I read, sometimes, of copperheads among you up North but not exactly this kind I guess (perhaps worse). Is Negro James in that part of country now days? If he is tell him I answered his letter he wrote me a year ago and tell me if he ever got mine. Does Your brother William stay with Johnson Kent yet, and how does he prosper? Nancy Jane, where is she and how does she get along? Does Ed or Uncle Lawtons folks come up often, or does our folks go down there? I must write to Joel to-morrow, he goes to school yet I suppose: when I get time I will have to write to Ed. You get but little time to go fishing and boating I reckon. be a good steady boy and do as well as you can: dont get in the habit of wrangling and using bad language but when your passions get aroused keep cool, and you will never regret it. Write to me occasionally and I will try and answer your letters. I am well supplied with stamps at present I was lucky enough to get 25 envelopes like this just before leaving camp which cost $1,00. only. But I must close. Farewell.

To Clinton Pangburn Esq.

Ira S. Pettit
Co. F. 1st Battallion
11th U.S. Inf. 2nd Brigade
2nd Div 5 corps.

Saturday 13: On guard; post No. 3, 2nd relief. Ordered at 4 P.M. to strike tents and prepare to move. A heavy thunder shower prevailed from 6 until 8 o'clock after which we started and marched until nearly midnight towards Warrention.

Sunday 14: Again took up our line of march at 10 A.M. and kept it up until after dark. Fine traveling: made a good distance.

Monday 15: Started at sunrise and marched until 3 P.M. following the railroad nearly the whole way. Reached Warrenton Junction. Very hot: some died from sunstroke. The march was rapid.

Tuesday 16: On guard. Very hot. We lay still the whcle day. Straglers come in by the hundred. Yesterday we crossed the plains of Mannassas (as I was told) and saw where skirmishing had been done, graves of the slain &c. Here are old fortifications.

Wednesday 17: Again started before sunrise and continued the tramp moderately until 4 o'clock P.M. passed Centreville A.M. where extensive fortifications were erected. Tremenduous falling out of the men; We could not begin to keep up to part of the straglers. Awful dusty.

Thursday 18: Went 2 miles last night to arrest a citizen. They gave us milk to drink &c. Camp Near Gum Spring,* V.A. No march to-day, which gives us a chance to rest from our weariness and the straglers to catch up. Hot and very dry: we are greatly put to it for good water. Through the mercies of divine Providence I have thus far stood the marches well.

Friday 19: Rained finely last night. We again started at six o'clock and marched six miles. A sharp cavalry skirmish took place to-day near where we are camped. Had a pleasant march.

Saturday 20: Camp Near Aldie, V.A. On guard last night and to-day: it rained a heavy shower last night, and to day is lowry and showry.

Sunday 21: This hardly appears like a sabath day. Heavy cannonading nearly all day off towards Snicker's Gap. A fight must be progressing. A division of our (the 5th) corps was sent out in light marching order.

Monday 22: We have a plenty of good water; beeves are slaughtered every day and we draw rations of fresh meat every night; but we are short on for pork and salt. Supply trains have started to Centreville for rations.

Tuesday 23: This is an open country where we are now. We are greatly in need of soap to wash our clothes. A man sentenced to be hung for manslaughter, which deed he committed two years ago, is put in our charge: He is to be executed next friday.** Detailed for guard.

---

*Now named Arcola.
**See diary entries of June 25, 1863, and July 11, 1863. Also see page 361.

147

Wednesday 24: On guard, post No. 4, 2nd relief. All the tents throughout the camp are being placed in regularity and things righted up which looks like making a stay, but it is a surer sign of leaving.

Thursday 25: Again detailed for guard, (only one night in bed) post No. 2, 2'nd relief. The man sentenced to be hanged to-morrow is reprieved. Lowry and misty.

Friday 26: Revalie this morning at 2 o'clock and the command was on the move at daylight! A heavy mist all day and we marched until after sunset: passed through Leesburg, crossed the Potomac and we are now in Maryland.

Saturday 27: Windy and cool: some muddy. Marched again at daybreak. I saw Capt. Cothran's Battery M. 1st N.Y. Art'y and the 111th P.V. 12th Army Corps. which I have long looked for. We passed through Fredrick M.D. and encamped a few miles from there. Fine country and crops are good.

Sunday 28: Did not march to-day. Many are coming up who fell out on the march. We waded sevral large streams both days and many suffer much from sore feet in consequence of getting them wet. Detailed for guard. Mail came in this P.M. Got a letter & 2 papers from Sister Lucina.

Monday 29: Marched again: passed near Fredericktown M.D. and crossed a large arched bridge:* Good McAdadamised road and fine weather to march. Encamped a little after sunset. Maj. Gen. Hooker is now relieved from the command of the Army of the Potomac by Maj. Gen. Meade of the 5th Army Corps.

Tuesday 30: Muster day: started in good season: passed through the villages of Liberty, Union Town, and

---

*This stone arched bridge carried the Old National Pike (now U.S. 40) across the Monocacy River southeast of Frederick, Maryland, until World War II. It was popularly known as Jug Bridge. The jug-shaped monument has been moved to the south limits of Frederick, and the inscription states that the 4 arches, 63' span structure was built 1808-1809. The Toll House on the west bank is today a residence.

Frizzleburg. Encamped at sunset. Gen. Sykes now commands our Corps and Brigadier Gen. Ayres commands our Division. Col. Burbanks our Brigade.

Note:

As the Eleventh Regiment made its way laboriously toward Gettysburg, it was never far from violence, and Stuart's Cavalry was often responsible for it.

"Stuart's loss in the battles of the 17th, 19th, and 21st of June was 65 killed, 279 wounded, and 166 missing; a total of 510.

"The Federal loss at Aldie and Middleburg, on the 17th of June, was 505. Colonel J. I. Gregg reports a loss of 127 in the battle of the 19th of June, and Generals Gregg and Buford report a loss of 188 on the 21st of June. Colonel Vincent lost 7 on the same day. The total Federal loss in these three engagements was, therefore, 827."*

Jeb Stuart crossed the Potomac River at Rowser's Ford, near Seneca, on June 27, 1863, to enter Maryland on his ride around the Union Army.

*McClellan, H. B. *I Rode with JEB Stuart, Life and Campaigns of Major-General J. E. B. Stuart.* Edited with an introduction by Burke Davis. Bloomington, Indiana: Civil War Centennial Series, Indiana University Press, 1958. p. 314.

JULY, 1863

Wednesday 1: Took up our march early and got into Pennsylvania at 10 A.M. we went near Hanover: Stoped quite a spell for rest and dinner. A large force of Rebs are going before us: we saw many dead horses and a few graves where a sharp skirmish took place yesterday.

Thursday 2: Started last evening an hour before sunset and marched until midnight. Started again at daylight and marched until 10 A.M. The enemy are giving us battle and hard fighting is now in progress. We are two miles from Gettysburg in Adams Co. P.A.

Friday 3: The fight renued early and the cannonading terrible all day! much heavier than at Chancellorsville but not so much musketry is heard. We captured Longstreet and 2500 prisoners of war. *(Ira has drawn lines through the preceding sentence.)* The enemy have gave away. Our regiment lost more than in any other engagement.

Saturday 4: No firing! not even national salutes. The enemy are on the retreat. I took a walk over part of the battlefield where our line of battle fought: saw the dead bodies of many of ours.

Sunday 5: The Pioneers and other details of men are burying the dead. Took a more extensive tramp over the rocky and marshy field and saw many of the enemy's slain.

Monday 6: A heavy shower prevailed yesterday which is a God-send to the wounded soldiers. Marched last night from sunset until mid-night in pursuit of the enemy; dark and slippery. Started and shifted sevral times but finally settled down for the day. An occasional shower of rain which will impede the enemys rapid retreat.

Tuesday 7: The battle of Gettysburg is a glorious achievement of the Army of the Potomac. Marched again from early morn, and went in to camp somewhat late.

Wednesday 8: Rained last night; and to-day it poured in torrents but we were on the march notwithstanding until 3 P.M. over a rocky and miry road and over a high mountain. Flowing water to wade. Went barefoot most of way.

Thursday 9: Passed through Frederick yesterday and went into camp within sight of the place, from whence we started this morning; crossed over South Mountain and halted before sunset where we remained. Left a letter to Georgie with a citizen to put into the office.

Friday 10: Shoes were issued this morning amid great cheering, which we were greatly in need of. Marched, well shod, with a squeak squeak for about 3 hours. Some cannonading at a distance. 2 regts sent out on a reconoisance.

Saturday 11: Caragan who was pardoned from the gallows was sent to duty yesterday. He belonged to the 6th regular inf. On guard. We lay near Antietam Creek. The troops are manouvered in line of battle, skirmishers thrown out &c.

Sunday 12: Moved a mile or so last night. Washed my shirt and took a bath in Antietam Creek. Marched 2 or three miles starting at noon. Our men are moved forward cautiously. A heavy shower took place and we went into camp. Got a letter from home and sent one to Edward.

Monday 13: Cloudy and showery. Our troops are engaged throwing up breastworks to fall back upon in case they are driven in the impending engagement. Lines of battle are formed, skirmishers thrown out and cautious movements made. A little skirmish firing is all.

Tuesday 14: Sent a letter to R. Tenny and commenced one to cousin Fanny. The Rebs have stole away from us and recrossed the Potomac! Marched towards where they were enmassed, saw their defences. Rainy and we have a damp berth.

Wednesday 15: On guard. Took line of march early and went back; recrossing South Mountain and encamped not many miles from the foot of it. Hot: so much stragling is seldom seen. Both men and animals are greatly fatigued. Saw Battery M. 1st N.Y. and Wm. Holmes but had little time for conversation.

Thursday 16: Enjoyed a peaceful rest and marched early again but went into camp by noon not far from Berlin* which is on the Potomac. Came through Burkitsville and are now in sight of Petersville.

Friday 17: Rained last night and to-day. Started this P.M. crossed the Potomac into V.A. on pontoon bridges and encamped after dark.

Saturday 18: Started early again and made but 10 miles. Sent a letter to cousin Fanny and bought 2 cigars on the way. Hot; went into camp early.

Sunday 19: Marched only 5 miles. Jayhawked a couple of sheep and had a fine meal of mutton. On guard.

Monday 20: Marched from morning until noon, made 12 miles. Hot and a hard march. Much stragling. Followed the range of mountains apast Snickers gap. Saw a large body of Kilpatrick's Cavalry.

Tuesday 21: We lay still to-day which gives us a fine opportunity to rest and straighten up. I washed clothes for our officers.

Wednesday 22: Marched at noon but made only 5 miles. Fawcett and I led the horses. Division headquarters at a fine house where many swarms of bees were kept and quite a number of slaves.

Thursday 23: On guard. Decamped in good season: before starting I bought a canteen of milk and some biscuit at the house. Entered Mannassas Gap: had a sharp skirmish! Some cannonading. At dark the affair ceased.

Friday 24: Rocky, O Jehu! Our troops were formed into lines of battle and advances cautiously made but the

---

*Now called Brunswick, Maryland.

enemy are found to have retreated into the valley. Quite many were killed and wounded in the skirmish yesterday. Marched part way through the gap and encamped for the day.

Saturday 25: Started early. Marched out of the gap and onward until a little past noon. Fawcett and I led the horses. Took a good wash and washed a shirt. Blackberries are abundant which we lay into.

Sunday 26: Hot. Rained last night holding the dust at bay. Marched again in good season; passed through Orlean; halted at 1, o'clock P.M. We again led the horses: I like the job. Lots of slaves in these parts.

Monday 27: Marched six miles: passed through Warrenton and went into camp in a pleasant spot. I never before saw blackberries in such abundance. Rainy. On guard.

Tuesday 28: Our rest was not disturbed this morning by revallie! We lay still to-day, feasted on berries and enjoyed a peaceful rest. A pleasant and delightful day. Received a letter this evening from cousin Marvin Serg't Maj 111th P.V. 12th A.C.*

Wednesday 29: Rained last night. Cloudy, windy, cool and delightful. Have fine times among the blackberries.

Thursday 30: Wrote a letter to Georgie, and sent $5,00, home in it. Cool and delightful.

Friday 31: Rec'd a letter from cousins Daniel and Debbie Sitterley and wrote one in reply. On guard: post NO. 2, 1st relief.

---

*See page 336.

153

AUGUST, 1863

Saturday 1: Sent the letter which I wrote yesterday. Very hot: we keep in the shade; We are supplied with water from an elegant spring near the house of a large plantation.

Sunday 2: Ordered to move our tents in allignment: we also made bunks and shades. I now tent with Nelson. Hot. We have a fine stream to bathe and wash our clothes in, and quite satisfied to remain here.

Monday 3: Very hot. Bowers are being built over the Gen.'s division headquarters and camps regulated. We were issued one days ration of loaf bread! The blackberries are about played.

Tuesday 4: Orders to march were rec'd last night at sunset; and by dark we moved off over rough roads but the moon soon lighted our pathway: made about 6 miles, and to-day 2 more and pitched tents.

Wednesday 5: A heavy thunder shower prevailed yesterday P.M. making it very nasty on this red clay soil. We were detailed all for fatigue to build officer's bunks and to clean off a place in the woods for division headquarters. Exceedingly hot

Thursday 6: Had orders to march again last night the general call was sounded and we struck tents: but the order was countermanded. Marched 5 miles this morning to the banks of the Rappahannock at Beverly Ford.*

Friday 7· On guard; post No 2, 1st relief. The boys have fine times plunging into the dirty Rappahannock.

---

*Near town now called Remington, Virginia.

Saturday 8: Washed my shirt and pants. The corps headquarters are pitched near us. Camp Near Beverly Ford V.A.

Sunday 9: We were paid up to the 1st of July. Some sutlers have come in. Received a letter from R. Tenny. Drew rations of loaf bread.

Monday 10: Wrote a letter to Aunt Lucy and sent five dollars.

Tuesday 11: Many rumors afloat that the Regulars are to leave the field to replenish their thined ranks. Conscripts will soon come in to fill those of the volunteers.

Wednesday 12: Wrote a letter to cousin Joel and inclosed $10,00 for him to hand to father. Took a bathe in the Rappahannock.

Thursday 13: Received a letter late this evening from Sister Lucina and Cousin Jane: also an Intelligencer containing a list of the conscripts in our section.

Friday 14: 1st and 2nd Brigades 2nd Division 5th Corps. All the regulars of the Army of the Potomac to leave the field. We started early and marched to Rappahannock Station, took the cars from thence and arrived at Alexandria at sunset.

Saturday 15: Having a high time in Alexandria. Very hot weather. Spending our money freely for the good things. Spent $4,00 foolishly for a hat and fixings.

Alexandria V.A.
Aug. 15th 1863,

Dear Father—

The regulars of the Army of the Potomac are taken from the field. We got abord the cars at Rappahannack Station near Beverly Ford yesterday and arived at the above place last night. It is now nearly sunset we will perhaps in a few hours get abord a transport and sail for N.Y. at least we think we will go there; but it may be to Albany, Boston, Charleston or some other seaport.

Different regiments will go to different places. Conscripts are rapidly being brought in to swell the ranks of the volunteers; the object is to replenish ours also and recruiting officers will soon be sent out, probably. I received Lucina's and Jane's letter of the 8th also the paper containing the list of Conscripts a perusal of which gave me much pleasure. You bet we're having a good time to day.

More Anon.
Ira.

Sunday 16: The 1st Brigade are on board of transports and we expect to be soon and be off for I know not where. Very tiresome to lay around in town these hot days; and wait in suspense.

Monday 17: Sent a letter to father. We moved in front of an ancient church and churchyard where Washington attended divine service. Saw the house* wherein Col. Elsworth was assassinated.

Tuesday 18: We got on board the steamer Daniel Webster last evening and this morning at 4, o'clock steamed off adown the Potomac. Saw Washington City, the Washington monument and Mount Vernon.

Atlantic Ocean Aug. 19th/63.

Dear Father:—

I am now on the blue ocean many miles from sight of land I have just had a fit of seasickness causing me to "heave Jonah" but I am now over it. I can now devour four mens rations as it causes a keen apetite. I intend to take a cabin dinner for I feel like geting the full worth of my money. I wrote to you sunday last while in Alexandria that the Regulars were called from the field to recruit up. We left Beverly Ford on the 14th and were marched to Rappahannock Station where we took the cars and arrived in Alexandria on the evening of the same day. At sunset

---

*The Marshall House.

156

on the 17th we went aboard the Steamer Daniel Webster. She steamed a short distance down the Potomac and lay at anchor until four o'clock the next morning. We passed Ft. Washington Mt. Vernon Aquia Creek and many places which I remember of seeing as we went down from Washington to the Camp last Winter. Aquia Creek has been destroyed, wharf, railroad and bridges, by the rebels, while we were in persuit of them so as to embarrass as much as possible our privilege of again having it for a base of supplies; but we had shiped off all the cars and valuable property. Night came upon us and we had not yet entered the main ocean from Chespeake Bay; but this morning no land is to be seen by the naked eye nor any time during the day. It has thus far been a very delightful trip save when the wind breezes somewhat too briskly, causing the noble steamer to rool heavily and many of us to stick our heads over the rail and cast into the sea. Yesterday while making down the river an unladen schooner attempted to cross our track; the machinery was stoped that she might succeed, but the streamer struck her fair in the side and centre! We backed off from her and she filled in five minutes and tiped on her beam ends but did not sink. Our steamer's bow was damaged and the water made its way in a little but the carpenter soon repaired the leak. I was aloft at the time she struck, I saw what was like to happen and made fast; we felt the shock but slightly, but if the schooner had been heavily laden we might have went down also.

Wednesday 19: Ran into a schooner yesterday and sank her. No land in view any time to-day. Windy; the boat rools heavily; many of us are seasick and "heave Jonah."
Thursday 20: Saw a Seahorse this morning. Arrived and moored in New York harbor before noon. Encamped in Madison Park. On the whole we had a safe and pleasant passage. I profited by it.

Aug. 21st:—We arrived safely yesterday at 10 A.M. in New York City. We are in Madison Square; We know how to appreciate such times as we are now having: rations are brought to us, cooked, every meal time. Times are now quiet here and the draft is going on: we expect some trouble in geting the conscripts off. Maj. Gordon is here to-day. We may go to Ft. Independence after the draft. I rec'd Lucina's and Janes letter of the 9th also the paper containing a list of the drafted. I expected father, to send you $20,00 of my last pay. I have sent you a $10,00 note and you will find a five herein inclosed. I have spent more than I wish I had; but, I thought I must have a taste of some of the good things for sale. I have a plenty of money left but I cannot send any more until we are again paid off which will perhaps be within twenty five days. I intend to go and see old Horace before long. But I must close. Direct as usual, but leave off the division.

Yours &c.

Ira S. Pettit

Co. F. 11th U.S. Infantry.

Friday 21: Sent a letter to Father with 5,00, inclosed. We buisy cleaning up our arms and accoutrements. We now get exelent rations cooked and brought to us.

Saturday 22: We all pitched our tents this morning and policed up the ground. On guard, post No 1, 3d relief: guard mount at 10 A.M. The draft is progressing quietly.

Sunday 23: The fine Parks of this City are being badly mussed up by our encamping in them. Took two swims in the East River. I now know how to appreciate our present good times.

Monday 24: Wrote a letter to cousin Marvin D. Pettit Sergt. Maj. 111th P.V. Two of our boys are absent on a spree.

Tuesday 25: Detailed For (standing) orderly at Division headquarters. I relieved Graw who is confined under guard for geting tipsey.

Wednesday 26: A large suply of clothing is being brought

here to Division headquarters, and sent off to the regiments.

Thursday 27: Wrote a letter to Mr. Wm. Holmes Battery M. 1st N.Y. Artillery. City life goes better every day: get rations of butter and cheese, comparitively high living.

Friday 28: All the Provost Guard have gone to the regiment and to their respective companies, except those on guard and myself.

Saturday 29: I am orderly no more. The remainder of us joined our companies this noon. New dress uniforms, scales &c. are being issued. Rained. Camp near Joness Woods East 71st Street New York City.

Sunday 30: On guard post No. 6 2d relief. Guard mount, 10 o'clock A.M. Maj. Gordon command this camp. We are within 100 yards of East River. Opposite to us is Blackwells Island upon which is a Lunatic Assylum, Poor House, Penitentiary &c.

Monday 31: Monthly inspection and muster day. Dress parade this evening. Turned out in our new uniforms and scales!

Note:

The *Daniel Webster*, which Ira boarded on August 17, 1863, had been used by the Sanitary Commission in one of the commission's many services to the soldiers during the Civil War.

"The commission proved its value during the Peninsula campaign of 1862. The transfer of troops to this new and somewhat malarious country soon brought on an amount of sickness with which the Governmental agencies were unable to deal. With the approval of the medical bureau, the commission applied for the use of a number of transports, then lying idle. The Secretary of War ordered boats with a capacity of one thousand persons to be detailed to the commission, which in turn agreed to take care of that number of sick and wounded. The *Daniel Webster*, assigned to the commission April 25, 1862, was

159

refitted as a hospital and reached the York River on April 30th, with the general secretary, Mr. Olmsted, and a number of surgeons and nurses.

"Other ships were detailed, though great inconvenience was suffered from the fact that several were recalled to the transport service . . ."*

*Francis Trevelyan Miller, Editor-in-chief. *Prisons and Hospitals. The Photographic History of the Civil War. In Ten Volumes.* Thomas Yoseloff, Inc. United States of America. Castle Books. New York. 1957. p. 336.

SEPTEMBER, 1863

Tuesday 1: Wrote a letter to Mr. Daniel Sitterley. We get no such rations here as we did in Madison Park: have been on hard tack for a few days past.

Wednesday 2: We have drill an hour in the morning and an hour in the evening: Dress parade at sunset. Loaf bread has come around again.

Thursday 3: Wrote two letters one to father and one to Mary Jane. We have drawn A tents throughout the camp. Received a letter from cousin Fanny.

New York   Sept. 4th 1863.

Dear Father:—

I have at length taken steps to recover the $10,00 ten dollars which was lost by mail last April.

You will have to place your name at the bottom of the last article. You will present it to any of your favorite bankers in Lockport or elsewhere and the Cashier will place his name in the vacant place where it reads "You will please pay to the order of"

I presume that you have received my two last letters, one mailed at Alexandria V.A. and the other in this City. We were dismissed from the Provost Guard last friday and joined our respective companies. I just received a letter from cousin Fanny Brown. I have a letter nearly finished to Sister Mary Jane. But I will write no more at present.

Please let me know the result of this business article as soon as possible by taking your time for it.

Your's &c.
Ira S. Pettit.

Direct
> Co. F. 11th U.S. Infantry
> Camp Near Jonses Woods East 71st Street N.Y.

Friday 4: Very fine weather nowadays; nights are rather cold. Cookhouses are being built and our accommodations will soon be ample.

Saturday 5: On Guard; to run with the Prisoners and not to walk post. Hillman, one of the prisoners, stole off.

Sunday 6: Robinson a prisoner also escaped last night. Serg't. Creighton, commander of the Guard, is put under arrest. Inspection this A.M. Dress-parade in Jones' Woods this evening.

Monday 6: Drill hours are one before breakfast, and from 10 o'clock A.M. until noon. Jones' Woods a great place for Picnics, Excurtions, Festivals. 1st Sergeant Whitton is now Sergeant Major, and Sergeant Chase is our 1st Sergeant.

Tuesday 8: A sore on my foot causes it to swell so that I cannot wear a shoe: do not drill nor go out on parade. A man was found dead this P.M. in the river! Was probably murdered.

Wednesday 9: Exceedingly fine fall weather: no showers have taken place in some time. Another picnic in Jones' Woods. No ceasation of Band music.

Thursday 10: Rumors afloat that we are to leave here for the field. What then will our new uniforms scales and fixings amount to! Captains Rusell and Layton have gone on the recruiting service.

Friday 11: On Guard; post No. 4, 3^d relief. At sunset the general call was sounded, tents were struck, baggage packed and we were marched in style to the wharf at which we landed a distance of three miles.

Saturday 12: We lay on the wharf last night and to-day. This evening at dusk we got aboard the ferry boat and were taken to Amboy Station where we immediately took the cars for Philadelphia. Maj. Gordon commands the 11th now.

Sunday 13: Got off the cars in Philadelphia this morning at twilight and enjoyed a rich breakfast at the relief association house; after which we soon started by rail for Baltimore which place we reached at 3 P.M. and took supper there.

Monday 14: Arrived in Washington from Baltimore last evening after dark and took another good meal at the Soldier's Retreat before we retired. Heavy shower. Took boat for Alexandria this P.M. and encamped back of the Town near fort Ellsworth.

Tuesday 15: We lay close to the railroad. Many conscripts are on their way to the front. I went up to Fort Ellsworth.* Gen. Ayres came in with more troops. Dress-parade this evening.

Wednesday 16: No orders in regard to what disposition is to be made of our regiment. Drew rations. Loaf bread. Hot and show'ry. Dress parade at sunset.

Thursday 17: We have tolerable easy times but are waiting in suspense.

Friday 18: Rain fell in torrents. On Guard post No. 5 1st relief. Guard mount at 10 A.M.

Saturday 19: Done some washing and put things in order.

Sunday 20: Inspection of everything at 8 A.M. Took a walk up to fort Ellsworth again. Nights are uncomfortably cool since the rain. New shelter tents were issued. I drew one. Pleasant day.

Monday 21: Again for the Field! Started early by rail (2nd 11th & 47th regulars) and reached Culpepper V.A. at 2 P.M. where we joined our Division and Corps. Camp Near Culpepper V.A.

Tuesday 22: Wrote a long letter to Sister Lucina. Beautiful country hereabouts and a delightful Autumn. Lieut. Ritner is now Provost Marshall, and Lieut. Huntington has charge of our Company.

---

*Fort Ellsworth was located about two miles from the Potomac River, west of Alexandria.

Headquarters 2ᵈ Div., (Regular) 5th Corps, U.S.,
Camp of 11ᵗʰ Infantry Near Culpepper V.A.
September 22ⁿᵈ 1863

Sister Lucina:

We are again in the field after an absence of a little over a month. The last letter I have had from home was yours and cousin Jane's of Aug. 8ᵗʰ and 9ᵗʰ which was received on the night of 13ᵗʰ but a few hours before leaving Beverly Ford for Alexandria. While in the latter place I wrote a letter to father, and two more while in New York and received one from cousin Fanny and wrote letters to Mary Jane, cousin Marvin, and Mr. Wm. Holmes. I also wrote to aunt Lucy while at Bev. Ford. The last we were paid was Aug. the 9ᵗʰ of which I sent home $15,00, and $5,00 of my old pay. Mr. Murray also gave me a paper good for the certificate lost in the mails last Spring which I sent to father in my last letter. Most of our division were again paid off in Newyork and we were to be paid the day after we left the City but were off too soon. It is probable that you have got some of my many letters and answered them but for some reason they have not yet been received. I would have written more but I was reduced to a single red stamp which I have reserved for a long time so that when it was finally decided upon where we were to be placed I could write and let you know and whenever you wish to hear from me send a stamp and direct F. 11. 2ⁿᵈ Div. 5ᵗʰ Corps. I might have reserved much more but we were to get our dues soon, sure as we thought, and we did not dream of being recalled so soon. The following is the disposition made of my last pay. $15,00, sent home; lent $2,00, paid 3,00 for a hat, gilt band, letters, figures and bugle, like a dunce, as soon as we got in Alexandria and when we got into New York we all had to draw regulation uniform hats. also fine coats and brass scales to wear on the shoulders like epaulets. But all these fancy things are of no account to us here. O we cut a swell in New York. Dress-parade and guard mount was worth seeing! The Band of 11ᵗʰ Infantry is the most accomplished of any in the service. The Provo. Guard was dismissed and we are now to our companies. Maj. Gordon now commands the regiment and Major Jones has gone to Fort Independence. I forgot to state that I also wrote a letter to cousin Joel Aug. 12th and directed it to Lake Road P.O. not knowing that he had returned to school until the evening of the next day when I got your's and Jane's letters. If I had stamps plenty I should have before now written to Grandfather and answered Jane's letter. I wrote to Daniel Sitterley while in N.Y. I stated in my letter dated (Atlantic Ocean) about our trip on the steamer Daniel Webster from Alexandria to New York, but forgot I think to make mention of the sea horses I saw just before entering N. Y. Harbor. They showed themselves above the surface as far as the shoulders and had every appearance of a horse. Beyond sight of land the water is a deep indigo blue much diffrent color than shore water. We returned to Washington by rail where we remained one day and night and stayed in those same barracks which we stoped in last winter on our way out here: you can see them in the picture I had taken and sent from there last winter. We started from N.Y. on the evening of Sept. 12th and reached Alexandria the 14th where we remained until yesterday when we started early on the cars and came to this place in good season. Conscripts are constantly pouring in and our forces are being rapidly increased. One days march would bring us in contact with the Johnny Rebs. O, Lucina the Autumn here is delightful! Time passes rapidly here. While in New York it seemed almost as long as the whole Summer campain. The ground is just as soft to lie on here as in the great City; we can make it much more comfortable by gathering grass or boughs to lie on. New tents and other clothing have again been issued: nights are geting quite chilly. I would like to get a letter from home please write every two weeks until I get one. Send a newspaper occasionally, I was pleased to read the list of conscripts in your last. Do you ever read in the papers anything about our regiment? did you see our list of killed and wounded. I presume you know that Capt. Barri died from wounds received at Gettysburg as you inquired if he was my captain yet. He was captain of co. B. my captains name is Caleb Rodney Layton. He is now on the recruiting service. 1st Lieut. Joseph M. Ritner commands the company. David H. Hazzard is our 2nd Lieutenant. Those were shocking accidents which you mentioned. In my letter to Mary Jane I congratulated uncle Elisha's folks on our new cousin. I am sorry to learn that the spring wheat crop is so poor. Did mother make her intended visit to the East? How did you manage things during her absence? I hope she had a safe and pleasant trip and happy visit. I can immagine Father you and Jane all into the parlor around the big table writing to me and Joel seated in the easy chair reading my letters about wading the Rapidan &c. That was a glad piece of poetry which you cliped from the Tribune and sent me. I would like to see the new mowing machine. I was surprised to see Harrison's and Clark's names in the list of the drafted. Why dont Emory write to me? has he got to come shure? I should think that he would be exempt. If he has to come I would be happy to see him in the 3^d brigade of our Division with the N.Y. Vol's. where we could see each other every day. another long and dismal Winter is before us: both armies are busy fortifying; there may be a great battle this fall before stormy weather sets in. Tell me in your next who of our friends are obliged to come to the field. I would gladly welcome Some of them into our ranks as fellow soldiers. Stiles Mix's name I noticed in the list. I noticed a telegraph dispatch in the N.Y. Herald some time ago of the destruction of the Steamer Zimmerman by fire while at her moorings Niagara C.W. it stated that two perished in the fire. Fanny wrote me a good letter. She spoke of aunt Susan's and Mrs. Batchelors visit and how glad she was to see them. I suppose now-a-days the hum of the machine can be heard in every direction and the poor fellows are working in the disagreeable dust. Has it not been vexing for the boys to milk twice a day all summer in fly time exposed to merciless switchings of the cow's fly-fighters? Now are the days of corncutting. soon will come husking and cold fingers, diging and picking up dirty potatoes. Do the fairs promise to be any thing? How is the fruit crop, the butternut trees my poplar. Your likeness is now before me and pretty fair picture too. I have kept it as neat and clean as when you inclosed it into the letter. It is yet in the same paper. Jane wrote that you promised her one of my photographs if I was willing: not any objections at all. Had we got pay in New York I would have got a number more taken. I have a good supply of things in my housewife it is a good one. I keep that bible yet; it is in good order and I peruse it often. Now when you write again try and think of uncle William and family. I will write to them as soon as I can. It must be a hard blow to Mr. Mix and family to lose Harriet and Mary. Tell me more about them in your next. Henry and Electa where are they and how are they geting on. Does it seem like a long time since I took my leave from home? I feel well paid by what I have travelled and seen besides the money I get for all I have sacrificed and endured. God has shown great mercy to me as He promises to all who love him and keep his commandments. Be not weary in well doing: be patient with those you have to deal with although it may be trying in the extreme and nothing will be lost in the end. My desires to see Washington, Mount Vernon, the Ocean &c &c have been well gratified. We spent a good time in Alexandria. I saw the house in which Col. Ellsworth was assassinnated and the old church where Washington used to attend divine service. There are very old graves in the church-yard. I copied some of the inscriptions from the tombstones. "Eleanor 8th wife of Daniel Wren. Died Apr. 1st 1798 aged 132* years." One of his wives who died at the

---

*The number '1' is apparently a prankster's addition to the originally engraved age, and is easily discernible to this day. The church to which he is referring is Christ Church in Alexandria.

age of 20 the following poetry was on the stone inscribed.

> "All you who come my grave to see
> As I am* you soon may be
> Repent and turn to God in time
> For I was taken in my prime."

On another of a young man.

> "Go my dear youth obey the call of Heaven
> Thy sins were few we trust they are forgiven
> Yet oh what pen can paint the Parent's woe
> God only gives the balm who struck the blow."

Adieu.

This letter is full enough of such as it is so Wishing peaceful times to you all I will close. Farewell.

Your Brother Ira S. Pettit
Co F. 11th U.S. Infantry.
2nd Div. 2nd Brigade
5th Army Corps.

(For the first time, Ira draws an iron cross. The symbol in the center of the cross is presumed to be a five without the top, since the iron cross was the insignia of the Fifth Corps. The flag of the First Battalion of the Fifth Corps was a red iron cross on a white background.)

Wednesday 23: Sent the letter which I wrote yesterday. We are under marching orders: eight days rations are being issued. Inspection of everything this evening.
Thursday 24: I mounted guard as supernumerary. Mac-Mahn who deserted us last winter is now caught and confined in our guard house.

---

*Ira omitted "now."

Friday 25: On Guard post No. 1, 2nd relief. Guard mount at 5 P.M.

Saturday 26: Burns* a deserter from our regiment was just brought in to us. To-day we have quite a guardhouse full of prisoners.

Sunday 27: Brigadier review by Lieut. Col. Green. Frost last night. The Paymaster is in camp. We signed the rools this evening.

Monday 28: Division review by Gen. Meade and Secratary Stanton. We were paid this P.M. I rec'd $23,13, $00,62 charged for belt and plate.

Tuesday 29: Brigade and battalion drill every day. I am excused in consequence of galled feet and painful boils. Received a long and exelent letter this evening from Mr. Wm. Holmes Batry M, 1st N.Y. Art'y.

Wednesday 30: Monthly regimental inspection and review. 1st Lieut. Hartwell is now our company commander. Pleasant.

---

*See page 366.

169

OCTOBER, 1863

Thursday 1: Detailed for guard tonight.
Friday 2: On guard: post No. 3, 3ᵈ relief. Rained sevral smart showers. 1st Lieut. Bentzoni arrived in camp this P.M. from fort Independence.
Saturday 3: A clear sky again. 1st Lieut. Bentzoni who arrived yesterday is to take charge of our co: viz; Co. F. 11th U.S.I.

(And the next page, covering days 4, 5, 6, 7, 8 and 9, has been torn from the diary.)

Camp Of 11ᵗʰ U.S. Infantry Near Culpepper V.A.
Oct. 6ᵗʰ 1863.

Dear Sister Lucina:

Your's mailed Oct. 1ˢᵗ was joyously received last evening. I could plainly immagine you all solitary and alone seated in the 2ⁿᵈ side seat from the stage pening in a hurry that letter. I appreciate your punctuality in replying to my last. These five stamps are worth much to me. I am lousy with money for we were again paid off one week ago yesterday but it would not buy stamps for there are none here consequently those five added greatly to the value of your letter. Four days ago I received a long captious and interresting letter from Holmes dated at Kellys Ford V.A. and last saturday night I had another from Cousin Marvin! He had been promoted to 2ⁿᵈ Lieutenant. He has been sick but has now recovered and doing duty again. We supposed that no drafted men would be sent into our ranks but in this we were mistaken: last sunday fifty were brought to our regiment and distributed to the sevral companies. Substitutes are selected for us as far as possible. We lay exactly where we were when I wrote my last. We have our camp slicked up finely. Since then Gen. Meade and staff have been here and a grand review of our division took place. It was big satisfaction to know that my money all got home safely; and, now I'll send some more. This string of 5^s is *yours*. I cannot accuse you, Lucina, of injustice for not writing to me sooner. Accident after accident seems to happen in that section. The capsizing of that schooner was a shocking affair. It is funny that among all who were enrolled on the conscript list on our street that none had to go! I laughed when I read your statement. I'm glad they cant draft me, a'int you? Where does Stiles, Bill, Lute and Marcus get all their money to *buy* themselves clear!!! I am glad to learn that you are attending school this fall. You *deserve* to for doing so well while mother was absent on her late visit East. Attending to your studies must absorb nearly all of your time. I hope that Mr. Martin will succeed in collecting the money that paper calls for. Mr. Murray told me if I found any thing wrong about it to speak to him about it. It was indeed a great loss to our regiment to lose so exelent an officer as Captain Barri. First Lieutenant Charles Bentzoni came here last friday from fort Independence and took command of our company. I got a picture taken yesterday which I will enclose with $5,25. You will see that I am *shaved*; It cost $1,00. I intend to get another taken to send in my next also: do with them what you like. Oweing to the unusual brevity of this letter I expect to be detailed to go out on picket and stay three days; but no more for this time; so, Adieu.

Your Brother Ira.
F
11
U.S.I.

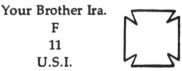

(On a separate piece of paper, included with this letter, Ira has written, "I did not hear of Reubin Pierce's Death.")

Saturday 10: Revalie sounded at one o'clock this morning then the general call. Were issued eight days rations and hurried into the ranks, leaving many good things; and marched off. Went only 5 miles and returned this evening.

Sunday 11: The command left early; we marched from Culpepper, crossed the Rappahannock and encamped at Beverley Ford. The enemy following and shelling in our rear.

Monday 12: Crossed back over the river at early dawn and prepared for battle marching in line quite a distance towards Culpepper and encamped.

Tuesday 13: The Command was aroused at midnight and we got silently away and crossed the river again and took another rest until morn. then marched all day towards Centreville. Cannonading in the rear.

Wednesday 14: Unsteady marching back and forth all day long, and until late this evening making at last towards Centreville. I tired and exhausted fell out with others and lie down just before the command halted. Much stragling many of whom the enemy picked up.

Thursday 15: We arose early and soon found the regiment. The command took up line of march seasonable: we passed through, and encamped four miles east of Centreville a slight shower prevails.

Friday 16: Rainy. Straglers are constantly coming in. Rations are being issued sufficient to keep the eight days on hand! All but the eight days rations we have got though. I washed some clothes.

Saturday 17: Decamped last evening at dusk and marched two miles or more back towards Centreville in torrents of rain, and remained there until this morning, then came on to the place. Signal Corps at work all day. An occasional cannon shot can be heard.

Sunday 18: Marched back to the very spot from whence we came night before last. Rations again issued this evening for two days only.

Monday 19: The whole army appears to be on the move.

172

We took up our line of march at early dawn again passed through Centreville and after a hard journey went into camp on the old Bull Run battlefield; Saw numerous traces of the old conflicts. Detailed for Picket.

Tuesday 20: Revallie this morning at 2 o'clock and off the Army moved at rapid gate through rough ways and stringing along in the dark. A halt after an hour's sun then at 1 P.M. moved on until an hour before sunset. Made about 12 miles in all.

Wednesday 21: A day of rest. Received an excelent letter from home. Nearly everyman is out of rations. Camp near New Baltimore.

The remaining pages of the diary had been torn out before its return to the Pettit family. The following is an accounting of the 11th Regiment's activities from October, 1863, to June 16, 1864, at which time the siege operations against Petersburg and Richmond commenced and lasted until April 2, 1865, according to Frederick H. Dyer:*

October 9-22, 1863: Campaign of Maneuvers, "The Bristoe Campaign."

November 7-8, 1863: Advance to line of the Rappahannock.

November 7, 1863: Engagement, Rappahannock Station.

November 26 to December 2, 1863: Campaign, Mine Run. Actions at Locust Grove, Payne's Farm, Orange Court House or Orange Grove, Robertson's Tavern and New Hope Church.

May 5-7, 1864: Battle of the Wilderness.

May 8-21, 1864: Battles of Spottsylvania Court House, Laurel Hill, Ny River, Fredericksburg Road.

May 22-26, 1864: Operations on line of North Anna River, and engagements.

---

*Frederick H. Dyer, *A Compendium of the War of the Rebellion*, Vol. II: *Chronological Record of the Campaigns, Battles, Engagements, Actions, Combats, Sieges, Skirmishes, etc., in the United States, 1861 to 1865* (copyright 1959, by Sagamore Press, Inc.; New York: Thomas Yoseloff), pp. 923, 926-27, 933-34, 938-41, 944.

May 26-28, 1864: Operations on line of the Pamunkey River.

May 28-31, 1864: Operations and engagements on line of the Totopotomoy River.

June 1-12, 1864: Battles about Cold Harbor.

June 1-3, 1864: Battle of Bethesda Church.

June 16-18, 1864: Assaults on Petersburg.

June 16, 1864 to April 2, 1865: Siege operations against Petersburg and Richmond.

The monthly 'Record of Events' of the Eleventh Regiment found in the National Archives, Washington, D.C., M-66, Roll 124, Aisle 10, Tier 34, Drawer 4 (10-34-4), corroborates Dyer and Pettit:

"October, 1863: Regiment took part in the engagement at Rappahannock Station, and fell back with the Army to Centreville. Returned to Rappahannock and encamped near Peols Mills, doing picket duty.

"November, 1863: Remained on picket duty at Peols Mills until 26th, then marched to Mine Run, Virginia, and bivouacked in front of enemy.

"December, 1863: December 2 retreated from in front of enemy at Mine Run, crossed the Rapidan and halted at Cattlett's Station two days. Then, on command, moved fourteen miles to Bealton Station and camped until 27th. Then, on orders, marched down the Orange and Alexandria R.R. to Bristow Station, Virginia.

"January, 1864: Remained camped on R.R. near Nokesville until 3rd. Then went to Alexandria to guard trains rest of month."

(No record of events appears from February and March, 1864.)

"April, 1864: Regiment engaged in guarding trains. On 24th, transferred to Bealton Station."

(No record for May, 1864.)

"June, 1864: On being flanked June 2, regiment fell back

174

one half mile and constructed works, remained until June 6, then marched six miles and camped near Allen's Mills until 11th. Then crossed Chickahominy at Long Ridge on 12th and camped near Charles City Court House. On June 16 crossed James River on transports and arrived in front of Petersburg daybreak June 18. Engaged enemy under heavy fire, and at night threw up entrenchments, occupying these until 28th, when relieved and retired a mile to rear for remainder of June."

(No record for July or August, 1864.)

"September, 1864: Engaged during September holding position on right side of Petersburg and Weldon R.R. On 30th left and took part in engagement near Globe House, Virginia, and also October 6, 1864.

"October, 1864: On October 4, marched to right and remained in position on left of Petersburg and Weldon R.R. remainder of October.

"November, 1864: The Command left the Army of the Potomac November 1, and proceeded to Fort Hamilton, New York Harbor, arriving November 6. Went to Baltimore, Maryland, November 23; then to Camp Parole, December 5 and performed garrison duty rest of December."

DECEMBER, 1863

Camp Of 11th U.S. Inf't'y.
Near Bealton Station VA
Dec. 21st 1863

Dear Father: It is perhaps some satisfaction to get a letter from me with the assurance that I am in good condition although it be unusually brief. I sent a letter to Lucina on the 9th on which day we were paid and inclosed five dollars for her to hand you to give to uncle William and tell him that I sent it to Him. I also wrote another on the following day and directed it to Mother with five dollars more. I have been detailed with many others of our regiment to make corduroy roads since I wrote the last and consequently I have had no favorable opportunities for writing since. In this letter you will find another V. I have left yet to send you a neat sparking "bran fired new ten dollar bill"! I would like to send it as it is but hardly dare risk it. I will either get it split and send it at twice or send the whole by that bank operation again and pay a quarter for being safe. I will try and have another letter reach you by New Years. Probably you are enduring very cold weather about these times. It is pretty snug here too, but no snow has fallen yet: we have fixed up our tents comfortable with a small fire place at one end to prevent the snug embraces of "Jack Frost" good hard wood is abundant and we would all be quite content to remain here all winter. Old "Smoke John" goes bounding past us laden with supplies for troops to the front. We have been fed on loaf bread ever since we came here. I presume we will make another move to the rear before making a final winter rest. Father, for rabbits this country beats all yet. It is quite amusing as we often encamp in or near the woods when we first march in to see the terrified creatures go bobing around not knowing which way to escape! But their chance for escape is always slim, they are generally caught alive in our hands as they go bounding through the ranks amid many shouts of "catch im! catch im!! there he goes!!!"" Last Spring before the battle of Chancellorsville a large ammount of clothing was boxed up and sent to Washington except overcoats and marked the co, regt. &c so as to be returned when called for. I turned in my uniform coat and a half dozen pair of white gloves which are of no account here; also a good sized book. Last friday night our boxes came to hand all right each receiving his own and much other belonging to those slain in battle which was cast lots for. Had we got it while in N.Y. to save drawing new ones it might have been quite a profit to us. We prophesy small pay next time as we have each a big clothing bill to foot and all we have drawn over our allowance will be deducted. I have drawn a new overcoat, $9,50 Blanket $3,50. Tent $1,75 Uniform coat in N.Y. $7,50 Hat $2,04, and a change of other garments. When we were paid at Culpepper 62 cents was taken from each man's pay for throwing away the cartridge box strap and brass plate we slip it on the waist belt like the cap box: it is more convenient and makes less harness. That is all I have had stoped from me yet.

An occurrance took place in this Division last friday between the hours of 12 and 1 o'clock P.M. which you will no doubt read of in the newspapers. Viz: The shooting of John McMahn of our regiment (and of our old company) for desertion. The whole Division turned out under arms and were formed into a square to witness the execution. I was on guard and also on post at the hour and had not a fair sight at it for a few obstacles but it was quite near and I heard the volley. All the rest of the guard not on post were taken out to see the example.

I was well acquainted with McMann, Four others was sentenced to be shot with him but were reprieved and sent to duty. One was Burns of the same old Co.

McMann's case was an extreme one; pure desertion (He was a rough case) re-enlisted as a substitute and happened to be sent straight to this regiment where he was recognized immediately. He left us after the Chancellorville fight. He has now received his just deserts. But I will close for this time and go to dinner. I expected to croud what I had to write on ½ sheet but could not.

Wishing you a Merry Christmas I bid you farewell.

Ira S. Pettit

P.S. I received a long letter from cousin Clarrissa last saturday night: only three days coming. Ira.

F.
11
U.S.I.

(Information concerning Private John McMann's court martial and execution appears on page 356. Also see diary entry dated September 24, 1863.)

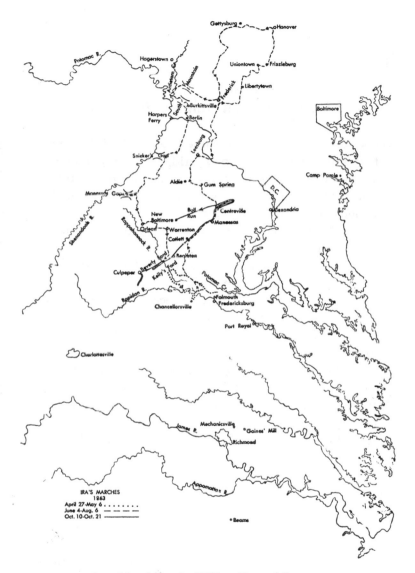

Map drawn by William Howard Ray.

Chronology of
Marches and Encampments—1863

February—April: Encamped three miles behind the line—two miles from a railroad bridge crossing Potomac Creek, north of Falmouth, Virginia. Erected fortifications at R.R. bridge and served in picket lines maintained three to five miles away.

April 27: Marched westward from camp shortly after noon for ten miles.

April 28: Marched from 3:00 p.m. until after sunset.

April 29: Crossed Rappahannock on pontoon bridges early in day at Kelly's Ford, proceeded south across Rapidan, wading it by moonlight.

April 30: Marched back and forth, seeking favorable place to attack.

May 1: Engaged enemy a little before noon. Battle of Chancellorsville ensued. Fell back a mile in the evening.

May 2: Moved two miles toward United States Ford a little before sunrise.

May 3: Retreated across Rappahannock at United States Ford on pontoon bridges.

May 4: Fell back several miles.

May 5: Started back toward camp about 3:00 p.m., halted by heavy rain and nightfall.

May 6: Arrived in camp north of Falmouth by noon, in rain.

June 4: Started at dawn and marched ten miles to United States Ford.

June 13: Marched from 8:00 p.m. 'til midnight toward Warrenton.

June 14: Marched a good distance, from 10:00 a.m. until after dark.

June 15: Started at sunrise, marched along railroad 'til 3:00 p.m., arriving at Warrenton Junction.

June 17: Marched from before sunrise (passing Centreville before noon) until 4:00 p.m., camped near Gum Spring (Arcola), Virginia.

June 19: Marched six miles and camped near Aldie, Virginia.

June 26: Marched from daylight until after sunset, through Leesburg and across the Potomac.

June 27: Marched at daybreak, and encamped a few miles from Frederick, Maryland.

June 29: Passed near Fredericktown, crossed a large arch bridge, encamped after sunset.

June 30: Started early, passed through Liberty, Uniontown, and Frizzellburg.

July 1: Crossed into Pennsylvania (near Hanover) at 10:00 a.m. Rested, and marched further from an hour before sunset until midnight.

July 2: Resumed march at daylight, engaged enemy about 10:00 a.m., two miles from Gettysburg.

July 3: Heavy fighting continued.

July 5: Pursued enemy from sunset until midnight.

July 6: Rain impeded retreat and pursuit.

July 7: Marched from early morn until late.

July 8: Marched in downpour through Frederick.

July 9: Crossed over South Mountain.

July 10: Marched three hours (in new squeaky shoes). Camped near Antietam Creek.

July 11: Moved a mile at night.

July 12: Moved forward two or three miles with caution.

July 13: Cautious movements and skirmishes.

July 14: Marched toward vacated Rebel defences.

July 15: Recrossed South Mountain, camped near foot of it.

July 16: Marched during forenoon through Burkittsville to Berlin (Brunswick), on Potomac (in sight of Petersville).

July 17: Crossed Potomac in afternoon on pontoon bridges.

July 18: Marched ten miles.

July 19: Marched five miles.

July 20: Marched during forenoon (twelve miles), followed mountain range past Snicker's Gap.

July 22: Marched five miles.

July 23: Entered Manassas Gap. Sharp skirmish, including cannonading.

July 24: Pursued enemy cautiously part way through Manassas Gap.

July 25: Marched back out of Manassas Gap.

July 26: Marched through Orlean. Halted at 1:00 p.m.

July 27: Marched six miles, through Warrenton, and encamped.

August 3: Marched six miles at night.

August 4: Marched two more miles.

August 6: Marched five miles to Beverly Ford on Rappahannock.

August 14: Entrained at Rappahannock Station for Alexandria.

September 21—October 9: Encamped near Culpeper, Virginia.

October 10: Marched off with eight days' rations, went five miles, and returned to Culpeper.

October 11: Marched early from Culpeper, and encamped across the Rappahannock at Beverly Ford. (Enemy in pursuit.)

October 12: Recrossed Rappahannock to do battle, and marched quite a distance toward Culpeper.

October 13: Aroused at midnight and retreated across Rappahannock again. Rested until morning. Marched all day toward Centreville, with cannonading in rear.

October 14: Marched back and forth all day long, working back to Centreville, exhausted.

October 15: Arose early, passed through Centreville, and encamped four miles east.

October 16: Marched two miles back toward Centreville at dusk.

October 17: Marched on to Centreville.

October 18: Marched back to encampment four miles east of Centreville.

October 19: Marched at dawn back through Centreville, and encamped on old Bull Run Battlefield.

October 20: Moved on about 2:00 a.m. until dawn, then again in the afternoon, for a total of twelve miles to encampment near New Baltimore, Virginia.

EIGHTEEN HUNDRED SIXTY-FOUR

The last entry remaining in Ira's diary was recorded on Wednesday, October 21, 1863. By then the Army of the Potomac often dined on hard tack, but that was of banquet quality compared to what was yet in store for Private Pettit.

We know from other sources that in October, 1863, the Army of the Potomac forced Lee's Army back to the Rappahannock. On November 7, 1863, General Meade advanced to the river and precipitated the battle which forced Lee to retreat across it. There were more skirmishes before both armies went into winter quarters.

The Eleventh Regiment camped for a time at Bealeton Station, Virginia, during and after these engagements, then at Catlett Station and finally at Alexandria. From January through April, 1864, the Eleventh Regiment was assigned guard duty, riding the supply train between Alexandria and Culpeper.

The latter part of April, 1864, found the Army of the Potomac prepared for a spring offensive from which there would be no steps back.

By May 5, 1864, Private Ira Pettit was once again in those 'extensive forests,' called the Wilderness, and there on May 12, his birthday and a day of heavy fighting, he received a head wound.

After he left the Wilderness, Ira marched beside Enoch Pettit, of the One Hundred Fifty-first New York Volunteers, from Fredericksburg to Port Royal, Virginia. (Port Royal was a supply depot of the Union Army.) On May 30 he helped to guard a wagon train to army headquarters, which was by this time near Mechanicsville, Virginia, not far from Richmond. On June 2 he reported to his regiment which was in line of battle.

187

Shortly after greeting his comrades and receiving and reading his mail, the Rebels charged and captured Private Pettit and twelve other members of Company F, as well as thirty-two other men of the Eleventh Regiment.

The end was close at hand. These captives were taken first to Richmond, probably Libby Prison, and from there they were sent to Andersonville Stockade, Sumter County, Georgia.

There remain only two letters after April 22, 1864, from Private Ira S. Pettit, datelined Camp Sumter, Andersonville Station, Georgia, and although dated June 21, 1864, and July 8, 1864, and bearing the marks of censorship, their postmarks were January 18, 1865, Old Point Comfort, Virginia.

JANUARY, 1864

Camp Of 11th U.S. Inf'ty.
Alexandria VA
Jan. 13th 1864.

Dear Father:

Yours of the 4th was gladly received on the 10th showing an unusual delay of three days, as I generally get your letters in three days after being mailed. You have probably been unaware of where I have been since I wrote my last which you write of geting safely. Well we have moved camp twice since; first we went from Bealton Station to Catletts Station, staying just one week then came by rail to the above place. We are encamped near the depot in commodious A tents. Our duty is now to guard the train from here to Culpepper. It takes nearly one half the regiment one day and the other half the next. A large number goes out on each train, armed and pieces loaded ready to fire into Moseby's band if they make a dash at us. I like it very much. Our regiment *happened* to have a streak of good luck in getting the job. You may believe father that I now get a plenty of riding on the railroad enough to make up what I did'nt get while at home. Every other day almost an hundred miles and back! and get pay too instead of paying for it. It again extends beyond the Rappahannock; a new bridge is built across the river. It would do you good to travel the route a few times to see the extensive fortifications on the plains of Bull Run and Mannassas and the often disputed grounds between us and the enemy; also where cars have been burned and the track destroyed repeatedly. On our retreat from Culpeper last fall they also played Jessie with things destroying all the bridges &c

piling the ties, then placing the iron on the piles so it rested in the centre then set them on fire, the iron becoming heated would bend; some is twisted around trees and many other queer contrivances to spoil it. But it takes but a short time to replace it and make it in good runing order as it now is, and O what a business is done on it! A great many three years men who have served two years are being discharged on conditions of reenlisting for three years more and are now on their way home on a 35 days furlough; sometimes a whole regiment at once; the 86th N.Y. have just gone on the above conditions.

It does me much good to have you write to me. You are the only parent I have living. Well it appears that another five dollars has made a miss-go. *Let it went.* I must expect to lose some. I have five more I meant to have sent but guess I will keep it until next payday unless I arrive at a diffrent conclusion when I mail this letter tomorrow. I am now where I can express it safely to you. When paid last, after collecting a few debts, I have over $50,00 twenty of which I meant to reach home and give five to Uncle William besides. I had a good time on it Christmas and New-years: spent more than I ought to perhaps. I got the last letter Lucina wrote a few hours after I sent my last. The ground is now covered with snow and there is quite a wintry appearance but no such severe cold as you write of. You quote hay at a very high figure but you would not wonder at it if you knew how much it takes to feed our horses and mules. But I must lay this aside until to-morrow for it is nearly 10 AM. at which hour I must leave with the rest of the detail on a train and attend to this to-morrow.

Your boy.   Ira

Jan. 14th/64
P.S. I am now on pass in the town and sit as I write this in the Marshall House where Col. Ellsworth was assassinated. Had a safe and pleasant trip yesterday. I guess I will

keep this $5,00 until we are again paid. The rools have gone to Washington to be approved and will soon return.   Ira.

Note:

The Old Town Holiday Inn, Alexandria, Virginia, reached its completion on October 6, 1975. This new Holiday Inn, containing two hundred and twenty-eight rooms, covers an entire block facing King Street between Pitt and Royal Streets, which includes the area where once stood the Marshall House. On May 24, 1976, the bronze plaque which had graced the preceding building was installed on this new inn. The plaque informs passersby:

"THE MARSHALL HOUSE
stood upon this site, and within the building
on the early morning of May 24, 1861,
JAMES W. JACKSON
was killed by federal soldiers while defending
his property and personal rights, as stated in
the verdict of the coroner's jury.
He was
the first martyr to the cause of Southern
Independence. The justice of history does
not permit his name to be forgotten.
Not in the excitement of battle, but coolly,

and for a great principle, He laid down his
life, an example to all, in defense of his
home and the sacred soil of his native state.
VIRGINIA

erected by the sons
and daughters of
Confederate Soldiers."

Who was the real hero of the day depends upon one's perspective.

As one of his contributions to the security of Washington, D.C., Colonel Elmer E. Ellsworth (accompanied by his Fire Zouaves) proceeded to enter the tavern of James W. Jackson in Alexandria, Virginia, on May 24, 1861, and to remove the Confederate flag which graced the tavern's roof.

Mr. Jackson, who apparently had some notions about the sanctity of private property as well as the Confederate cause, took somewhat seriously this invasion of his inn and removal of his flag. Thereupon he shot Colonel Ellsworth and in turn, was shot by another Zouave.

As many young Yanks hastened to enlist in the Union army they may have dreamed themselves into the same heroic aura that suffused the late Colonel Ellsworth.

APRIL, 1864

Camp of 11th U.S. Infntry
Alexandria V^a
Apr. 12th 1864.

Dear Father:—

It is now evening: I have just been relievd from Camp
Guard and had time enough to hurry down to the office of
Adam's Express Co. and put twenty five dollars under
way; for which I received a receipt. I directed it to you the
same as my letters. I did not pay the freight on it. We were
again paid off last evening, I received $23,75. Before we
were paid on the 29th of Feb. and I expressed to you $15,00.
on the 3^d of March. Only one letter have I received since
and that was a good one from cousin Emory. He stated
that you had got the certificate and not a word have I heard
about it since, whether you ever got the money or not.
However I will not write in a censureing manner for I
cannot but think that you have written to me concerning
it, but I have never received any satisfaction in regard to
it. I received that School Catalogue and letter which
Lucina sent me and I wrote a long answer to it; mailed it
March 26th I have not now the leisure to write any thing
more than what pertains to this little business matter.
Suffice it to say that we still remain here. The weather is
pleasant and happier times cannot be realized by soldiers.
I am in the best of health. Plese write as soon as you get
this even if you have sent me a letter an hour before. After
waiting a due length of time, I shall look for a letter from
you with great anxiety. I inclosed one of the new kind of

$20,00. treasury notes and a V. let me know particularly whether you get the same money which I sent.

No more at present.
This from your grateful Boy. Ira.
Co. F. 11th U.S. Inf.
Alexandria V.a.

P.S. The money Clerk says that the package will be forwarded to the office of the company nearest to you which I suppose is in Lockport: They will then notify you from that place. I directed it as he advised me to Wilson. The clerk's name is P.M. Pettit.

Camp of 11th U.S. Infantry,
Alexandria V^a
Apr. 22nd '64.

Sister Lucina:—

I received yours and father's letter of the 17th this morning, and read it with much satisfaction, to know that you had received my last. Quite likely that by this time you have received the money which I expressed to you $25#. I also received the other letter which you and Pet. wrote and found it very interesting. Then Mary Mitchel is dead too! Very sudden was it not I noticed her name in the list of lady students in the School Catalogue. Tell Lucretia that one of our corporals (namely): Pulaski Jerome seems to know something about her whether she is acquainted with him or not. When he found I was from Wilson he inquired if I knew of W^m. Barnard and if he was not connected by relation to Mr. Aceley Williams. He said that when the latter lived on the Ridge road in the town of Gaines he knew a girl who lived with him by the name of Lucretia Mitchel. He says that She and Miss Odell used to be togather a considerable. Corporal Taylor of co. "E" on hearing my name inquired if I was from York State. He said he knew many Pettits in Saratoga Co. where he lived. He spoke of Jonathan, Grandfather, Cousin William, the

Nash'es and particularly Sam. Does Father know of any Taylors thereabouts? Last monday I received a letter from cousin Fanny and one from cousin Dudley. Last wednesday I received one from Mary Jane. She wrote to you at the same time and you speak in your last of receiving it. Yours and Clinton's came to hand on the 15th To-day I have written to Mary Jane and sent her two photographs of two negatives. I will also send you two of the same. My eyes never took well in a picture yet. I had 12 taken for $4,# an equal number of each kind. I think that money clerk is no relation to us, but he is a young and a smart man and among the "upper tens". I have done business with Him twice, he saw my name on the packages and to whom they were adressed then wrote them both on the receipts. Says another clerk "there's your namesake."— "Yes I see" he remarked; and made no further inquiries nor did I. but perhaps I may if I have another occasion in the office. Rumors were afloat that we were to be relieved by some of the Invalid Corps as all the ablebodied troops here and elsewhere have been: but, it is now pretty certain that will remain here on duty yet for some time. Everything indicates an offensive movement of the army. Troops are pouring in constantly and Sutlers are being sent away. No more furloughs are to be granted, Beeves are car'd to the front by thousands so that the supply waggons need not be laden with meat rations on marches. The sick too are being sent away. Three cases of small Pox has recently broke out in our own company but they were not extreme. It is a little prevalent in this place but seems not to be alarming. But I will bring this letter to a close.

Respectfully from your brother

Ira.

F

11

U.S.I.

JUNE, 1864

Camp Sumpter Near Andersonville Station Georgia.
June 21st 1864.

Dear Mother,
   I am now a prisoner of war. I marched side by side with Enoch Pettit from Fredericksburg to Port Royal. There we separated on Monday, May the 30th and I help guard a waggon train to army headquarters which was near Mechanicsville Va. On the 2nd of June I reported to my regiment which was with the command and in line of battle. I was handed Lucina's letter and photograph, one from Fanny and Clarrissa, and one from Harvey U. Pease. Just had time to read them and had a good talk with the boys before the enemy made a charge on our right flank and captured myself and 12 others of our company! We were taken to Richmond on the 3d. On the 8th we left Richmond and reached this place on the 14th. I am in good health and spirits and get a plenty to eat. My wound is hardly yet propperly healed.
   If you wish to write to me adress Ira S. Pettit, Prisoner of War, Co. F., 11th U.S. Inf. Via: Washington, D.C. Camp Sumpter near Andersonville Station Georgia.
   Respectfully from Ira to his mother.
   Caty J. Pettit.

Ira S. Pettit.

P.S. In your directions add: Detatchment Seventynine-one Sergeant Meade's squad.

The preceding letter is addressed in a plain envelope to:
>Mrs. Clinton Pettit
>Wilson, Niagara Co., New York
>By the way of flag of truce,
>Washington, D.C.

Note:

When Henry Wirz took command of Andersonville Stockade he grouped the men into squads of ninety. Three squads, or two hundred and seventy men, made up a detachment. The detachments were numbered sequentially, starting with those located at the north end of the stockade beside the gate.*

Of course the squads of each detachment were numbered 1, 2 and 3; therefore, Private Pettit at first belonged to the 79th detachment, 1st squad (mess), i.e., 79-1. This must have put him some distance down the north slope, possibly near the marshy area which bisected the prison from east to west.

By July he had been changed to detachment 57-1. One's detachment number must have been changed frequently due to the gaps made by deaths, transfers of prisoners to other stockades and other phenomena prevailing in the prison.

---

*McElroy, John. *This Was Andersonville*. Edited with an introduction by Roy Meredith. New York: Bonanza Books, 1957. p. 20.

JULY, 1864

Camp Sumpter
Near Anderson Station Georgia,
July 8th 1864.

Dear Father:—

I am now a prisoner of war. I returned to my regiment on the 2nd of June. The command was in line of battle on the Mechanicsville pike. I received a letter from Lucina with her photograph; one from cousin Clarissa, and one from Harvey U. Pease. I had not been back four hours scarcely, before the enemy turned our right, and twelve of our company besides myself were captured. We were in Richmond until the 8th and arrived here on the 15th by rail. It is very hot but we have a shelter which affords a protection from storms and from heat a shade. We get a plenty to eat and I have been in good health and spirits until after the fourth of July; since I have had the diarrhoea which makes me very weak. I can get around and hope soon to recover. About 10 of the 2nd Mounted Rifles are here. We now belong to the 57-one detachment instead of 79-one. or in other words detatchment 57. first mess. I wrote a letter to Mother from here on the 21th of June. Direct your letters as follows:—

Ira. S. Pettit (prisoner of war)
Washington D.C. Co. F. 11th U.S. Infantry.
Via flag of truce.
Camp Sumpter Georgia. Detatchment fiftyseven-one.
Respectfully from your boy.
Ira.

The above written is contained in a brown envelope and addressed thusly:

> "Mr. Clinton Pettit
>
> Wilson, Niagara County
>
> N.Y.
>
> Via flag of truce and Washington D.C.
>
> From a prisoner of war."

NOVEMBER, 1864

U.S. SANITARY COMMISSION
Camp Parole, Annapolis Md.
November 28th 1864.

Mr. Pettit

Sir—You undoubtedly have been waiting for a long time to hear from your Son Ira. It is my painful duty to inform you of his death. He died at Andersonville Ga., on the 18th of October.

Your Son was captured on the 2nd day of June near Mechanicsville Va. together with 45 others of the Regt. I was a tentmate of his as long as I was in Andersonville Prison.

After we were captured, we were taken to Richmond, where we remained till the 8th of June, we then were sent to Georgia, which we reached on the 15th. About the beginning of August Ira got the Scurvy in his mouth, and at the end of the month in his legs. In the middle of Sept. he also got the Diarhea, which I think was more the cause of his death than the Scurvey. On the 28th of Sept. I left the prison for Savannah Ira not being able to accompany us. On the 8th of Nov. I heard of his death from a young man by the name of Phelps* belonging to the 11th Pa. Cav. This man also had posession of your Son's Diary and various other articles. It was my intention to try and get the Diary from Phelps, but before I could see him a second time he had taken the oath of allegiance to the rebels, and gone out of the Stockade. About the last of August your son told me

---

*See page 268.

it was his wish that in case he should die, I should take charge of his Diary and send it home, but me not being with him at the time of his death it was impossible for me to do so.

I was paroled on the 19th inst. I had the scurvey very bad, but since I have arrived in Yankeedom it has nearly disappeared.

If you want to write to me I will try and answer all your questions. As in a few days I am going home on a 30 days furlough you may address:
Saxonburgh, Butler County Pa. If you write after the expiration of 30 days direct Co. F. 11th U.S. Infty.—1st Battalion Camp Parole, Annapolis Md.

Your Son never despaired and was willing to lay down his life for his country if necessary, which declaration he very often made.

Yours truly
Edmund Riedel*

---

*See page 257.

DECEMBER, 1864

Saxonburgh
Butler Co. Pa.
Dec. 31st 1864.

Miss Lucina Pettit

Dear Miss—Yours of the 6th inst. I have recd. I will try to answer your questions in regard to your Brother.

I cannot exactly tell when he was taken with the Scurvey-I believe sometime in August. At first it only troubled him while eating, but about in the middle of September it had drawn up both his legs so, that it was with great difficulty and pain that he could walk. About the 17th or 18th of Sept. he also was taken with Diarrheaa, and that in it's worst form, which I believe, was mostly the cause of his death. He confidently expected an exchange to take place about the beginning of Sept., and he often told me that he was bound to live till then. When the expected exchange did not come off, he said he would gladly lay down his life if it done his country any good;—he did not want the Government to disgrace itself by acceeding to the terms of the rebels.

When your Brother got so that he could not walk about very well, I done his cooking for him, also the other tentmates tried to make it as comfortable as possible to him. On the evening of the 28th of Sept. when we had to leave him (he being unable to accompany us) he felt very bad, but said he would keep up courage to the last.

I do not know if I ever can get Ira's Diary, as Phelps has joined the rebel ranks; if ever an opportunity offers I would gladly do it.

I did not hear anything of Ira after I had left him, until Nov. when I was informed of his death by several, but as I was unable to move for I too had the Scurvey—I could not hunt up Phelps, and when I sent somebody for him he had already joined the rebel army.

Ira never got any medicine, although he often went to the Hospital at Sick call.

Our own men had to carry out the dead, the rebels then buried them—but so many died sometimes that corpses would have to lie 3 or 4 days before being interred.

On the 12th of May your Brother was wounded in the head and was away from the Regt. until the day of his and my capture—the 2nd of June near Mechanicsville, Va. If Ira had been one hour later he would not have been captured. In Richmond we were nearly stripped of everything, I however, had the luck to smuggle my woolen Blanket through with me to Andersonville and had give shelter for 7 of us! And we were lucky too!

Next Tuesday I have to return to the Regt. as my furlough will then be out.

Your Brother was a good friend of mine—may I not call you so? I remain, with great respect.

Edmund Riedel

If you wish to write more (which I would like my friend's sister to do) Address:

Co. F., 11th U.S. Infty.
Washington
D.C.

Chronology of
Marches and Encampments—1864

From mid-December, 1863, to January 5, 1864: Encamped near Bealeton Station, Virginia.

January 5—12: Encamped at Catlett Station, Virginia.

January 13—April 22: Served as guard on trains between Alexandria and Culpeper, Virginia.

May 12: Incurred head wound.

May 29: Marched from Fredericksburg to Port Royal, Virginia.

May 30—June 2: Served as guard on wagon train to Mechanicsville, Virginia, where captured on June 2.

June 3—8: Held in Richmond, Virginia.

June 15, 1864: Arrived by rail at Camp Sumter near Anderson Station, Georgia.

EIGHTEEN HUNDRED SIXTY-FIVE

I pledged allegiance

Private Ira S. Pettit had been turned into a stockade covering little more than twenty acres of sandy, barren soil, surrounded by twenty-feet-tall pine trunks which had been slave-hewn and stood side by side, anchored some five feet into the ground. The prison population, during his sojourn there, at times reached more than thirty thousand men.

Probably everything that Private Pettit had seen before this seemed purely academic in comparison. His head wound had hardly healed, and again, we might surmise that he could have contracted tuberculosis. The handfuls of unbolted cornmeal and the lack of ordinary vegetables soon produced within him scurvy and diarrhea. We might suspect that maggots had infested his yet unhealed head wound. No doubt he became afflicted with the pints and quarts of lice that thrived on all the men.

Being unable to walk, Ira had had to remain at Andersonville when the Rebels started moving prisoners en masse during the autumn of 1864.

The precise day cannot be determined with absolute certainty, but it appears most likely that it was on October 18, 1864, that the soul and spirit, which had inhabited a five feet, six and one-half inches physical structure called Ira S. Pettit, scaled the heights of those twenty-feet-tall pine palings, and escaped the insufferable swamp of misery called Camp Sumter.

OCTOBER, 1865

New York Oct 24th 1865

My Dear Freind

I am happy yet sad, happy to think I can add one joy to your sorrow, and sad that it is my painful task to state that the diary was put in to the hand of my friend, who brought it to me for me to get it to you, if I could find you. The enclosed is all that your dear brother gave to him (a fellow prisoner) a day or two before he died. He was sensible and asked as favour for him to take it and deliver to his folks, if he was fortunate enough to escape. The young man was named William E. Mott* of the fourteenth Conn Volunteers he was eight months a prisoner and was transfered from one prison to another until he escaped and joined Shermans Army, when coming through the South. Mr Mott came home on furlough in April last—then gave it to me and I should have sent it to you then, but I did not fully understand where he got it from, until he was discharged and came home for good, for he was transfered to another regiment after his furlough expired and kept some time longer. He has now gone to California, he left here the 16th of Oct, he is an Orphan and a fine worthy young man, he saved nothing of his own but kept the diary through all, now if it adds one mite to your happiness to receive it, I will answer for him as well as for myself, we are well paid, or shall feel that we are if we can hear from you that you have got it safe, for though of a small amount it must be very dear as a last relic from one

---

*See page 249.

who died in that never to be forgotten prison, please write when you get this and let me know that you have got it. If it ever happens that you come this way or any of your folks, call and see me and I will receive you as friends

yours in haste
Mrs. John Gregory

I send you the photograph of Mr Mott as taken last April, and the change after paying the postage

Note:

Since neither the letter from Mrs. Gregory nor the envelope in which it was sent to Clinton Pettit provided a return address and since Mrs. Gregory included 'change,' one must conclude that Mr. Pettit had already written to her and had sent postage to her to bring the diary home.

[The illustrations which preceded this page in the original edition may be inserted elsewhere in this edition.]

Our Father,

These notes, diary, and letters remain in a hand-hewn wooden box, passing haplessly from one keeper to another.

The cause for which Ira Pettit believed he died has been challenged and championed in tribal councils and courts of supreme justice; in speeches and declarations; in hearings and decisions; by tests, bans, treaties; by riots, marches, war; in victory, compromise, surrender; all in the trappings of civilization.

Tomorrow, man will fraternize with yesterday's enemy.

Almost nothing is forever, but perhaps a quince or a poplar tree still graces a yet serene spot in Wilson, Niagara County, New York, United States, North America, Planet Earth, Universe.

Art Thou in Heaven?

EPILOGUE

A FEW ANDERSONVILLE ALUMNI

Andersonville Prison was a deformed brain-child conceived by many motives, born in a bed of expediency, and nutured upon despair. A delinquent juvenile, it matured rapidly into an habitual criminal, casting a dark shadow upon the soul of the Confederacy.

It was not the first such mutant of man's handiwork, possibly not the worst, and certainly not the last. Man has not bred out the evil within his own morality. And it may be that evil is a natural and integral phenomenon in the make-up of man, existing only to the extent of each individual's comprehension of it.

Disclaimed by its progenitors, Andersonville inevitably became an orphan that lay at the doorstep of necessity in the neighborhood of humanity.

the Ides of March

The train trip from Richmond, Virginia, to Andersonville Stockade, Camp Sumter, Georgia, usually took about
six days. John McElroy, Company L, Sixteenth Regiment,
Illinois Cavalry (attached to Cumberland Gap, Tennessee),
had been among that first load of prisoners in February,
1864, and years later he described the coming of March,
1864, to Sumter County, Georgia.

"The fuel and building material in the stockade were
speedily exhausted. The later comers had nothing whatever to build shelter with.

"But, after the Spring rains had fairly set in, it seemed
that we had not tasted misery until then. About the
middle of March the windows of heaven opened, and it
began a rain like that of the time of Noah. It was tropical in
quantity and persistency, and artic in temperature. For
dreary hours that lengthened into weary days and nights,
and these again into never-ending weeks, the driving,
drenching flood poured down upon the sodden earth,
searching the very marrow of the five thousand hapless
men against whose chilled frames it beat with pitiless
monotony, and soaked the sand bank upon which we lay
until it was like a sponge filled with ice-water. It seems to
me now that it must have been two or three weeks that the
sun was wholly hidden behind the dripping clouds, not
shining out once in all that time. The intervals when it did
not rain were rare and short. An hour's respite would be
followed by a day of steady, regular pelting of the great
rain drops.

"I find that the report of the Smithsonian Institute gives
the average annual rainfall in the section around Andersonville, at fifty-six inches—nearly five feet—while that of
foggy England is only thirty-two. Our experience would
lead me to think that we got the five feet all at once.

231

"We first comers, who had huts, were measurably better off than the later arrivals. It was much drier in our leaf-thatched tents, and we were spared much of the annoyance that comes from the steady dash of rain against the body for hours.

"The condition of those who had no tents was truly pitiable. They sat or lay on the hill-side the live-long day and night, and took the washing flow with such gloomy composure as they could muster."*

*McElroy, John. *Andersonville: A Story of Rebel Military Prisons.* Toledo, Ohio: Published by D. R. Locke, Blade Printing and Paper Co., Electrotypers, Printers and Binders, 1879. p. 152.

Private John A. Cain

John A. Cain and Ira S. Pettit in all probability never knew one another, and only indirectly did their lives overlap.

Although his motives may sometimes appear ambivalent, the enigmatic aura which surrounds the history of John A. Cain becomes irrelevant in its pathos.

For a few hours on August 23, 1861, twenty-nine year old John A. Cain belonged to Company E, Fourth Regiment, New Jersey Infantry Volunteers. He enrolled that day as a musician (fifer) for a period of three years at Trenton, New Jersey. His presence was not in evidence after August 23, and records indicate that he did not answer roll call after enlistment. Company muster rolls, dated August 31, 1861, list him as having deserted at Trenton before joining the regiment.

In San Francisco, California, on February 13, 1863, John A. Cain, by now thirty years old, was enlisted by Captain C. S. Eigenbrodt into one of the companies being recruited for the Massachusetts Cavalry. Private Cain was described as standing five feet, six and one-fourth inches tall, with blue eyes, black hair and fair complexion. His occupation was given as that of a farmer, and his *home of record* at the time of this enlistment was New York City. Muster rolls listed his birthplace as New Jersey.

Companies E, F, L, and M, Second Regiment, Massachusetts Cavalry, were organized at San Francisco in February and March, 1863, and left the state on March 21, destined for Readville, Massachusetts, where they joined the regiment as the California Battalion on April 16, 1863. Private Cain was a member of Company E.

By the middle of May, 1863, Companies E, F, G, H, I, L, and M were in Washington, D.C., participating in its defences. After June 23, their duties during the remainder of 1863 included patrol duty in the rear of the Army of the Potomac and reconnaissance and skirmish operations in the nearby Maryland and Virginia countryside, spasmodically spurred on by a wistful desire to capture John Singleton Mosby. Operating from Vienna, Virginia, after October 9, 1863, they scouted Gum Spring, Annandale, and Tyson's Cross Roads, made a reconnaissance to the Blue Ridge Mountains and took part in picket attacks.

They spent much of January, 1864, around Ellis and Ely's Fords, scouting Aldie and Circlesville. And on February 22, 1864, as a detachment of the Second Massachusetts Cavalry and a detachment of the Sixteenth New York Cavalry scouted near Dranesville, Virginia, they were attacked by a party of Confederate Cavalry scouts. Those who escaped the Rebels' attack continued to Farmwell on their way to Muddy Branch.

When the Confederates departed this scene of battle on February 22, 1864, they took with them fifty-seven new prisoners. Ten Union cavalrymen lay dead upon the field, and seven other Union cavalrymen carried wounds into camp that night.

Private John A. Cain was one of those fifty-seven prisoners. He was taken to Richmond, Virginia, on February 29. Departing Richmond on March 4, 1864, for Camp Sumter, Georgia, about a week's train-ride away, Private Cain arrived at the stockade at Andersonville on March 10, 1864.

Private Cain's prisoner-of-war memorandum indicates that he was admitted to the hospital for treatment at Andersonville on January 4, 1865, for pleuretis and on April 13, 1865, for scorbutis. Quite ill by then, Private Cain was paroled from prison at Jacksonville, Florida, on April 28, 1865. (A total of thirty-three hundred prisoners were paroled through Jacksonville.) From Jacksonville he was taken to Camp Parole, Annapolis, Maryland, and placed in St. John's College Hospital for medical treatment.

It becomes quite evident from subsequent events that Private Cain was one of those thousands who was shuttled back and forth from Andersonville to Savannah, to Millen, and back again to Andersonville during the last four months of 1864.

From St. John's College Hospital on June 3, 1865, Private Cain corresponded with the Secretary of War. His letter to the Honorable E. M. Stanton read, in part: "Deeming it my duty to myself and my country, I here send you a partial list of Union prisoners who left the Stockade prison at Camp Lawton near Millen, Ga. on, or about the 10th of November last; and is supposed to have taken the 'Oath of Allegiance' to the late 'Confederate Government.' Should this be of any service to you in bringing them to justice I shall consider myself amply compensated for my trouble, I am, sir, your most humble and obedient servant, Jno. A. Cain, Co. E, 2 Mass Cav., Ward 8, St. Johns College Hospital, Annapolis, Maryland.

"List of Prisoners of War, who left the stockade at the Solicitation of rebel authorities at Millen, Ga. on, or about the 10th, November 1864 for disloyal purposes.

"... Wm. E. Mott, F., 14 Conn; ..."

Private Cain's list contained the names of one hundred and thirty-four persons, and in nearly all cases he listed the company, regiment, and state or Federal unit in which the individual had served. Aside from William E. Mott, Company F, Fourteenth Regiment, Connecticut, Private Cain listed two other men from the Fourteenth Regiment's Company F, Connecticut, and four members from Companies A, B, L, and M, Second Massachusetts Cavalry, who allegedly embraced allegiance to the Confederate government on that day.

On July 7, 1865, at Fairfax Court House, Virginia, in

poignantly familiar territory, John A. Cain was honorably discharged from military service with the rank of corporal. He stayed for a time, after his discharge, at New Boys Home,* 7th Street, Washington, D.C. Before he left it forever, there was yet another service John A. Cain would perform for the United States.

On September 22, 1865, John A. Cain took the witness stand for the prosecution in the trial of Henry Wirz, former commandant of the Andersonville Stockade Prison, Camp Sumter, Georgia.

"September 22, 1865. John A. CAIN, for the prosecution: I was in the military service of the United States; I enlisted in the California cavalry battalion, at San Francisco.

"Condition of the Prisoners in the Stockade

"I was taken prisoner the 22d February, 1864; I was taken to Richmond, Va., and remained there three or four days, long enough to be searched and have everything taken from me and the rest of us. I was taken from there to Andersonville, and arrived at Andersonville on the 10th of March, 1864; it was raining very hard when we arrived there, about two o'clock in the morning. We were drawn up in line four deep, about 1,000 of us, and were marched through water about knee deep; a great many of the men were very sick and feeble; they were forced to walk through that mud and water about knee deep to the

---

*One of the many humanitarian services performed by the Sanitary Commission was to provide a home for discharged soldiers: "A 'home' was established in Washington to give food and lodging and proper care to discharged soldiers. Those in charge were always ready to help soldiers to correct defective papers, to act as agents for those too feeble to present their claims at the pension office or to the paymaster, and to protect them from sharpers and the like. Lodges were established near the railway stations to give temporary shelter. Two nurses' homes were established, but these were largely used as temporary shelter for mothers or wives seeking their wounded sons or husbands."[1]

[1] Francis Trevelyan Miller, Editor-in chief. *Prisons and Hospitals. The Photographic History of the Civil War.* In Ten Volumes. Thomas Yoseloff, Inc. United States of America. Castle Books. New York. 1957. p. 340.

stockade, a distance of about half a mile; they were turned loose into the stockade; it was raining hard and we were without shelter and we did not know where to go; they were ordered to fall in the next morning to receive orders how we were to proceed while there. Being very dry I started to the swamp to get some water; in the dark I fell into a hole headlong; however, after some difficulty, I found the water and got a drink and started back; I came across several shebangs, as we called them, rudely constructed tents and covers made out of pine boughs and poles; they were a poor excuse for covering; the rain was beating on the men who were lying under them; the men were very emaciated and sick, as I thought; some were groaning. We had some little talk with them; they told us that we had no shelter and that we would have to do the best we could. I went upon the shady side of a large tree and stood up and sat down as best I could until morning; it rained until daylight. When daylight came, I can hardly describe the scene that I beheld—men lying around in all directions sick, very sick and feeble; most of them were Belle island prisoners. It did not matter about the health of the men; it seemed to me that the healthiest of the men took sick as quick, if not quicker, than some of those who were weak. Two of my own comrades—stouter or heartier men never lived—took sick the next day; I did not know from what cause unless it was from change of water; we had to carry one of them in a blanket to the hospital. This hospital was only a few boards thrown together very temporarily to shed the rain off those very sick lying in there; they were lying in their own filth, with nobody to take care of them. When I visited the hospital to see my own comrades, men would appeal to me to help them to the sink, or to give them a drink of water, or a piece of bread or something of that kind; I very nearly got sick at the stomach and had to leave the place. About ten o'clock that day I was ordered to the other side of the stockade; the place was very steep, rising up from the swamp; it could not be called a hill—it was a bank, inclining at an angle of about forty degrees; I was allotted to a place on that bank that was very difficult for a sick man or a weak man to ascend without good help, without two men to help him; I was obliged to lie there until I was taken to the hospital. I got scurvy and diarrhoea after a while; I was obliged to lie there without shelter; we sat by a fire which a hat would cover up, made of pitch-pine roots; I sat there for twenty hours at one time in the rain; it rained a great deal during the month of April. We could not cook what raw rations we got; I very often mixed up meal and ate it raw for want of wood and cooking utensils. We got a little more than a pint of meal; that was before Captain Wirz took command; we got a little better than that after he took command. The rations consisted of about a pint of meal and a half a pound of very coarse beef; we took it to be mule flesh; it looked more like horse or mule flesh than beef; we got about a teaspoonful of salt; that was our rations for twenty-four hours; I very often ate my beef or mule flesh raw; I just picked the bones. In that condition I lay on that side of the hill until about the 23d of May, when I became so weak that I could not get up to roll-call in the morning. Captain Wirz's sergeants ordered all the sick to fall in every morning, if they had to be carried up; I very often got some of my comrades to help me up this hill, and in many instances I fainted away when I got up. One time at the top of the hill I fainted away and was conveyed temporarily to a little tent, consequently missing the roll-call; the sergeant asked where I was; they could not find me; and he ordered my rations to be stopped that day; it was neglect of some comrades for not having me up. I finally got discouraged and made up mind to die; I did not wish to be any more trouble to my comrades, and I went over to the gate and was successful in getting to the hospital; that was a little after the hospital was moved out of the stockade, about the 23d or 24th of May, I think. What transpired in the stockade after that I cannot say,

238

except as I might see the victims of Wirz's cruelty come to the hospital. I was paroled as a nurse, or was allowed the privilege of nursing; we had no more liberty than any of the rest of the sick; I was very often allowed to go to the gate to help sick men off the wagons or ambulances, or to carry the men on stretchers. I had an opportunity there of seeing the cook-house and of seeing the rations taken out, and of hearing news of the inner part of the stockade.

"Shooting of Prisoners by the Guards

"I kept a memorandum of the events that transpired there. By reference to that memorandum-book I can tell about men being shot there by the sentinels; I can recollect, without referring to the memorandum, the case of three prisoners who were shot by the sentinels. About the middle of April, 1864, (witness refers to his memorandum-book and gives the date as the 23d of April) an insane man was shot; he was considered insane by us; he would go around among the debris of the swamp and pick up undigested food, beans and meat, that had passed through men; I have often myself tried to turn him from it, telling him to go to his quarters and let that alone, or something to that effect, which made me form the conclusion that he was insane or crazy; he was very emaciated. He was one of the Belle Island prisoners. I know something about a man being shot on the 2d of May; I do not know that I saw him before he was shot; he was a man of dark complexion; I took him to be a German; he belonged to a Pennsylvania regiment; I do not know his name; I was told he was an insane man; he was near the hospital, or rather on the southeast corner of the stockade where the hospital was located first; I do not recollect seeing Captain Wirz then; I did not see him on the other occasion, April 23d; my tent was in the middle of the stockade, and if there had been anything of that kind occurring, by the time I could get there through the crowd of men it was all over. I know something about a guard at

239

the hospital shooting a man; the entry in my memorandum of the 25th of July is, "Rebel guard shot a sick Union prisoner for coming near his fire." His leg was amputated near the thigh; he died; I cannot say when; I did not see him when he was shot; it was done about nine o'clock in the morning; I had been at his fire before he was shot, and I was there about ten minutes after he was shot; I heard the report and got up, and heard the man moaning very piteously; I went down to where he was; they had just carried him into the tent; I heard him make a statement the next day; the guard had their line inside on this end of the swamp hospital; it was very common for us to go down and sit near the fires and converse with the guard and trade with them; there was no order against that; I often went down and warmed myself, and heated soup and mush and corn-meal coffee; we used to call it conscript; this man said he went down as usual and sat near the fire, and that the first thing he knew, the guard, without any warning, drew his musket and shot him.

"Q. Do you know anything of a man that was shot on the day following, the 26th of July?

"A. I heard the shot, but did not see the man. Not long afterwards the man was brought into the hospital; I did not see him after he was brought in; some time in July; I recollect it without reference to my diary; it was about the middle of July; his name was John Burke; he belonged to the sixty-ninth New York volunteers, Colonel Corcoran's old regiment; he was brought to my place where I was nursing; I had five tents to take care of, three in a tent; he was sent to me to take care of; the ball went in the right cheek, cut off his tongue, cut out his upper teeth, passed out through his left jaw, and cut three of his fingers nearly off; he was sitting in his tent at the time, smoking his pipe, when the ball went in and struck him. That man died; he made a statement to me when he was aware he could not live; he said he was starving to death; he could not eat what he got, and could not get anything better to eat; I made a requisition on the doctor's steward for suitable food; in some instances it was to be had, but he could not get it; this man died in consequence of gangrene getting in his tongue, and breathing through it, the doctor said, was the cause of his death; he died about a day after being removed from my charge; he was sent to the surgical ward, but it was too late.

"By the COURT: The man stated how he came to be shot; he said he was lying in his tent, and that the guard fired at a man right on the dead-line, missing the man and hitting him. I know the date when John Burke died; about the 25th or 26th of July, I think.

"General Cobb's Speech

"General Cobb was at Andersonville about the 2d of May, and made a little speech to us, not very gentlemanly or encouraging to us. I do not recollect seeing Governor Brown, of Georgia, at Andersonville there at that time, but General Cobb made some allusion to a remark which Brown had made, that he would not have us there any longer, as we were a nuisance to the country; General Cobb made this remark to some of the men; he said that Governor Brown said he would not keep us there any longer; that we were a nuisance to the country, and that if Jefferson Davis did not move us he would move us on his own responsibility, or something to that effect.

"General Winder Orders the Guard to shoot Prisoners

"General Winder visited the hospital after I was sent there; I know something about his ordering men to be shot about the 20th of July; I was standing at the gate; there had been no dead-line established inside the hospital, never; in fact there was no dead-line except right in front of the gate; in order to keep the gate clear he ordered the guard to shoot any damned Yankee who would trespass on the dead-line; it was only a mark sometimes made in the dust with a bayonet; he said,

241

further, "Any Yankee son-of-a-bitch you catch bathing in that creek down there shoot him." The nurses and attendants had a parole at that time; the pass was taken away from us, and we were refused the privilege of bathing in the creek; we bathed below the hospital; we had a ditch dug through one end of the hospital for washing-water, and a sink at the lower end; it was a tributary of Sweet Water branch; I did not see any reason why I should not be allowed to bathe there; it was all swamp waste land beyond that.

"Shooting of Prisoners by the Guard

"Cross-examined by COUNSEL:

"John Burke spoke very inaudibly and incorrectly, but I could understand him; he wrote on paper at different times the things he wanted. The man that was shot at the fire, was shot as he stood at the fire. He went there to warm himself, as usual, as there were no orders against it. It was very chilly on the evening of the 25th of July, especially to a man in his condition, especially in rainy weather, and with no blankets. Referring to my memorandum of the 9th of August, in reference to John Burke, the entry is, 'Burke, who was shot in the face, is dying for the want of proper nourishment.' That is what he told me the evening before he was removed from my care to the surgical ward.

"THE ASSISTANT JUDGE ADVOCATE submitted to the court the entry in the hospital record in the case of John Burke, showing that he died of dysentery on the 10th of August.

"WITNESS. Burke had no dysentery; I will state to the court that I am crippled myself now from the effects of my imprisonment.

"Condition of the Prisoners in the Stockade

"When I arrived on the 10th of March there were twenty-two thousand prisoners in the stockade, I think;

the hundred that I was assigned to was the 25th hundred; that was before the stockade was enlarged; at the time I was transferred to the hospital there were 18,000 or 20,000 prisoners in the stockade; Captain Wirz came there about ten days or two weeks after I had got there; there were about 14,000 or 15,000 prisoners there then; I helped to carry the sick from the stockade to the hospital myself on stretchers; there was a doctor in charge to receive men who were brought to the hospital gate, and such men as he thought fit to be admitted to the hospital he had carried in; I cannot say that I saw any other man eat undigested food, except the insane man I have mentioned, although I heard of it; I think no person but a crazy man would do it.

"General Winder Orders the Guard to Shoot Prisoners

"I think it was about the 20th of July that General Winder gave the order to shoot men. (Witness refers to his diary) The entry is, 'General Winder orders the guard to shoot every Yankee son-of-a-bitch caught trespassing on the dead-line or bathing in the river.'"*

Thus ended the testimony of Private John A. Cain in the trial of Henry Wirz. Wirz's sentence, death by hanging, was duly executed on November 10, 1865, on a gallows in the yard of the Old Capitol Prison. It is conceivable that John Cain was one of those who witnessed it.

Sometime after this incident, Mr. Cain moved from Washington, D.C., to Boston, Massachusetts, and 1868 found him a resident of Yarmouth, Nova Scotia. The scourge of scurvy and its sequelae plagued him in its ever-progressing agony.

From Drs. Farish and Farish, practising surgeons in the town of Yarmouth, Province of Nova Scotia, by way of the U.S. Consul's Office there, came the following statements to the Bureau of Pensions, dated January 22, 1869:

---

*Executive Documents, The House of Representatives, 2nd Session of the Fortieth Congress, Executive Document No. 23. *Trial of Henry Wirz.* Washington, D.C. Government Printing Office, 1868. pp. 393-4-5-6.

243

"We have carefully examined John A. Cain . . . the following is the present physical condition of the disability for which the pensioner states he was originally allowed his pension. The hip joint is distorted from swelling of the surrounding parts and is stiff, permanently fixed. The thigh cannot be bent upon the hip nor the leg but very slightly on the thigh. He is unable either to sit or stand, but is forced to keep the horizontal posture in bed, with the leg in the extended position. He suffers constant and severe pain in the hip and thigh, which is much aggravated by the least pressure or motion. There is also numbness and pain in the lower part of the spine. These symptoms have existed in nearly their present severity for nine months and to a less though severe degree for several months previously, and are daily increasing. At present his every want has to be attended to by his nurse, as he lies stretched helplessly on his back. The pensioner states that the disease was contracted in active service, while in the line of duty and in confinement as a prisoner of war, and we believe the exposure and hardships consequent upon such confinement to have been the original and sole cause of the disability. As above declared, we believe the present state of the disability to be permanent . . . From Documents in his possession he has been a captive in the Southern States for 14 months."

The preceding statements were signed by Dr. G. I. Farish, Dr. I. C. Farish, and J. M. Merrill, U.S. Consul Agent, all of Yarmouth, Nova Scotia.

John A. Cain died on February 25, 1869.

Perhaps his fleeting enlistment in Company E, Fourth Regiment, New Jersey Infantry Volunteers, had discouraged John Cain's return to that state, and it could be supposed that his removal to Boston, Massachusetts, was motivated by a search for the four members of his Second Regiment, Massachusetts Cavalry, whom he asserted had taken allegiance to the Confederate government at Camp Lawton, near Millen, Georgia.

One might wonder if his decision to go finally to Nova Scotia was caused by fear of retaliation from some of those whose actions he had disclosed to the War Department, or from sympathizers of the late Henry Wirz.

There could have been a rejection of, or a disillusionment in, the country that had in its own needs for existence indirectly ended his.

And his odyssey could have been nothing more than a frantic search for a doctor whose skill and knowledge would grant him a reprieve from impending doom. But whatever conclusions are drawn from the information known can only be speculation, and must depend upon the charity of those who speculate.

Raiders! Raiders! Raiders!

On May 22, 1864, five acres of land outside the stockade were set aside for hospital facilities. Private John A. Cain, by now suffering from diarrhea and incipient scurvy, was paroled to the hospital to serve as a nurse, and was thereby spared the horrors *within* the stockade during the remainder of his stay at Andersonville.

Inside this 'City of Death' the raiders ran rampant. These miscreants, who were also known as N'Yaarkers, had become the prison's crime syndicate, and by mid-June had flourished as lustily as all the other pestilences left unchecked. Policing of the prisoners within was left entirely to the inmates. What they did to each other as long as they stayed within the dead-line mattered not to the guards or the commandant of the prison. This lack of organized, authoritative resistance led the raiders to believe themselves invincible.

These raiders (or N'Yaarkers) were not a phenomenon new or unique to Andersonville. Many of the general populace had already encountered them at Richmond.

"Our N'Yaarkers," swift to see any opportunity for dishonest gain, had taken to bounty-jumping, or, as they termed it 'leppin' the bounty,' for a livelihood. Those who were thrust in upon us had followed this until it had become dangerous, and then deserted to the Rebels. The latter kept them at Castle Lightning for awhile, and then, rightly estimating their character, and considering that it was best to trade them off for a genuine Rebel soldier, sent them in among us, to be exchanged regularly with us. There was not so much good faith as good policy shown by this. It was a matter of indifference to the Rebels how soon our Government shot these deserters after getting them in its hands again. They were only anxious to use them to get their own men back.

"The moment they came into contact with us our troubles began. They stole whenever opportunities offered, and they were indefatigable in making these offer; they robbed by actual force, whenever force would avail; and more obsequious lickspittles to power never existed—they were perpetually on the look-out for a chance to curry favor by betraying some plan or scheme to those who guarded us."[1]

"With each long, hot summer hour the lice, the maggot-flies and the N'Yaarkers increased in numbers and venomous activity. They were ever-present annoyances and troubles; no time was free from them. The lice worried us by day and tormented us by night; the maggot-flies fouled our food, and laid in sores and wounds larvae that speedily became masses of wriggling worms. The N'Yaarkers were human vermin that preyed upon and harried us unceasingly."[2]

"By the middle of June the continual success of the Raiders emboldened them so that they no longer confined their depredations to the night but made their forays in broad daylight and there was hardly an hour in the twenty-four that the cry of 'Raiders! Raiders!' did not go up from some part of the pen, and on looking in the direction of the cry one would see a surging commotion, men struggling, and clubs being plied vigorously. This was even more common than the guards shooting men at the Creek crossing."[3]

"The proceeds of these forays enabled the Raiders to wax fat and lusty, while others were dying from starvation. They all had good tents, constructed of stolen blankets, and their headquarters was a large, roomy tent, with a circular top, situated on the street leading to the

[1] McElroy, John. Andersonville: A Story of Rebel Military Prisons. Toledo, Ohio: Published by D. R. Locke, Blade Printing and Paper Co., Electrotypers, Printers and Binders, 1879. p. 112.
[2] Ibid., 220.
[3] Ibid., 222.

South Gate, and capable of accommodating from seventy-five to one hundred men. All the material for this had been wrested away from others. While hundreds were dying of scurvy and diarrhea, from the miserable, insufficient food, and lack of vegetables, these fellows had flour, fresh meat, onions, potatoes, green beans, and other things, the very looks of which were a torture to hungry scorbutic, dysenteric men. They were on the best possible terms with the Rebels, whom they fawned upon and groveled before and were in return allowed many favors, in the way of trading, going out upon detail, and making purchases."[4]

The mean strength[5] of Federal prisoners held at the Andersonville Stockade during the month of June, 1864, was twenty-two thousand, two hundred and ninety-one men.[6] As the population of the stockade grew in appalling numbers, there were always those of 'raider' mentality and inclination in each new group of arrivals, whose presence merely reinforced the already heady atmosphere produced by this successful reign of terror.

And so it was that in mid-June, 1864, William H. E. Mott, Edmund Riedel, and Ira S. Pettit passed through those gates into the midst of this crowded crime wave that was nearing its crescendo.

---

[4]McElroy, John. *Andersonville: A Story of Rebel Military Prisons*. Toledo, Ohio: Published by D. R. Locke, Blade Printing and Paper Co., Electrotypers, Printers and Binders, 1879. pp. 223, 224.

[5]Mean strength was calculated by adding together the number of prisoners present at the first, middle, and last of each month, and dividing the result by three.

[6]Executive Documents. The House of Representatives, 2nd Session of the Fortieth Congress, Executive Document No. 23. *Trial of Henry Wirz*. Washington, D.C. Government Printing Office, 1868. p. 636.

Private William Henry Edward Mott

William H. E. Mott enlisted on July 17, 1863, in the Fourteenth Regiment, Connecticut Infantry, at Hartford, Connecticut, for three years, as a substitute for Reverend Nathaniel H. Lewis. Private Mott was five feet, five inches tall, with hazel eyes, a fair complexion and brown hair. His occupation was listed as that of a *sailor* and his age as *nineteen*.

Through letters to the Pension Office, Washington, D.C., half a century later, Mr. Mott explained the circumstances that brought about his military experience.

"Dear Sir   In regard about my certificate of my Berth, it will be Doubtfull if I can find eny statment ove my Bearth when I was Bornd ore where I was Bornd at but I think I herd my Mother say that I was in N.Y. city have sent on to see if it was on the Regster The first I remembr living was Wickford R.I. soon after we moved to Fairhaven Mass Mother died there when I was 8 years old and soon after Father died. the six children scattered two Brothers and one Sister I have not seen sence then tryed find them when I come out of the army but could not so you can see how I am fix and I think you will find houndreds of Soulders will be in the same fix.

"As I wer in R.I. State Reform School at Proverdence city R.I. James M. Talcot Superendent of the School at that time 1863 had A friend N. H. Luomes was Drafted A Hartford conn and they hird me to go as A subtuttet for him at $5,00 A month for three years, after I come out the army I was hired to work in the shoe shop at the school.

"As they have my name and age registered at the school

249

if that will do I will send and git A statement filled or you can send to the Reform School and get my age at Proverdence city R.I. as I Listed out ove the school W. E. Mott co F. 14 C.V. co D. 2" conn H.A. Pension 1040795."

The preceding letter was received by the U.S. Pension Office on March 3, 1913, and was followed on April 29, 1913, by another.

"Pension Department In regard about my age from the school at Proverdence city R.I. I know I wer older then they clame I am. As I we Perfect stranger to the Judge and court at New Port R.I. I clamed I was pass 18 years old at that time 1861 but the Judge thort I was not so old, so he must have put my age down lest so to get me in the school, as I wer not known at New Port R.I. as I had jest come from New Bedford Mass. my mother dided when I was 8 years old as I had no home or eny one to look after me they sent me to the school When I Listed 1863 I was pass 19 going on 20 when I Listed at Hartford I am not sure Whether I gived my age or the Officer From the school as the Officer come up with me to take me back to the school if I did not pass I did not have eny thing to say as I wer pushed in to tak another man place N. H. Loumes A Preacher as he was drafted. As there was no fight in him I was taken out R.I. in Conn. I cant see how it was don. I never got A doller when Listed but was to $5 a munt when I come home but if I had got killed as soon as I got to the front I suppose he would never had to pay eny think I think I was put in the army cheep dont you think so cant you find out my age by my Army Discriptive List I suppose I will have to stand to the school age as I cant do eny thing better co F" 14 conn co D" 2 conn H.A. W E Mott."

Reverend Nathaniel H. Lewis' moral code and sense of civic duty had made an immeasurable impact upon William Henry Edward Mott, in the youth of his life, even without the formalities of church ritual.

No information is given in Mr. Mott's files concerning the reason for his appearance before a judge in Newport,

Rhode Island, but he had found a home at the school from that day, September 21, 1861, until July 27, 1863. The officer who had accompanied him to Hartford, Connecticut, returned to the State Reform School at Providence, Rhode Island, alone.

Returns of the Fourteenth Regiment, Connecticut Infantry, acknowledged that Private William E. Mott was gained as a recruit at Cedar Run, Virginia, on August 11, 1863. The gaps left in the Union Army at Gettysburg were being filled.

During September, 1863, the Fourteenth Regiment advanced from the Rappahannock to the Rapidan. It participated in the Bristoe Campaign in October and the Mine Run Campaign in late November and early December. After those affrays it remained at Stevensburg, Virginia, until April, 1864.

In the comparative calm of winter quarters during late February, 1864, Private Mott contracted a case of measles.

Grant's Army of the Potomac started on its journey to Appomattox one early morning in May, 1864, although at the moment it was unaware of its exact and final destination. This army, whose polish paled the morning dew that rolled truculently off its boots and lay the early morning's dust, began its journey through a thick, second growth forest in search of Robert E. Lee's Army of Northern Virginia.

Beyond that wilderness, Robert E. Lee, whose army had been washed in its own blood, seasoned by the salt of its own tears, and inspired by its own history, would not wait for the sophisticated and manicured Army of the Potomac. With the speed and agility of a moccasin in water, Lee's army plunged into this wilderness to meet that army and to fight it wherever it was found.

In the bloody and fiery confusion that came to be known as the Battles of the Wilderness, William H. E. Mott became disconnected from the Army of the Potomac. Various records of the Fourteenth Regiment recorded various theories of his departure. On May 4 he was reported to have deserted on the march, and on May 6 it was recorded that he deserted at Wilderness. Finally, the company muster rolls stated that he was taken prisoner at the Battles of the Wilderness on *May 6, 1864,* thereby accounting for him, statistically, from desertion.

Wherever and whatever the circumstances of his departure from the Fourteenth Regiment, the Rebels took possession of his corporal limits at Wilderness/ Fredericksburg, Virginia, on *May 8, 1864.*

Private Mott was confined at Richmond, Virginia, on May 9, 1864, and on June 8, 1864, he was sent to the Andersonville Stockade, Camp Sumter, Georgia. Confederate records do not provide any information concerning the terms, time, place or manner under which they dismissed William Mott from their custody.

The information provided by Private John A. Cain in reference to Private Mott was duly noted in the appropriate categories of the War Department's military files, and note was also made that Mott reached the Union lines on March 20, 1865, at New Bern, North Carolina.

According to Mrs. John Gregory of New York City, Private Mott had come 'home' in April, 1865, on furlough after having spent eight months as a prisoner, and having been transferred from one prison to another. Mr. Mott would later assert to the Federal government that he had spent over ten months in Andersonville, after which he had escaped and joined Sherman on his march through the South.

Private Mott had been granted a furlough shortly after he reported to the Union authorities, and was ordered to return to his regiment in thirty days.

Along with all the veterans and other recruits of the Fourteenth Regiment, Connecticut Infantry, Private Mott was transferred to the Second Regiment, Connecticut Heavy Artillery, on May 30, 1865. Private Mott's presence or absence was not stated on his muster and descriptive roll of men transferred. The Second Regiment, Connecticut Heavy Artillery, was mustered out on August 18, 1865.

Twenty-one years later Mr. Mott would apply for a copy of his discharge certificate.

It is possible that Mr. Mott went to California in the autumn of 1865, as Mrs. Gregory indicated, but Mr. Mott's itinerary of his life, according to his own recollections, was that he had lived in Providence, Rhode Island, 1866; California, 1866-1867; Guam and China, 1868-1869; and from 1870 until 1903 at Stockton, Hanford, and Whitmore, California, and the Napa County Veterans' Home.

On October 9, 1874, William H. E. Mott married Nancy Hatler at Stockton, California. They became the parents of six children—Philip H. Mott, Addie A. Mott Guill, Electa A. Mott Pritchard, Clarence E. Mott, Minnie V. Mott Dennison, and Margaret E. Mott Jamison. Mr. and Mrs. William H. E. Mott were divorced at Redding, California, in 1889.

December, 1886, appears to be the first contact Mr. Mott made with the government after his military service. Identifying himself as a lumberman at Whitmore, California, William E. Mott made application for a copy of his military discharge certificate. According to his notarized statement, his original certificate had been lost in March, 1869, when his cabin near Visalia, Tulare County, California, burned. (Although Federal files did not contain a copy of a discharge certificate for William E. Mott, the government apparently conceded the once-existence of such a document on the grounds of a sworn statement by Yad N. Smith, Captain, Company D, Second Regiment, Connecticut Heavy Artillery, that Private Mott was mustered out on August 18, 1865, at Fort Ethan Allen, Virginia.)

In 1891 Mr. Mott applied for a veteran's pension, alleging that he had been ruptured at Andersonville

253

Prison while digging stumps for fuel, and that he had become deaf from exposure.

At Red Bluff, California, on June 22, 1892, a Pension Claims Board report indicated that Mr. Mott suffered from a hernia rupture and *slight* deafness of the right ear and *very slight* deafness of the left ear.

Mr. Mott had been attacked in the late 1880's by an unknown assailant who had smashed his head and left him for dead. This injury probably did not do much to improve his hearing ability. Miraculously, he had survived this onslaught. Mr. Mott also had a badly mangled left hand which he credited to an accidental shotgun blast during a hunting expedition in November, 1874.

To the extent that the West was wild during that period of its history, William H. E. Mott appears to have had a constitution equal to it.

His pension applications listed his occupation as that of a farmer and laborer. Farmer, laborer or lumberman would have been rugged vocations for anyone with the afflictions which Mr. Mott alleged he received while in Andersonville Prison.

On January 9, 1899, Thomas Baldwin, a resident of the Veterans' Home in Napa County, California, submitted a general affidavit on behalf of claimant W. E. Mott to the U.S. Pension Office, presumably for the objective and unbiased enlightenment of that office as it considered the service-connected disabilities alleged by Veteran Mott:

"I Know the claimint and Know that he was a member of Second conn Heavey artillery of the Same Regt that I belonged I belonged to conn B. & the claimant Blonged to conn D of the Second conn Heavy artillery as he had been in the 14th Regt of the conn vols Inf, & was taken prisoner and was in andersonville prison before he came in our Regt & after being Discharged we have been Separate until we met here in the Veterans Home & Since we met here I Know that he is the man that he So Represents himself to by circumstances that he tells of that occured while we was in the Service that I know of occuring and a person not being there could not Know except being present at the time. Now as to the time & place when and where his Disabilities occured I Know that they occured while in andersonville prison by his Statements to me Since he came here in the Home I did not Know that he was Ruptured while in the army as we was in Diffirnt companies while in Service and I further declared that I have no interest in said case and am not concerned in its prosecution." Signed, "Thomas Baldwin."

William H. E. Mott's final residence was at the Pacific Branch National Home for Disabled Volunteer Soldiers, where he died of arteriosclerosis and chronic interstitial nephritis on March 9, 1926. His means of livelihood, at the time of his death, was a Federal pension in the amount of $72.00 per month.

By the time death came to call upon this orphaned son of Gilbert and Mary Mott, he was blind in his right eye and totally deaf.

In the notification of William H. E. Mott's death, which was sent to the Commissioner of Pensions, Washington, D. C., from the Pacific Branch National Home for Disabled Volunteer Soldiers, dated March 12, 1926, it was stated that Mr. Mott was single and had *no relatives*.

On May 26, 1926, a letter was directed to the Pension Department in Washington, D.C.: "Dear Sir—My father W. E. Mott passed away Mar 9th 1926 at Soldier Home Los Angeles. His pension he received previously to his death I am informed is to be returned to Wash. am I informed correctly or did it go to Estate on what date do veterans receive their pay check. If my father had pension in possession and not cashed is it to return to the Dept. There are no minor children nor widow nor dependent mother nor father in this case. Very truly, Mrs Electa Pritchard nee Mott."

On June 5, 1926, a letter was directed to Mrs. Electa Pritchard of 698 Joost Avenue, San Francisco, California, from Winfield Scott, Commissioner of Pensions, Washington, D.C.: "Madam: In response to your letter of the 26th ultimo in the case of William E. Mott, certificate No. 1,040,795, I have to advise you that payment was last made by this Bureau to March 4, 1926, through the Soldiers' Home. Inquiry relative to any sum which may have remained in the hands of the Treasurer of the Home, at the death of the soldier, should be addressed to that official, as this Bureau has no control over such fund. From March 4, 1926, to the date of death, inclusive, is a period known as the accrued pension and such unpaid pension is not an asset of the estate, nor is it chargeable with the debts of the estate. The only circumstances under which this pension can ever be paid are set forth under the act of Congress approved March 2, 1895, a copy of which is enclosed."

Military records covering his tour of duty did not indicate that there was a deterioration of Private Mott's physical adaptability to prison life in such horrendous surroundings for whatever period of time he was there. Apparently, only later in life did he suffer from the effects of Camp Sumter. His orphan background may well have served to strengthen his physical stamina and to hone his ingenuity to a fine edge.

Private Edmund Riedel

Edmund Riedel was an ordinary man.

There is no indelible impression of his existence in the quiet town of Saxonburg, Pennsylvania, where Private Edmund Riedel was born on January 16, 1844, and where he found the young lady who was to share almost thirty-five years of his life.

The Evangelical Lutheran Church in which Edmund Riedel and Emmaline C. Franke were married on September 5, 1869, stands mute and dignified at the east end of Saxonburg's Main Street, where ministers of a now different Protestant denomination lead members of their congregation through the tenets of their faith.

Leaving an agrarian background, Edmund Riedel went to the nearby City of Pittsburgh, Pennsylvania, to earn his livelihood as a saddler. It was there, on May 2, 1862, that he enlisted as a private in the United States Regular Army. On May 12, 1862, he was mustered into Company H, Eleventh Regiment, Regular Infantry.

This gray-eyed, blonde-haired young man, who stood five feet, seven and one-half inches tall, and whose fair complexion would resent the scorching Georgia sun, had just begun his journey to the Andersonville Stockade.

Although there appears to be no recorded diagnosis of his illness, Private Riedel was hospitalized from August, 1862, until September, 1863, at Philadelphia, Pennsylvania. This hospitalization precluded his participation at Chancellorsville and Gettysburg. But on September 27, 1863, Private Riedel was found fit for duty and was sent to his company encamped near Culpeper, Virginia.

Private Riedel was with the Eleventh Regiment during the action along the Rappahannock in the autumn of 1863. It is likely that he witnessed the execution of Private John McMann, near Bealeton Station, Virginia, on December 18, 1863.

In the spring of 1864 at the battles in the Wilderness Private Riedel became even more intimately acquainted with the subtle complexities of making war. As the fighting at Cold Harbor got under way, Private Edmund Riedel was taken captive by the Confederates in the Gaines' Mill area near Mechanicsville, on June 2, 1864.

On June 8, 1864, Edmund Riedel, Ira Pettit, and William H. E. Mott were among those who left the Richmond prison(s) where they had been temporarily held, and boarded the cars that were destined for Anderson Station, near Americus, Georgia. (Why Private Mott was held in Richmond for thirty days, rather than the usual few, is not known, and it is not known in which of Richmond's prisons he was held. It is possible that he was in the same one with Privates Riedel and Pettit, and it is equally possible that he was held in Castle Thunder or other of Richmond's prisons.)[1]

As the Rebels began their shuffling of large numbers of prisoners in September, Private Riedel was dispatched from Andersonville. He was evidently well enough to stand upright, but on what other basis he was among those chosen to be moved on September 28, 1864, is not known. That he was sent to Savannah, then Millen, then back again to Savannah where he was exchanged on November 18, 1864, is consistent with consequent information and incidents.

Probably filled with awesome anguish and anxiety, Private Edmund Riedel made his exodus from Andersonville Stockade on that early autumn evening of 1864, and gained a passport to almost sixty more years of life.

---

[1]See page 246.

By November 26, 1864, Private Riedel was safely within the Union lines at Camp Parole, Annapolis, Maryland. He was sent on furlough to his home in Butler County, Pennsylvania, on December 4, 1864, returning to St. John's Hospital on January 6, 1865, and to his regiment on January 14, 1865.

The Eleventh Regiment had been moved to Fort Hamilton in New York Harbor on November 2, 1864. Following assignment at Baltimore, Maryland, on November 18, the regiment was sent to Annapolis on December 5, where it was on duty at Camp Parole until January 26, 1865. Leaving Annapolis, the Eleventh Regiment was stationed at City Point, Virginia, near General Grant's headquarters until March 8, 1865.[2] On March 2, 1865, Private Riedel was honorably discharged there.

Following his discharge, Edmund Riedel lived in Pittsburgh, Pennsylvania, until November, 1865. From then until July, 1867, he was a resident of Cincinnati, Ohio. In July, 1867, he returned to Saxonburg, Pennsylvania, for two months, and from September, 1867, until his death, Mr. Riedel's residence was Trenton, New Jersey, where he lived for many years at 563 Chestnut Avenue.

Although he had not lost his expertise as a saddler, Mr. Riedel was employed as a foreman in a wire rope factory in Trenton.

With the birth of Walter A. Riedel on May 23, 1886, the Riedel family had grown to nine members. Mr. and Mrs. Edmund Riedel were also the parents of six other children: Charles E., born July 19, 1870; Elvira A., born June 21, 1872; Edmund J., born August 29, 1874; Emma S., born May 10, 1876; William O., born May 23, 1878; and Ida E., born February 8, 1883.

By the end of January, 1905, this family had been diminished by four. On May 30, 1882, Charles E. Riedel

---

[2]Dyer, Frederick H. *A Compendium of the War of the Rebellion.* Des Moines, Iowa: The Dyer Publishing Company, 1908. p. 1713.

had died, Ida E. Riedel had passed away in October, 1885, Edmund J. Riedel died in January, 1904, and on January 24, 1905, the Riedels lost Emma. On June 8, 1914, Mrs. Emmaline C. Riedel, at the age of sixty-eight, joined these four children in death.

Edmund Riedel remained a widower after Emmaline's death until his own demise on September 8, 1923, at the age of seventy-nine.

Mr. Riedel had enlisted in the army while Major General George Brinton McClellan was in command of the Army of the Potomac, and he lived in the State of New Jersey during the years (1878-1881) that General McClellan had served it as governor. In 1885 Mr. Riedel interred his daughter Ida in Riverview Cemetery, Trenton, at very nearly the same time General George B. McClellan was placed to rest there.

William O. Riedel the third son of Edmund and Emmaline Riedel passed away on March 25, 1946. He was interred in Riverview Cemetery, Trenton, New Jersey, near Mr. and Mrs. Edmund Riedel and Charles, Ida, Edmund J., and Emma.

Mr. Riedel had received a veteran's pension from the United States government under the Pension Acts by continuing legislation, as these acts set out provisions on the basis of length of military service and age of veteran. He made no claims to fame or allegations of heroism, and he lodged no complaints of war-caused infirmities upon the conscience of that government.

Edmund Riedel was an extraordinary ordinary man.

". . . as sure as I goes to hell,
   and I know I goes there."

so said Henry Wirz, the prisonkeeper, as he went about
wielding the heavy hand of unbridled power upon the
prisoners for whatever they did or for whatever he
imagined they might do that would impinge upon his
volatile emotions. As he sent sick men to the stocks and
chain gangs, as he set dogs upon those who had tried to
flee, as he ordered to be shot any who infringed upon the
'deadline,' as he kicked and stamped the sick for being
unable to stand or walk, as he cut off rations to the already
famished men and, on occasion, even shot those who
incensed him, he may well have had reason to think so.

As the trial for his trespasses against his fellow creatures
came upon him, Henry Wirz was found to be in a physical
condition in some ways no better than some of his former
prisoners. Less than two years after he had first entered
Andersonville Prison armed with a pistol, the guards who
surrounded it, the approbation of those who sent him
there, and his own comprehension of how to deal with
those who came into his care, Henry Wirz was described
by two men of medicine in the presence of the court that
had brought him before it to account for his deeds.

"October 24, 1865. At the request of counsel for the
accused, Dr. C. M. Ford and Dr. John C. Bates made in the
presence of the court, an examination of the physical
condition of the prisoner.

"By consent of the judge advocate,

"Dr. C. M. FORD was called as a witness for the

*Executive Documents. Printed by order of the House of Repre-
sentatives during the Second Session of the Fortieth Congress, Executive
Document No. 23. *Trial of Henry Wirz*. Washington, D.C. Government
Printing Office, 1868. p. 112.

defence, and being duly sworn, was examined as follows:
   "By COUNSEL:
Q. State what is your position.
A. I am acting assistant surgeon in the army of the United States, in charge of the hospital at the Old Capitol.
Q. Have you, during some time past, been in the habit of seeing the prisoner?
A. Yes, sir; since June, I believe, ever since his imprisonment, he has been under my care when sick.
Q. Have you during that time examined his right arm, and have you examined it to-day?
A. Yes, sir.
Q. What do you find to be the present condition of his arm?
A. It is swollen and inflamed, ulcerated in three places; and it has the appearance of having been broken. In addition to that, I believe that portions of both bones of the arm are dead.
Q. State your professional opinion as to the strength of his arm in its present condition? Would he be capable with that arm of pushing or knocking down a person, or using any heavy or even a light instrument in doing so?
A. I don't know that I can answer that question entirely. I don't know how much strength he has in the arm; but I should think him incapable of knocking a man, or lifting a very heavy instrument of any kind, without doing great injury to the arm.
Q. Have you examined also the prisoner's left shoulder?
A. Yes, sir.
Q. State what you found to be its condition.
A. There is a very large scar on the left shoulder, and a portion—about half, I should suppose—the outer half of the muscle of the shoulder. The deltoid muscle is entirely gone—I suppose from the wound; it has been carried away, only the front part of the muscle of the shoulder remaining.
Q. How does that influence the strength of the arm?

A. It prevents in a great measure the action of the deltoid muscle, the use of which is to elevate the arm. It would prevent the perfect elevation of the arm. It has no influence at all on the flexion of the arm at the elbow, or striking out with the fore-arm from the elbow; it does not have any material effect as to that.

Q. How do you find the fingers of the prisoner's right hand?

A. I believe that two fingers, the little finger and the next, are slightly contracted; not permanently so, I believe. I am not positive, but I think I could straighten them. The contraction is due to the injury of the nerve leading down to the fingers.

Q. Have you examined the legs of the prisoner?

A. I have.

Q. What do you find to be their condition?

A. I find both of them covered with dark brown scars, as if they had been ulcerated at one time.

Q. Do you find traces of his having had the scurvy?

A. Yes, sir.

Q. State your professional opinion as to the bodily strength of the prisoner, so far as regards his ability to do any injury to any one?

A. He is now in a very prostrated condition; and I should not think him now capable of doing much violence to any one in the present condition of his system.

Q. Taking into consideration the general condition of his arms, legs, and bodily frame, do you think him capable of exerting himself to any extent in doing injury to anybody, pushing a man down, or anything of that kind?

A. I believe that he might push a person down, but I do not think he would be apt to exert himself to do any act of violence, because in doing that he would be very apt to do injury to himself.

"By the JUDGE ADVOCATE:

Q. In what you have said, you speak of the prisoner's present condition?

A. Yes, sir.

Q. The opinion which you give has no reference to the condition in which he was a year ago?

A. No, sir.

Q. From the symptoms presented, can you reason back and tell us what was his condition in 1864?

A. I should not think the right arm was any better in 1864 than it is now. The scurvy, if he was suffering from it then, might make the wound worse. Scurvy or similar disease will often cause fractures to open again after being reunited.

Q. Can you say with certainty what was the prisoner's condition a year ago?

A. I cannot; but the external appearances would indicate that there had been a very extensive injury to the bones and the tissues.

"By the COURT:

Q. Can you say whether the wound has ever healed, and this is the second breaking out of it?

A. No, sir; I do not know; I first met the prisoner in June, when he came to the prison. The wound was then in very nearly the same condition as now.

"The PRISONER. In 1863, my health failing, I asked a furlough to go to Europe, and received it after an examination by the chief surgeon at the hospital at Richmond. I went to Europe and had my wound operated upon in Paris. The doctor there thought that all the dead bone had come out. After spending several months in Switzerland, I returned to England, and from there to the Confederate States. On shipboard, three or four months afterwards, the wound broke open again, and has been in its present condition since February, 1864.

"By consent of the judge advocate,

"Dr. JOHN C. BATES, being recalled, was examined as a witness for the defence.

"By COUNSEL:

Q. You have heard the opinion just given by Dr. Ford;

264

give us your general opinion about the state of the prisoner's health.

A. I have the advantage of Dr. Ford in having seen the prisoner at Andersonville; but while there I never examined him professionally. I noticed on several occasions that he had difficulty in using his right arm. I never inquired what was the matter. As I stated some time since, he was feeble in September, 1864, and did not look like a man enjoying the best of health. The impression of some of the medical gentlemen at Andersonville (you can take it for what it is worth) was, that there was in his system a constitutional syphilitic taint. For that reason, I asked him to let me examine his shanks. There is, it seems to me, an intermingling of the scorbutic and syphilitic taint. When this first manifested itself I do not know. I agree with Dr. Ford in all that he has said; there is nothing from which I would dissent. I concur in his opinion in reference to the left shoulder, the destruction of a portion of the deltoid muscle, and also in his opinion in reference to the right arm, the inability to use it with any considerable degree of force in lifting or striking. He could not use the right arm very extensively, without injury to the bones, which are partially destroyed.

"By the JUDGE ADVOCATE:

Q. May not a man disabled in the arm so that he cannot strike out straight, without danger of injury to himself, be still able to use a pistol with great effect by exercising the wrist?

A. In the case of injury or partial destruction of the main muscle of the shoulder, he might use the arm from the elbow; but the upper portion of the arm would remain partially inactive.

"By COUNSEL:

Q. Would it cause the prisoner any pain if he should use a pistol or any instrument, by striking from the elbow with his right arm?

A. I should think so; considering the condition of the

265

bones and the ulceration, it might be a serious injury to them."*

With the clinical eye of a physician Henry Wirz could easily prognosticate the outcome of his orders, and with the detachment of a foreigner, who had lost his personal fortune in this war and who had received a debilitating wound in one of its battles, he could seek requital with the blessings of his superiors, unhampered by an indigenous love or loyalty for either side; but not unlike those upon whom he could vent his own agony and frustration he, too, was vulnerable.

If Henry Wirz committed none of those alleged atrocities, at least the testimony of those who accused him had the virtue of consistency.

The vaccines that had been given to many of those who could not show well-defined vaccination scars had by now taken on the symptoms of secondary syphilis. The surgeons treated these virulent sores by cutting off the limbs. Then a deadly gangrene raged in the stubs left from these amputations.

The life that clung so tenaciously to the bodies of these starving men aroused itself sufficiently to unite in an effort to rid itself of the torment of the raiders. After a skirmish of revolutionary proportions within the stockade between the raiders and their surviving and indignant victims, six of the leaders of this many-tentacled beast of prey were tried for their crimes and found guilty as charged. The sentences of death by hanging, reached by a verdict of their peers, were put into effect on July 10, 1864. And Henry Wirz did not heed the prophetic moral of this desperate anger.

Amidst the anguished turmoil of that skirmish and those trials, Private Ira S. Pettit dutifully wrote his father

---

*Executive Documents. Printed by order of the House of Representatives during the Second Session of the Fortieth Congress, Executive Document No. 23. *Trial of Henry Wirz*. Washington, D.C. Government Printing Office, 1868. pp. 803-4-5.

on July 8, providing him his most recent detachment address.

The faces of Ira Pettit, William Mott and Edmund Riedel were among those that had carpeted the north and south hillsides of the stockade that July 10, 1864, as the prisoners viewed yet another way to die at Andersonville. Frederick M. Phelps was not then in the stockade, but fate had already headed him in that direction.

Others of those raiders who were tried and found guilty of lesser crimes were sentenced to run a gantlet formed by their victims who assailed them with whatever contrived weapons they could lay their hands upon. Some survived. Some did not.

A comparative peace reigned. The rains that had come down for more than twenty of the thirty days in June abated in July.

Death, however, took no respite. One thousand, nine hundred and fifty-two men abandoned their ragged and emaciated bodies to the sandy soil of Sumter County, Georgia, during the month of July, 1864.* Even as those six raiders thrashed the fetid atmosphere in their final assault upon life, men lay dying in their holes in the ground, beneath their blanket tents or under the burning sun. The nearby pine trees, encouraged by that sun, lifted their branches ever higher toward the Georgia sky.

Bringing with him his varied experiences in the Army of the Potomac and some of the accoutrements of Company E (or Company F), Eleventh Pennsylvania Cavalry, Private Frederick M. Phelps came into that stockade on or about July 23, 1864.

---

*Executive Documents. Printed by order of the House of Representatives during the Second Session of the Fortieth Congress, Executive Document No. 23. *Trial of Henry Wirz.* Washington, D.C. Government Printing Office, 1868. p. 636.

Private Frederick M. Phelps

War provides occasion for the intrinsic fiber of the individual to be laid bare.

The intention here is neither to indict nor to pass moral judgement, but rather a compelling desire to correct and set forth an accurate, coherent and continuous record, in order to provide an objective view of the actual military activities of a young man who, perhaps unwittingly, played a part in the life of Private Ira S. Pettit.

No one argues that Private Frederick M. Phelps was a soldier of the U.S. Army during the Civil War. It is not disputed that he was a prisoner at Andersonville, Georgia. The circumstances of his capture, the length of time he spent at Andersonville, the manner of his release and the records of his enlistments are different matters.

If facts are irrefutable, Private Phelps' military record may be a classic example of the 'bounty-jumper' syndrome which consumed the time and attention of many young men in the United States from 1861 to 1865. For one or another reason there has been a failure to collate these facts or to scrutinize all his records simultaneously.

The only service of any significant value which Private Phelps may have rendered the U.S. Army appears to have been a minute diversion of the already greatly depleted resources of the Rebels for his care and detention while he was under their jurisdiction.

* * *

Private Phelps' military experience, so far as records thus uncovered reveal, began with his enlistment on

October 5, 1861, at New York City, to serve for three years in Company A, Ninetieth New York Infantry Volunteers. He was described as being five feet, four and one-half inches tall, with hazel eyes, light brown hair, and dark complexion. His age was given as nineteen years, his birthplace as Otsego County, New York, and his occupation as that of a farmer.

He was mustered in as a private on October 11, 1861, and transferred to Company D on February 1, 1862. On March 5, 1862, Frederick Phelps was discharged for "disability (youth and mental infirmity)"[1] at Key West, Florida. His age was listed as sixteen years at the time of separation from service.

Private Phelps had served the Union Army for almost five months. He acknowledged this term of service rendered his country in *some* of his applications for pension.

* * *

On July 17, 1862, the Governor of the State of New York issued a proclamation which provided a bounty of fifty dollars to be paid immediately to every private soldier who thereafter volunteered into the service of the United States.[2]

* * *

On the 23rd day of August, 1862, at Cortlandville, New York, Frederick M. Phelps enlisted for a period of three years in the One Hundred Fifty-seventh New York Infantry Volunteers. This time he was described as being eighteen years old, five feet, nine inches tall, with grey eyes, light complexion and brown hair. He claimed to have been born at Solon, New York. His means of livelihood had been farming.

He was mustered into Company K of the One Hundred

---

[1] Army of the United States Certificate of Disability for Discharge of Private Frederick M. Phelps, dated March 5, 1862.

[2] Phisterer, Frederick. *New York in the War of the Rebellion*. Albany, New York: F. B. Lyon Company, State Printers, 1912. p. 34.

Fifty-seventh on September 19, 1862, at Hamilton, New York. On September 25th of that year, the One Hundred Fifty-seventh Regiment left the state for Washington, D.C., to serve there until November 1, 1862.

Company muster roll and company returns record Private Frederick M. Phelps' desertion on October 11, 1862, at Camp Chase, Virginia.

Private Phelps had served the Union Army for three weeks. He did *not* acknowledge this term of service rendered his country in his applications for pension.

* * *

Frederick M. Phelps entered service for the third time on December 5, 1862, at Otsego, New York, by enlisting for three years in Battery A, First New York Light Artillery. Muster-in rolls gave his age as twenty-one years, and described him as having brown eyes, brown hair and light complexion. His birthplace was said to be Otsego, New York, and his vocation was said to have been painting.

He received, upon enlistment, clothing from the United States in the amount of thirty-four dollars and sixty-six cents and one hundred dollars in bounty pay.[3]

The muster and descriptive roll of a detachment of U.S. vols. forwarded, for the First Regiment, New York Light Artillery, dated February 10, 1863, at Albany Depot, New York, and the muster roll for Private Frederick M. Phelps of Battery A, dated February 28, 1863, both listed him as, "Deserted January 1, 1863, at Utica."

Private Phelps had served the Union Army an additional three weeks. He did *not* acknowledge this term of service rendered his country in his applications for pension.

* * *

Private Frederick M. Phelps had enlisted in the Union

---

[3]From Volunteer Descriptive List and Account of Pay and Clothing of Frederick M. Phelps, Company A, First New York Light Artillery. Office of the Adjutant General, National Archives, Washington, D.C.

Army three times in the State of New York within a fifteen month period, had compiled approximately six and one-half months' total service time, had received one disability discharge and had earned, to his credit, two charges of desertion.

What Mr. Phelps, a twice-successful deserter by now, did for the next thirteen months is not known.

* * *

In the Township of Clymer, State of Pennsylvania, on February 29, 1864, Frederick M. Phelps enlisted once again to serve as a soldier in the Army of the United States for a period of three years. He was mustered into service in the Eleventh Regiment, Pennsylvania Cavalry, on March 1, 1864, at Williamsport, Pennsylvania. (Bounty paid for volunteer enlistment in Pennsylvania in February, 1864, was three hundred dollars.)

His name was not taken up on muster rolls of the regiment, but his volunteer enlistment record indicated that he was mustered into Company F, Eleventh Regiment, Pennsylvania Cavalry, even though it appears that Private Phelps traveled with Company E most of the time.

After being dispatched from his draft rendezvous at Carlisle, Pennsylvania, on March 10, 1864, records of Private Phelps' whereabouts and activities from then until the end of the war became the subject of controversy and speculation, a controversy and speculation which was apparently never satisfactorily or decisively resolved, and may never be.

The descriptive list of deserters, dated August 7, 1864, at Jones Landing, Virginia, contained the following information: "Frederick Phelps, Pvt. Company E, 11th Regiment, Pennsylvania Cavalry (age—20 years; height—5 feet, 7 inches; complexion—light; eyes—hazel; hair—brown; born at Lawrence, New York; occupation—farmer) deserted at Point of Rocks, July 1, gone to enemy."

Private Phelps evidently served for four months during

this enlistment, bringing his total service time to approximately ten and one-half months, with a total of four enlistments and three charges of desertion. He acknowledged this term of service rendered his country in *some* of his applications for pension, but claimed capture, not desertion.

* * *

The anonymity which Private Phelps enjoyed during his stay with Companies E and F, Eleventh Regiment of the Pennsylvania Cavalry, would have served him well if his intentions had been to desert at good opportunity.

The prisoner-of-war memorandum for Frederick M. Phelps shows that he was captured on July 5, 1864, at Chester Station, Virginia. He was yet a long way from home, in a most sensitive area near the Confederate Capitol, and chances were, that on July 5, Private Phelps still wore Union blues.

By 1864 bounty jumping had become so commonplace that new volunteers were sometimes taken South under heavy guard. Desertion was also not so easily accomplished as it had been early on. Besides this, those who were deep in enemy territory were always faced with the possibility of falling into the hands of the enemy, even if they did extricate themselves successfully from their own regiments. And the Eleventh Pennsylvania Cavalry was in hostile territory. Private Phelps may not have taken all this into account on July 1, 1864.

Phelps was confined at Richmond, Virginia, on July 10, and sent as a prisoner to Andersonville, Georgia, July 16, 1864. His prison memo shows that he was admitted to the hospital on October 11, 1864, for *scorbutus* and released from the hospital on November 2, 1864. According to additional notation, he was sent to Millen, Georgia, on November 11.

After July 1, 1864, aside from the prisoner-of-war memorandum held in the Adjutant General's office, the

Federal government heard no more from Private Frederick M. Phelps for a number of years.

* * *

George E. Lemon, of Washington, D.C., a duly authorized attorney, submitted to the government a Declaration of Original Invalid Pension, dated January 24, 1883, on behalf of Frederick M. Phelps, age 37, a resident of Evart, County of Osceola, Michigan. This declaration was based *solely* on Mr. Phelps' service as a private in *Company E* of the Eleventh Regiment of the Pennsylvania Cavalry, in which he declared that he had been discharged from the Pennsylvania Cavalry at Richmond, Virginia, on or about the 20th day of July, 1865, by reason of expiration of service. (Private Phelps will again, later, identify himself with Company E.)

Justification for an invalid pension was based on his statement that he had contracted chronic diarrhea, rheumatism and scurvy, affecting his mouth and legs, while in the service and in the line of his duty at Andersonville Prison, Georgia, on or about August, 1864, and he further stated that he had had no hospital treatment, nor had he been employed in any other military or naval service than that of the Pennsylvania Cavalry at any time. (This is the *only* time that reference is made to scurvy in his applications.)

Since leaving the service, Mr. Phelps stated that he had resided in Clymer, Pennsylvania, and Evart, Michigan. He had worked as a painter since the war, having been a painter and farmer prior to going into the military service, according to his statements. He alleged partial disability as a result of all the afflictions resulting from this military experience.

The examining surgeon's certificate, dated April 25, 1883, stated that, "This man is well nourished, of good average weight, of good physical appearance. There is no tenderness over abdomen, no tympanitis, no heptatic disease or ____,[4] tongue normal, no symptoms indicating that scurvy has ever existed, no symptoms indicating rheumatism, no deformity, no atrophy of muscles, no heart disease. We do not rate him." This certificate was signed by G. V. Chamberlain, C. H. White and A. W. Miller, as examining surgeons.

* * *

Almost seven years had elapsed and on August 30, 1889, Phelps, represented this time by Attorney Lafayette Bingham of Washingotn, D.C., submitted another Declaration for Original Invalid Pension, listing *only* his service with the Ninetieth New York Infantry, Company D. *He gave his age as forty-four years, his residence as Avondale, Michigan, and his previous residence as Clymer, Pennsylvania.*

His claim was based upon chronic diarrhea and rheumatism contracted while a prisoner of war at Andersonville. He stated in this declaration that he had been *treated at camp distribution at New Orleans.* (He had been discharged from the Ninetieth New York Infantry for more than two years before he found himself in Andersonville.)

* * *

On October 29, 1889, George E. Lemon, Counsellor at Law, directed a memo to the Honorable Commissioner of Pensions, Washington, D.C., inquiring as to the status of the claim of Private Phelps, and stating that, "Bates History of Pa. Vols. shows the applicant to have been an unassigned man of the 108th (11 Cav.) Pa. Vols, mustered in Feb. 29, 1864, and marked not accounted for. Please call on the War Dept. for his service as above." Signed— George E. Lemon.

* * *

Under the auspices of J. B. Cralle and Company, U.S. Pension Attorneys of Washington, D.C., Mr. Phelps made

---

[4]Undeciphered cipher.

a declaration for pension on the 21st of December, 1891, from Tuscola County, Michigan. He claimed *no* military service aside from the Ninetieth New York Infantry (Companies A and D) from which he had been discharged at Key West, Florida, on the 17th day of March, 1862, and the Eleventh Pennsylvania Cavalry, *Company E*, from which he made no explanation of separation.

Justification for his claim was based on the allegation that he was wholly disabled because of chronic rheumatism, catarrh and general disability, all of which were incurred at Andersonville Prison on or about October and November, 1864.

* * *

From Tuscola County, Michigan, on the 28th day of January, 1892, another Declaration for Original Invalid Pension was submitted for consideration. Now Mr. Phelps' claim was based upon his service in Companies A and D, Ninetieth New York Infantry as well as service in *Company E*, Eleventh Pennsylvania Cavalry. He averred that he was discharged at the end of the war, and had since lived in Evart, Michigan, and Clymer, Pennsylvania.

Physical disabilities claimed in this declaration were rheumatism and diarrhea, which Mr. Phelps alleged had been incurred while at Andersonville Prison, and which he alleged had been caused by "drinking bad water and exposure." Frederick Phelps stated that he was treated in the hospital at "*Castle Williams, governors island,*" and again he claimed that he "*had no hospital at Andersonville.*"

Mr. Phelps reported his final discharge date as July 7th, 1865, and iterated that he had rendered no military or naval service other than as stated in the Declaration for Original Invalid Pension, dated January 28, 1892. (The Eleventh Regiment of Pennsylvania Cavalry was mustered out at Richmond, Virginia, on August 13, 1865, according to Frederick Dyer.)[5]

[5]Dyer, Frederick H. *A Compendium of the War of the Rebellion.* Des Moines, Iowa: The Dyer Publishing Company, 1908. p. 1563.

On December 11, 1912, there was transmitted to the Adjutant General's office, from the Honorable F. H. Dodds of the House of Representatives, the following: "Frederick M. Phelps states as he has the facts, he enlisted in A., 90 N.Y. Inf. on Sept. 5, 1861, was discharged for disability on March 5, 1862, at Key West, Fla., from Co. D, same regiment, to which transferred on Feb. 4, 1862. He re-enlisted in Feb., 1864, in Co. F, 11 Pa. Cav., captured a day or two afterwards at battle of Reams Station, Va., taken to Libby prison and retained there about two weeks; then taken to Andersonville and while there was in detachment 108, 3rd mess, and was released in May, 1865. Reached home in October, 1865, was in bad physical condition when he got out of prison and wanted to get home the war being over. Wants charge of desertion from second service removed. Requests that the matter be given consideration."

This memo from Representative Dodds elicited the following response, dated December 13, 1912:

"The records show that Frederick M. Phelps was enrolled October 5, 1861, and was mustered into service October 11, 1861, as a private, Company A, 90th New York Volunteer Infantry, to serve three years; that he was transferred to Company D of the same regiment sometime in January or February, 1862, and that he was discharged the service as a private, March 5, 1862, on a 'Surgeon's Certificate of Disability.'

"The records also show that Frederick M. Phelps was enrolled February 29, 1864, at Williamsport, Pennsylvania, and was mustered into service March 1, 1864, as a private for Company F of the 11th Pennsylvania Cavalry, to serve 3 years. He was received at Carlisle, Pennsylvania, draft rendezvous, March 3, 1864, and was sent to the 11th Pennsylvania Cavalry, March 10, 1864. His name is not taken up on the rolls of any company of the regiment, nor has anything been found to show the date on which he joined the regiment, but a regimental descriptive list of deserters for the month of August, 1864, shows him 'Deserted July 1, 1864, Point of Rocks, Gone to the enemy.'

"The records of prisoners-of-war show that he was captured at Chester Station, Virginia, July 5, 1864; that he was confined at Richmond, Virginia, July 10, 1864, and sent to Andersonville, Georgia, July 16, 1864, and was sent to Millen, Georgia, November 11, 1864. No further record of him has been found, nor has anything been found of record to show either the date or the manner of his separation from service.

"The War Department is simply the custodian of the records of disbanded volunteer organizations, and has no authority to alter or amend those records so as to make them show that this man was discharged the service of the United States or to issue a discharge certificate in his case." Signed by George Andrews, Adjutant General.

* * *

Company F of the Pennsylvania Cavalry's Eleventh Regiment battled at Reams Station on June 29, 1864, and not February or March, 1864, as Private Phelps' statement implied. But if Private Phelps were with Company E, which was in the same general area on June 29, he would have known about the Reams Station melee, and he would have been at Point of Rocks on July 1 as both Companies E and F high-tailed it into camp on the Bermuda Hundred Peninsula. More than that, he might have been impressed with the fervor exhibited by the Rebels as they "surrounded and badly cut to pieces"[6] Company F, and he would have heard about Company F's loss in *missing* men.

Most of all, Private Phelps would have known that he was originally and officially mustered into Company F, no matter which company he had been keeping. It is doubtful that Company E would have even noted his absence had he been with Company F at that time. Finally, it was more

---

[6]Excerpt from Company Muster Roll for Company F, Eleventh Regiment, Pennsylvania Cavalry for May and June, 1864.

277

than five days after he disappeared at Point of Rocks before the Rebels captured him at Chester Station, quite a few miles in the opposite direction of Companies E and F and Jones Landing where they had encamped.

Specifics are much more difficult to defend than generalities.

* * *

To additional inquiry from Mr. Dodds in reference to Private Phelps, the Adjutant General responded again on January 17, 1913:

"As set forth in the communication addressed to Mr. Dodds by this office on December 13, 1912, the records show that Frederick M. Phelps, Company F (who is also referred to as a member of Company E), 11th Pennsylvania Cavalry, was sent from Andersonville, Georgia, where he was in confinement as a prisoner of war, to Millen, Georgia, November 11, 1864. An examination of all records likely to afford any information relative to this man after that date (November 11, 1864) has resulted in failure to find any record whatever of him. In the absence of record evidence relative to his whereabouts and services subsequent to the date mentioned, this Department, which is merely the custodian of the records of disbanded volunteer organizations, has no authority to accept affidavits made long after the war to establish a record of him after that date, and consequently, has no authority of law to alter or amend the records so as to make them show anything other than what they now show with regard to the soldier in question or to issue a certificate of discharge in his case." Signed by George Andrews, Adjutant General.

* * *

Under the provisions of the Act of May 11, 1912, Mr. Phelps submitted yet another declaration for pension on the 27th day of May, 1913, based *solely* upon his service in the Ninetieth Regiment, New York Infantry, and stating his birthdate as *February 22, 1842*, at Otsego County, New York.

In this declaration he listed his several places of post-war residence as Cortland County, New York; Tioga County, Pennsylvania; Osceola County, Michigan; and Oakland County, Michigan. *For the first time*, Mr. Phelps acknowledged having been a resident of New York State after the war.

On July 24, 1913, a letter from the Department of the Interior, Bureau of Pensions, Washington, D.C., was directed to Mr. Frederick M. Phelps, Route 2, Evart, Michigan, as follows:

"Your claim for pension under the act of May 11, 1912 filed May 29, 1913, is rejected on the ground that you deserted from Co. E, 11th Pennsylvania Cavalry your last contract of service on July 1, 1864, and have never been honorably discharged therefrom, and therefore, have no title under said act." Signed by E. C. Triman, Acting Commissioner.

* * *

As records of Private Frederick M. Phelps unravel, one tends to feel that here may be life's counterpart to fiction's Second Lieutenant Salso.[7]

Where, when, and on what terms Private Phelps parted company with the Rebels is not known. If he suffered ill effects from his stay in Andersonville, it would appear that he survived them for a considerable time.

According to private correspondence concerning Mr. Phelps, he had married Lavina Stevens at McGraw, New York, and had become the father of a son and a daughter.

While living with a sister in the City of Pontiac, Michigan, Frederick M. Phelps died of heart disease on February 9, 1920. By then a widower, he had been employed as a watchman. According to his death certificate, his age was unknown, but his birthplace was recorded as *New Jersey*.

---

[7]Second Lieutenant Salso is the protagonist in a short story by the same name, written by Yury Tynyanov, whose existence is pure illusion created by bureaucratic paperwork.

Frederick Phelps' earthly remains repose in Oakview Cemetery, Royal Oak, Michigan. The stone which marks his grave bears the birthyear, 1842.

* * *

There is no evidence in the pension files that the government ever correlated or considered Private Phelps' enlistments in the One Hundred Fifty-seventh Regiment, New York Infantry Volunteers, or the First Regiment, New York Light Artillery, while deciding upon his repeated applications for pension.

* * *

Unlike Private John McMann, Frederick M. Phelps did not have to face the rattling of musketry at the hands of his fellow soldiers. He was never called upon to stand trial on desertion charges or to refute Private Edmund Riedel's reference to his alleged allegiance to the Confederacy. He did not avail himself of the re-enlistment from desertion provided by a Presidential proclamation, and it would seem that he had not intentionally planned a tour of duty at Andersonville. But it is hard to imagine that he was not occasionally visited by visions and dreams of the horrors he witnessed among his fellow prisoners at Camp Sumter, Georgia, that summer and autumn of 1864.

Information and quoted materials concerning Frederick M. Phelps have been taken from his pension applications file and his compiled service records found in the Office of the Adjutant General, National Archives, Washington, D.C., and are specifically identified in the reference section of this book. Substantiative records from states and individuals have also been listed in that section.

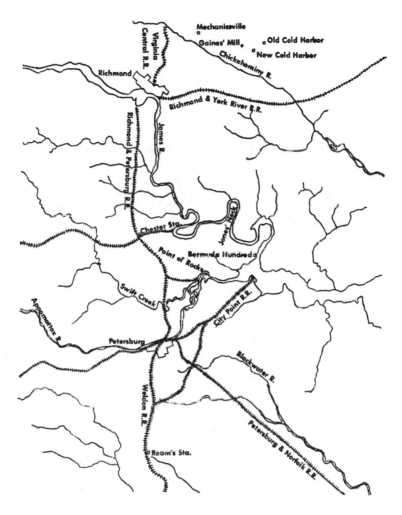

Map drawn by William Howard Ray.

Point of Rocks, Ream's Station, Chester Station, Virginia.

Map of area in which Private Frederick M. Phelps became separated from the Eleventh Regiment, Pennsylvania Cavalry, July 1, 1864.

281

"Well, this Southern Confederacy
is the d-----dest country to stand logs
on end on God Almighty's footstool." *

For the men who entered the stockade at Camp Sumter near Anderson Station, in Sumter County, Georgia, in 1864, there were innumerable possibilities.

Their chances were approximately one out of three that they would die there. They might successfully escape; it was claimed by some that three hundred and twenty-eight did. They could be murdered by fellow prisoners or shot by overly zealous guards. They could be torn apart by the hounds that tenaciously searched them out of the swamps, providing they had been able to escape the pine barricade which surrounded them and to elude drawing the attention of the guards. They were ever subject to the whims of Henry Wirz, to those who gave Wirz orders, and to those to whom Wirz gave orders.

If they placidly accepted their incarceration, they were still not immune from castrophe. There was starvation, scurvy, dysentery, gangrene, diarrhea, respiratory diseases, vaccines, amputations, flies, maggots, lice, insanity; and there was an army of billions of virulent bacteria stalking them relentlessly and indiscriminately. Those who were not buried there left Andersonville by various routes at various times.

The records of Confederate prisons are scarce and incomplete, but if one follows the journey taken by Private John McElroy an itinerant prisoner of the Rebels some insight into the over-all prison system may be gleaned, and some of the pieces of information contained herein

---

*McElroy, John. *Andersonville: A Story of Rebel Military Prisons.* Toledo, Ohio: Published by D. R. Locke, Blade Printing and Paper Co., Electrotypers, Printers and Binders, 1879. p. 523.

may seem to find their proper places. The following is a summary of his itinerary, as he related it in his book published in 1879:

On September 6, 1864, the Rebels announced to the residents of the Andersonville Stockade that there had been an agreement between their respective governments, and therefore, twenty thousand men were to be moved out for exchange. John McElroy was among the first to make the two-day, two hundred and forty mile trip from Andersonville to Savannah, Georgia.

This mass transfer was inspired by the ambitious activities of Bill Sherman rather than by any exchange agreement, and upon arrival in Savannah, the much chagrined prisoners were marched into another prison pen. According to McElroy, probably six to seven thousand of those who were moved out (many of whom were the old raider crowd) stopped at Savannah.

On October 11, 1864, orders came to the men in the Savannah Stockade that there was to be a transfer of one thousand prisoners. McElroy was again among the first who flanked out to take whatever advantage there might be in such a change.

They were taken to Millen, Georgia, about eighty miles north and west of Savannah, and five miles past Millen they were escorted into another stockade. An almost exact replica of Andersonville, this was Camp Lawton, and as they, these first arrivals, exercised their ingenuity and imagination in making themselves at home in this new stockade, the rest of those prisoners from Savannah, as well as more men from Andersonville, joined them.

Their stay at Camp Lawton lasted approximately six weeks. And according to McElroy's experienced guess, there were about six or seven thousand prisoners in residence at Millen also, including a strong contingent of raiders.

Shortly after the U.S. Presidential election in November,

1864, an incident worthy of note transpired at Millen. Private McElroy related it in detail.

"One day in November, . . . orders came in to make out rolls of all those who were born outside of the United States, and whose terms of service had expired.

"We held a little council among ourselves as to the meaning of this, and concluded that some partial exchange had been agreed on, and the Rebels were going to send back the class of boys whom they thought would be of least value to the Government. Acting on this conclusion the great majority of us enrolled ourselves as foreigners, and as having served out our terms. I made out the roll of my hundred, and managed to give every man a foreign nativity. Those whose names would bear it were assigned to England, Ireland, Scotland, France and Germany, and the balance were distributed through Canada and the West Indies. After finishing the roll and sending it out, I did not wonder that the Rebels believed the battles for the Union were fought by foreign mercenaries. The other rolls were made out in the same way, and I do not suppose that they showed five hundred native Americans in the Stockade.

"The next day after sending out the rolls, there came an order that all those whose names appeared thereon should fall in. We did so, promptly, and as nearly every man in camp was included, we fell in as for other purposes, by hundreds and thousands. We were then marched outside, and massed around a stump on which stood a Rebel officer, evidently waiting to make us a speech. We awaited his remarks with the greatest impatience, but he did not begin until the last division had marched out and came to a parade rest close to the stump.

"It was the same old story: 'Prisoners, you can no longer have any doubt that your Government has cruelly abandoned you; it makes no efforts to release you, and refuses all our offers of exchange. We are anxious to get our men back, and have made every effort to do so, but it refuses to meet us on any reasonable grounds. Your Secretary of War has said that the Government can get along very well without you, and General Halleck has said that you were nothing but a set of blackberry pickers and coffee boilers, anyhow.

'You've already endured much more than it could expect of you; you served it faithfully during the term you enlisted for, and now, when it is through with you, it throws you aside to starve and die. You also can have no doubt that the Southern Confederacy is certain to succeed in securing its independence. It will do this in a few months. It now offers you an opportunity to join its service, and if you serve it faithfully to the end, you will receive the same rewards as the rest of its soldiers. You will be taken out of here, be well clothed and fed, given a good bounty, and, at the conclusion of the War receive a land warrant for a nice farm. If you' ——

"But we had heard enough. The Sergeant of our division—a man with a stentorian voice—sprang out and shouted:

'*Attention, First Division!*'

"We Sergeants of hundreds repeated the command down the line. Shouted he: 'First Divison, *about*'

"Said we: 'First Hundred, *about* ——,' 'Second Hundred, *about* ——,' 'Third Hundred, *about* ——,' 'Fourth Hundred, *about* ——,' etc., etc.

"Said he ——, 'Face!'

"Ten Sergeants repeated 'Face!' one after the other, and each man in the hundreds turned on his heel. Then our leader commanded ——, 'First Division, *forward!* MARCH!' and we strode back into the Stockade, followed immediately by all the other divisions, leaving the orator still standing on the stump.

"The Rebels were furious at this curt way of replying. We had scarcely reached our quarters when they came in with several companies, with loaded guns and fixed bayonets. They drove us out of our tents and huts, into one corner, under the pretense of hunting axes and spades, but in reality to steal our blankets, and whatever else they could find that they wanted, and to break down and injure our huts, many of which, costing us days of patient labor, they destroyed in pure wantonness.

"We were burning with the bitterest indignation. A tall, slender man named Lloyd, a member of the Sixty-First Ohio—a rough, uneducated fellow, but brim full of patriotism and manly common sense, jumped up on a stump and poured out his soul in rude but fiery eloquence: 'Comrades,' he said, 'do not let the blowing of these Rebel whelps discourage you; pay no attention to the lies they have told you to-day; you know well that our Government is too honorable and just to desert anyone who served it; it has *not* deserted us; their hell-born Confederacy is *not* going to succeed. I tell you that as sure as there is a God who reigns and judges in Israel, before the Spring breezes stir the tops of these blasted old pines their _____ Confederacy and all the lousy graybacks who support it will be so deep in hell that nothing but a search warrant from the throne of God Almighty can ever find it again. And the glorious old Stars and Stripes-'

"Here we began cheering tremendously. A Rebel Captain came running up, said to the guard, who was leaning on his gun, gazing curiously at Lloyd:

'What in _____ are you standing gaping there for? Why don't you shoot the _____ _____ Yankee son _____ _____ ___ _____?' and snatching the gun away from him, cocked and leveled it at Lloyd, but the boys near jerked the speaker down from the stump and saved his life.

"We became fearfully wrought up. Some of the more excitable shouted out to charge on the line of guards, snatch their guns away from them, and force our way through the gates. The shouts were taken up by others, and, as if in obedience to the suggestion, we instinctively formed in line-of-battle facing the guards. A glance down the line showed me an array of desperate, tensely drawn such as one sees who looks at men when they are summoning up all their resolution for some deed of great peril. The Rebel officers hastily retreated behind the line of guards, whose faces blanched, but they leveled their muskets and prepared to receive us.

"Captain Bowes, who was overlooking the prison from an elevation outside, had, however, divined the trouble at the outset, and was preparing to meet it. The gunners, who had shotted their pieces and trained them upon us when we came out to listen to the speech, had again covered us with them, and were ready to sweep the prison with grape and canister at the instant of command. The long roll was summoning the infantry regiments back into line, and some of the cooler-headed among us pointed these facts out and succeeded in getting the line to dissolve again into groups of muttering, sullen-faced men. When this was done, the guards marched out, by a cautious, indirect manuver, so as not to turn their backs to us.

"It was believed that we had some among us who would like to avail themselves of the offer of the Rebels, and that they would try to inform the Rebels of their desires by going to the gate during the night and speaking to the Officer-of-the-Guard. A squad armed themselves with clubs and laid in wait for these. They succeeded in catching several—snatching some of them back even after they had told the guard their wishes in a tone so loud that all near could hear distinctly. The Officer-of-the-Guard rushed in two or three times in a vain attempt to save the would-be deserter from the cruel hands that clutched him and bore him away to where he had a lesson in loyalty impressed upon the fleshiest part of his person by a long, flexible strip of pine, wielded by very willing hands.

"After this was kept up for several nights different ideas began to prevail. It was felt that if a man wanted to join the

Rebels, the best way was to let him go and get rid of him. He was of no benefit to the Government, and would be of none to the Rebels. After this no restriction was put upon any one who desired to go outside and take the oath. But very few did so, however, and these were wholly confined to the Raider crowd."*

News came in mid-November that there had been an agreement worked out with the United States government for an exchange of ten thousand sick captives. The very illest of these were chosen, and many of them died enroute. Some of the men successfully feigned illness, and others who had money bought their way to freedom. Private McElroy estimated that about one-fourth of those at Millen went out at that time for a genuine exchange. Asserting that he had little acting talent and no money, McElroy remained at Camp Lawton.

Awakened by gunfire and the long roll of the drums one cold and rainy morning near the end of November, the prisoners were ordered to prepare to move. As they waited to board the train in the midst of a heavy downpour, some of them simply lay back down and died. Lying on the open cars as the rain continued to wash the face of the heavens and their unprotected bodies, others also found their souls set free. The train, with its dead, dying and half-alive freight, retraced its track to Savannah.

Savannah's stockade had been dismantled by this time, and when they arrived there, the prisoners were given a few crackers and marched to another train. After a few days of traveling slowly southward, they were unloaded at Blackshear, in Pierce County, Georgia, approximately eighty-six miles south of Savannah. They were marched into a pine woods and surrounded by a heavy guard. More

*McElroy, John. *Andersonville: A Story of Rebel Military Prisons.* Toledo, Ohio: Published by D. R. Locke, Blade Printing and Paper Co., Electrotypers, Printers and Binders, 1879. pp. 466-7-8-9, 470.

and more prisoners poured into Blackshear. The guessed population rose to between five and six thousand.

After a week's stay, the prisoners were told that the first thousand arrivals were to be taken back to Savannah for exchange, provided they signed a Non-Combatant's Oath. This simply meant that they could not perform any kind of military service until they had been properly exchanged. Feeling that he could stand no longer this outdoor prison life, Private John McElroy signed this oath.

Back again at Savannah these prisoners were marched through the streets and loaded onto another train. Going northward across the Savannah River, they were taken to Charleston, South Carolina; there had been no intention of exchange!

Marched through the streets and rubble of this city under seige, the prisoners were halted and encamped in a vacant lot. (Charleston was shelled from early August, 1863, until April, 1865.) Their sojourn there lasted only a few days. Boarding another train one night they headed northward again. Their destination now was Florence, South Carolina, and another but smaller replica of the stockade at Andersonville.

Some of those who had left Andersonville in September had been taken directly to Charleston instead of stopping at Savannah, and from Charleston on to Florence, after an outbreak of yellow fever in Charleston in October.

When those first prisoners came to Florence in October there had been no stockade, and about fifteen hundred prisoners had escaped by forcing the guard which had surrounded them. Subsequently, another stockade had been erected, and nearly all those who had escaped had been recaptured, and when Private McElroy arrived at Florence there were already about eleven thousand men held there.

The stories about the inhabitants of Florence were the same as those of Andersonville, but they were different, too

"One of the commonest of sights was to see men whose hands and feet were simply rotting off. The nights were frequently so cold that ice a quarter of an inch thick formed on the water. The naked frames of starving men were poorly calculated to withstand this frosty rigor, and thousands had their extremities so badly frozen as to destroy the life in those parts, and induce a rotting of the tissues by a dry gangrene. The rotted flesh fequently remained in its place for a long time—a loathsome but painless mass, that gradually sloughed off, leaving the sinews that passed through it to stand out like shining, white cords.

"While this was in some respects less terrible than the hospital gangrene at Andersonville, it was more generally diffused, and dreadful to the last degree. The Rebel Surgeons at Florence did not follow the habit of those at Andersonville, and try to check the disease by wholesale amputation, but simply let it run its course, and thousands finally carried their putrefied limbs through the lines, when the Confederacy broke up in the Spring, to be treated by our Surgeons.

"I had been in prison (at Florence) but a little while when a voice called out from a hole in the ground, as I was passing: 'S-a-y, Sergeant! Won't you please take these shears and cut my toes off?' 'What?' said I, in amazement, stopping in front of the dug-out. 'Just take these shears, won't you, and cut my toes off?' answered the inmate, an Indiana infantryman—holding up a pair of dull shears in his hand, and elevating a foot for me to look at.

"I examined the latter carefully. All the flesh of the toes, except little pads at the ends, had rotted off, leaving the bones as clean as if scraped. The little tendons still remained, and held the bones to their places, but this seemed to hurt the rest of the feet and annoy the man.

"You'd better let one of the Rebel doctors see this,' I said, after finishing my survey, 'before you conclude to have them off. May be they can be saved.'

"No; d——d if I'm going to have any of them Rebel butchers fooling around me. I'd die first, and then I wouldn't,' was the reply. 'You can do it better than they can. It's just a little snip. Just try it.'

"I don't like to,' I replied. 'I might lame you for life, and make you lots of trouble.'

"O, bother! what business is that of yours? They're *my* toes, and I want 'em off. They hurt me so I can't sleep. Come, now, take the shears and cut 'em off.

"I yielded, and taking the shears, snipped one tendon after another, close to the feet, and in a few seconds had the whole ten toes laying in a heap at the bottom of the dug-out. I picked them up and handed them to their owner, who gazed at them complacently, and remarked:

"Well, I'm durned glad they're off. I won't be bothered with corns any more, I flatter myself.'"*

And thus, their lives were.

Sometime during February orders came for a thousand men to prepare to move. McElroy decided to decline this invitation, and as one squad after another left, he flanked back. Finally, there were only eleven hundred men remaining, and they were paroled to stay inside or near the pen. The guards were taken off duty. McElroy later learned that those who left at this time were sent to Wilmington and then to Goldsboro, North Carolina.

On February 22, 1865, the remaining eleven hundred prisoners were marched over to the train, i.e., those who were able to march, and the sick were hauled to it on wagons. The very sick were left to die as successfully as they might. The train headed northeast out of Florence and continued its journey all night. In the afternoon of the 23rd, it stopped and reversed its direction. By the end of the next day the prisoners were once again at Florence for another short stay.

---

*McElroy, John. *Andersonville: A Story of Rebel Military Prisons*. Toledo, Ohio: Published by D. R. Locke, Blade Printing and Paper Co., Electrotypers, Printers and Binders, 1879. pp. 535-6-7.

Within a few days these last survivors of the eleven hundred who had been left at Florence were again loaded onto the cars, and two white flags led the train into the Union lines at a post west of Wilmington. Alongside a branch of the Cape Fear River the Rebels surrendered these men to Union soldiers of the Twenty-third Army Corps, United States Army.

As the troops of the Union's Western Army swarmed across Georgia, South Carolina, and North Carolina, the Rebels had gathered up their prisoners and scattered them in all directions. The trains ran back and forth, wherever there was track, in a manner not unlike a bag of mice suddenly set free.

And the trains left in their wake a string of dead whose final death rales had gone unheeded and unheard beneath the screech of unoiled wheels and the commands of Rebel guards.

The rationale characterized in the defence that Captain Wirz presented to the court to justify and/or ameliorate his heinous command of Andersonville Prison persuaded some to regard him as a scapegoat and to proclaim him a martyr. As they heard him interpret and re-design their testimony in a manner that exonerated himself, the former prisoners (who believed that they had glimpsed a raging monster inside this man) must have recognized in him at least one common human trait.

Henry Wirz had chosen to continue under his superiors rather than to risk the consequences of their discipline. By aiding and abetting, he contributed to the evil and became an active participant in it.

If his paying the supreme sacrifice for his own and their grievous sins made him a martyr, Henry Wirz stands not alone a victim of the system of jurisprudence devised by man. And if man had devised a system of perfect justice he would have long ago ceased to search for it in eternity.

blessed are they who survive
  —to inherit the spoils

As October, 1864, came upon the Andersonville Stockade there were still eight thousand, two hundred and eighteen prisoners within its gates. During that month four hundred and forty-four more captives were brought in. On the last day of that month there remained four thousand, two hundred and eight men.[1] Fortunately or otherwise, four thousand, four hundred and fifty-four prisoners had been transferred by Wirz or Winder or God to other quarters.

Private Ira Pettit's prisoner-of-war memorandum indicates that he sought admittance to the prison's hospital on October 11, 1864, complaining of diarrhea. His number for treatment and/or admittance was 14591, placing him eighth in line behind Private Frederick M. Phelps, whose number was 14583. Private Phelps, according to the hospital register, was admitted to the hospital that day, but according to that same hospital record, Private Pettit was returned to the stockade. Death for Private Pettit was still a week away.

The hospital register and prisoner-of-war memorandum further stated that Ira Pettit was admitted to the hospital on October 19, 1864, where he died on October 19, 1864, of scorbutus (hospital number 15249 and grave number 11170).

The prisoner-of-war memorandum for Private Phelps stated that he had been admitted to the hospital on October 11, 1864, for scorbutus, and that he was returned to the stockade on November 2, 1864, then sent to Millen,

---

[1] Record Group 249: *Records of the Commissary General of Prisoners.* *"Monthly Return—Andersonville,"* Vol. 110, Office of the U.S. Adjutant General, National Archives, Washington, D.C.

Georgia, on November 11, 1864, with "no further information."[2] as to parole or other disposition.

There is no hard evidence that Private Phelps was
suffering illness of any slight *or* significant degree. Even
though 'scorbutus' was noted on Phelps' prison
memorandum, a later medical examination stated that no
symptoms of scurvy's having *ever* existed were found.

Despite the prisoner-of-war memorandum there is the
real possibility that Private Pettit was never in the hospital
at Andersonville, while alive.

Private Phelps' admittance to the hospital, if indeed he
was admitted, could have been for any number of reasons
other than medical.

Private Phelps, on one occasion in his many applications for pension, stated that he received *"no hospital
treatment."*[3] On another occasion he alleged that he
received treatment in the hospital *"at camp distribution,
New Orleans.*[4] Finally he claimed that he received *"no
hospital treatment at Andersonville,"*[5] but was treated in the
hospital at *"Castle Williams, governor's island."*[6] (There is no
known record indicating that Private Phelps was ever at
Fort Independence, Boston Harbor. *But Ira Pettit was, and
Ira Pettit may have had memorabilia from Fort Independence.*
There is also no known record indicating that Private
Phelps was ever at New Orleans, but this will be
considered at more length later.)

To provide insight into the administrative operations of
the Andersonville hospital, an excerpt from the testimony
of one Confederate doctor at the trial of Henry Wirz is here
included:

---

[2] Direct quote.
[3] Declaration for Original Invalid Pension, dated 1/24/1883, from
Frederick Phelps.
[4] Declaration for Original Invalid Pension, dated 8/30/1889, from
Frederick Phelps.
[5] Declaration for Original Invalid Pension, dated 1/28/1892, from
Frederick Phelps.
[6] Ibid.

"So far as the names of the men and the diseases that they had, the hospital register was kept with great accuracy. If a man came to me I would diagnose his case, and send him to the hospital with a statement of the disease which I considered that he had. That was generally entered upon the register, but, perhaps, he would have half a dozen supervening diseases after he went into the hospital. The supervening diseases were hardly ever entered on the register, but generally only the disease with which he went from the stockade. I do not know what entry was made on the register when a man was shot in the stockade. I suppose the cause of death would be called 'vulnis sclopeticum;' that is the technical name for gunshot wound, and I suppose that would be the entry. Such an entry might be in the case of a man who had received wounds on the field of battle somewhere.

"Q. If a man in the stockade had been shot in the stockade, and the hospital register showed that he died of scorbutus, what would be the fact in that case?

"A. I do not suppose the register would show that, unless the man so shot was a patient, and under treatment for scorbutus at the time.

"Q. Examine the register now handed you, and examine it with some care, and state whether you recognize it, and whether it has any appearance of having been tampered with or changed since you saw it at the hospital.

"(Objected to by Mr. Baker until the book was proved, and objection overruled.)

"A. I recognize the book as being the hospital book kept at Andersonville. I see no marks that would indicate that it had been tampered with except some pencil marks on the margin, which I suppose are check marks.

"(The witness pointed out the marks referred to.)

"The hospital register was offered in evidence and accompanies the record.

"F. M. TRYON, clerk to the commission, a witness on

the part of the prosecution, being duly sworn, was examined as follows:

"Q. Examine the register and state what the pencil marks are.

"A. This book was given to me by Colonel Chipman to prepare an exhibit of the number of deaths, &c, which I did; and, in taking off the number of deaths I made the check marks referred to by the witness.

"The examination of Dr. AMOS THORNBURG was then resumed.

"Q. Examine the three indexes of the hospital register handed to you and see if you recognize them?

"A. I do; and, so far as I can see, they are all correct.

"The books were put in evidence by the judge advocate, and accompany this record.

"Q. I notice in this register very many entire columns representing that a patient was admitted, for instance, August 8, and died August 8, and in the column of remarks, 'died in quarters,' and again admitted August 9, died August 9, 'died in quarters,' and so on all through the book; what does that remark 'died in quarters' mean?

"A. I think Dr. Stevenson, perhaps would have to make a report of those cases, and they would have to be reported as having died of something, and as having died in hospital. I think, perhaps, there was an order that caused him to report them on the death register in hospital, and yet in the remarks they are put down 'died in quarters;' that means in the stockade. I never knew how he fixed up that difficulty. There were a great many things in reference to the hospital that I never could understand, and this was one of them. I suppose 'unknown' would be the entry in cases where the surgeon could not make out a proper diagnosis of the case. Those six men that were hung were marked as having died of 'asphyxia.' I do not recollect the date those men were hung, but I know they were all marked as having died of asphyxia. I asked the clerk in the hospital how he had entered those cases, and he referred me to the book, and showed me that he had marked them 'asphyxia.'

The JUDGE ADVOCATE. On page 110 of the Hospital Record there are given the names of six persons who died of asphyxia, and in the column of remarks, 'Tried by court-martial, and executed inside the prison;' that is the record.

"WITNESS. Those are no doubt the men who were hung.

"Q. I notice on examining this register that a large proportion of the patients recorded as having been admitted died in hospital, many of them, the day they were admitted, or immediately after, and that a few seem to be recorded as 'returned to the stockade.' Will you state to the court what your observation was with regard to the proportion that were returned to the stockade after being treated in the hospital?

"A. Well, I have no data from which I can state how many were returned to the stockade. The proportion, however, was small. Sometimes a man would come to the hospital and be treated there and relieved of his disease, but in the mean time some of the surgeons would become acquainted with him, and, perhaps, would have him detailed as a nurse, or, perhaps he would be detailed outside the stockade for some other business, and hence he was not returned to quarters. The proportion actually returned to quarters was very small. I never met among my own patients—those I had treated myself—any cases where I was unable to give a diagnosis of the cause of death, and where I had to report the disease as 'unknown.' I have met with patients after they were dead where I could not tell the cause of death. I have frequently seen men brought out of the stockade dead, and I did not know what they died of."[7]

[7]Executive Documents, the House of Representatives, 2nd Session of the Fortieth Congress, Executive Document No. 23. *Trial of Henry Wirz.* Washington, D.C., Government Printing Office, 1868. pp. 336-7-8.

Under cross-examination by Counsel, Dr. Amos Thornburg's testimony in reference to the hospital register continued:

"The hospital register was the property of the hospital outside the stockade. I think that no one in the stockade, or having control in the stockade, had anything to do with that book. That book was the property of the government. It was in charge of Surgeon White first, the surgeon-in-chief. Other surgeons could examine it any day they chose. I presume that if the other surgeons had brought up a list of names of persons having supervening diseases, they would have had the privilege of entering them. The surgeons would make their reports to the surgeon-in-chief, and from their report he would order the book to be made up. I don't know that any of the surgeons ever tried to have anything put in that book or alter it in any way. There was no rule on that subject that I know of. I think, though, it would have been presumption in any of the medical officers to have made an entry in the book without the permission of the surgeon in charge. The surgeon in charge is responsible for what was in it when he gave it up. If anything has been put in it since, I don't suppose he would be responsible. I have not seen anything that has been inserted since. I cannot recognize any of the handwriting in that book; it was done by the clerks.

"Q. Can you explain why it should be put in that hospital register that a person died in quarters?

"A. The only way I can account for it is this: the surgeon in charge would have to make a report to the medical director, and also reports to the surgeon general, and he would perhaps enter sick men in the book as in the hospital, when they were not. I think his idea was to draw as much commutation for the prisoners as he possibly could, and as we had a great many sick in the stockade, perhaps he would enter those in the stockade as being in the hospital. Those that were in the receiving and distributing hospital, which was one division of the

299

hospital, were in the stockade, and yet they were marked as in the hospital.

"When I said 'his idea was to draw as much commutation as possible,' I meant the surgeon in charge. I think it would more particularly apply to those in charge latterly, Dr. Stevenson and Dr. Clayton. I don't think, however, that Dr. Clayton would have made an entry that he could not have explained freely. Perhaps it would not apply so much to Dr. White."[8]

Under additional examination by the Judge Advocate, Dr. Thornburg testified:

"By the JUDGE ADVOCATE:

"Q. In cross-examination, in reply to a question as to what reason the surgeon in charge could have for making false entries in the hospital register, you said you supposed it was for the purpose of increasing the commutation. Explain what you mean; do you mean the hospital fund?

"A. Yes, sir.

"Q. Showing a larger number of patients?

"A. Yes. In a private conversation Dr. Stevenson told me that the more patients he had on his report, the more medicines and the more hospital fund he could draw. That was in the latter part of 1864. He often told me his plans, and what he aimed to do. That was one of them."[9]

The hospital's record of prisoner patients becomes suspect as it pertains to Private Pettit and Private Phelps in the light of this and other evidence.

More testimony apropos of the deaths occurring at Andersonville, which may have been wrongly reported, was elicited from Dr. Joseph Jones:

"In this collection of men from all parts of the world, every phase of human character was represented; the

[8]Executive Documents, the House of Representatives, 2nd Session of the Fortieth Congress, Executive Document No. 23. *Trial of Henry Wirz.* Washington, D.C., Government Printing Office, 1868. p. 339.
[9]Ibid. pp. 341-2.

stronger preyed upon the weaker, and even the sick who were unable to defend themselves were robbed of their scanty supplies of food and clothing. Dark stories were afloat, of men, both sick and well, who were murdered at night, strangled to death by their comrades for scant supplies of clothing or money."[10]

It is futile to speculate whether Private Pettit died with his possessions on him or perhaps even defending them. The actual circumstances of his death can never be established positively for those who choose to figment the endless opportunities to die at Andersonville.

* * *

Frederick M. Phelps stated to Edmund Riedel that Ira Pettit had died on October 18. It would have been by the remotest of possibilities that Phelps would have known what was recorded on the hospital register; therefore, one might assume that what he was stating was what he knew first-hand, or what he believed to be true.

It is possible that the hospital authorities did not know that Pettit was dead until roll call on the morning of October 19, or until Pettit's body was taken out to be sent to the dead house on that day. If this were the situation, it could have prompted the entry on the hospital register that he was admitted on the 19th and died on the 19th.

Had Private Phelps been in the hospital since the 11th of October, as a bona fide patient suffering of scurvy, it would have been unlikely that he would have had the opportunity to come into possession of Private Pettit's belongings, either before or after his death, despite prior arrangements, even if such arrangements had been made. In light of the usual robbing and/or stripping of the dead, it seems improbable that others would have sought out Private Phelps to endow him with whatever Private Pettit

---

[10] Ibid. p. 622.

might have worn or owned instead of appropriating such for their own purposes.

The divergence of interests, values, and experiences of Private Pettit and Private Phelps arouses a question as to whether Private Pettit would have committed his belongings to Phelps while yet alive, or as a legacy after death. Aside from their being in the same prison, it would appear that the only thing these two young men would have had in common was a mutual acquaintance with the State of New York.

Private Riedel stated that Private Phelps had Ira Pettit's diary and 'various other articles.' Private Mott, according to Mrs. Gregory, claimed that Private Pettit committed the diary to *Mott's* care a day or two before he died.

It is not known if Private Phelps searched out Private Riedel at Camp Lawton, or if it was Private Riedel who, in a frantic search for anyone with word from Private Pettit, found Phelps. Private Riedel and Private Phelps met at Millen on November *8*; and from Private John A. Cain's letter of June 3, 1865, one might assume that Private Mott was at Millen at that time also. It is possible and probable that Mott and Phelps came from Andersonville to Millen simultaneously.

Two days after Private Riedel's encounter with Phelps, i.e., November 10, 1864, and for some days thereafter, a number of men embraced the Confederate cause, according to Private John A. Cain and Private John McElroy.[11]

Rebel records for Private Phelps stated that he was sent to Millen on November 11, 1864, more than a week after leaving the hospital and three days after Private Riedel had seen him at Millen. Such notation on his prisoner-of-war records could have been as closely accurate as the hospital register which had alleged that Private Phelps was afflicted with scurvy. (One thousand men had been

---

[11]See pages 235, 287-88.

sent to Millen from Andersonville on November 3, 1864.[12]
It is not unreasonable to assume that Private Phelps was
among that contingent of prisoners.)

A thought that is difficult to suppress is that Private
Phelps, realizing at Millen that exchange was an imminent
contingency, and realizing that he could ill afford to risk a
direct encounter with Federal authorities, did take allegiance to the Confederacy.

There is a possibility that Frederick M. Phelps could
have returned to the Union's lines without arousing a
great concern or consternation on the part of the Union
officials, since there was now proof of a prison record with
the Rebels. It is possible that he would not have been
confronted with any of his other enlistments, and his
departure from Company E (or Company F) of the
Eleventh Pennsylvania Cavalry could have been debated.
Was he joining the Rebels (they did not acknowledge his
presence until July 5, and only then as a prisoner), or was
he *making a charge upon them* that day, July 1, 1864, when it
was recorded that he went to the enemy?

There is no evidence that the Federal government ever
took notice of Private Phelps' enlistments in the One
Hundred Fifty-seventh New York Infantry or the First
New York Light Artillery. The Federal government's
primary, and seemingly, only concern throughout the
years appears to have been that Private Phelps had not
returned to be officially discharged. However, Private
Phelps must have been under some apprehension that one
or more desertion charge(s) might confront his reappear-
ance; therefore, he could ill afford to chance exchange.
Frederick Phelps did not know how much the United
States authorities did not know.

Whether Private Mott had been separated by force (or
by choice) from the Union Army, while it was in utter

---

[12]Record Group 249: *Records of Commissary General of Prisoners.*
"*Monthly Return—Andersonville,*" Vol. 110, National Archives,
Washington, D.C.

confusion and under heavy fire in the Wilderness, remains unresolved with absolute certainty. If he did desert he had no way of knowing that he would eventually be recorded as having been captured, and therefore, he may have had, in his own mind, equal reason to be apprehensive of exchange.

If William E. Mott did take the oath of allegiance to the Confederacy on November 10, 1864, as alleged by Private Cain, and if Frederick M. Phelps did take the oath of allegiance to the Confederacy at that approximate same time, as alleged by Edmund Riedel, Mott and Phelps, if not already acquainted, could have become so during their orientation as newly converted Rebels. There is obviously small doubt that there was contact between Phelps and Mott.

There was no diary for 1864 returned to the Pettit family, but the chances appear more than fair that Ira Pettit would have kept one as long as he was humanly able to do so. In view of the historic events which transpired during late 1863, and during all of 1864, it also seems more than likely that such documentation, if it existed, would have been destroyed through or by Confederate censorship. The 1863 diary, as well as the two letters which Private Pettit had written inside the prison stockade (one to his step-mother and one to his father), held no intrinsic value to anyone other than the Pettit family and, more than this, they were readily identifiable. The envelopes containing Pettit's letters had censor marks, suggesting that they had passed through Rebel hands, and the 1863 diary had pages (which may have been unflattering to the Confederate Army) removed.

If Phelps and/or Mott had in their possession those two letters and the diary at the time they allegedly took allegiance to the Confederacy, it would be plausible that the Rebels would have read and censored them, and they could have completely destroyed any 1864 record at that time, had there been one. But in an environment of new converts among dedicated Confederates, it appears unlikely that the Confederates would have confiscated any benign contraband ('various other articles') from their newly acquired converts.

The mailing of Ira Pettit's letters in January, 1865, could have been nothing more than the result of poor postal service on the part of the officials at the Andersonville Stockade and the C.S.A. It could also have been a ghoulish prank by whatever kind of person it was who mailed them. Those letters were posted on January 18, 1865, at Old Point Comfort, Virginia, along the banks of the James River, the lower part of which takes on a broad, tidal, estuarial character on the edge of Chesapeake Bay.

It has been said by those who knew Private Phelps that he often spoke of the difficulty of working his way along a large and swollen river, *which he never did identify to his listeners,* but which they assumed was the Mississippi, as he made his way back to New York State after he had allegedly escaped the Rebel prison.

Floods during 1864, as reported by Hoyt and Langbein, were reported on three occasions during that year. "1864—MAY. 19 people drowned in Cherry Creek, Colo. JUNE. Arkansas and South Platte rivers, Colo. SEPTEMBER. City Creek, Utah;" [13] all of which were quite a distance from Andersonville, Georgia, for anyone traveling a route from Andersonville to New York State in November, 1864. The only major floods for the year 1865, according to that same study by Hoyt and Langbein, were in *March,* that year. Flooding was, according to them, "very extensive in western New York and Pennsylvania; upper Ohio, Susquehanna, Chenango, and Genesee rivers, with floods on Allegheny River exceeding all

---

[13]Hoyt, William G. and Langbein, Walter B. *Floods.* Princeton: Princeton University Press, 1955. p. 340.

previous record."[14] Mr. Phelps did not materialize in New York State until a number of months after the flood season in that area, and even alleged at one time that he was not freed from the Rebels until May, 1865.[15]

It becomes manifest that Private Phelps could have been referring to any one of those rivers during 1865, as mentioned by Hoyt and Langbein, but he could also have been referring to the estuarial character of the James River in the Old Point Comfort area of Virginia, which would appear to be in a swollen condition at anytime to those unused to estuaries.

The thought that he could have been referring to the Mississippi River could also be a consideration if, as he stated on his August, 1889, declaration for pension, he was treated at camp distribution at New Orleans where, in fact, some prisoners were exchanged.[16] Had this been the case, the Federal government would have provided his transportation home. But exchange is contrary to Phelps' alleged claim of having escaped, as well as to lack of any record of his exchange in the Federal files. Private Phelps appears to have been somewhat inconsistent in his inconsistencies.

One might recognize the possibility that Private Mott and Private Phelps could have traveled together for a time and for a distance after they departed the Rebels. It is possible that they left the Confederacy with the mutual consent of the Rebels, which happened in some instances; they could have escaped the Rebels after taking an oath of allegiance to the Confederate government; they could have been expelled by Confederate officials as undesirables, which also happened in some instances; or through their

[14] Ibid.
[15] See page 276.
[16] Lossing, Benson J., LLD. *A History of the Civil War.* Illustrated with reproductions of the Brady War Photographs by permission of the War Department, Washington, D.C. New York. The War Memorial Association, 1912. p. 430.

own devices, they could have actually successfully escaped the Rebel prison guards.

Whether Private Mott and Private Phelps traveled together or separately, they departed the Rebels without being officially turned over to the Federal government, and without being charged by their captors with escape. Rebel records gave no account of how or when Phelps and Mott departed their realm.

Purportedly, Private Mott had escaped and joined Sherman on his march through the South. Mr. Mott reconstructed a rather detailed explanation of his post-Confederate-prison operations, as he reminisced his military exploits against the South for the benefit of the pension office in his later years. He alleged that he had joined Sherman at Black Stock Court House, South Carolina. Black Stock, South Carolina, was a post village located fifty-three miles north of Columbia, South Carolina, on the Charlotte, Columbia, and Augusta Railroad.

It is not inconceivable that Private Mott could have joined Sherman's peripheral and/or supportive forces (infantry or cavalry) as they came through Columbia and the surrounding territory, providing he had been out of prison at that time and had been at that place. Sherman's Army had come into Columbia on February 17, 1865, transformed it into an inferno and promptly departed for Goldsboro, North Carolina.

If Private Mott did join Sherman's troops at Black Stock, no one took notice of him until March 20, 1865, at New Bern, North Carolina. And by that time much of Sherman's attention was being given to Johnston's forces as they exchanged the amenities of war in the final battle campaign at Bentonville, more than fifty miles northwest of New Bern.

William E. Mott would have found himself in precarious flight had he made his way to New Bern from Andersonville, Millen, or other of the Southern prisons, among the beleaguered and fleeing Rebels in the wake of Sherman's sweep through the Carolinas.

More records, however, appear in the files of the State of Rhode Island and the U.S. Adjutant General's Office at the National Archives, Washington, D.C., which are contrary to the narratives related by Mr. Mott concerning his post-prison contributions to Sherman.

On November 29, 1864, at Providence, Rhode Island, Private William Henry Edward Mott, alias Henry A. Mott, enrolled in the Fifth Regiment, Rhode Island Heavy Artillery. Again a substitute, Mr. Mott's Substitute Volunteer Enlistment Certificate reads as follows:

"I, *Henry A. Mott*, born in *Canada*, aged *twenty-six* years, and by occupation a *shoemaker*, do hereby acknowledge to have agreed with *Albert B. Collins*, Esq., of *Westerly, Rhode Island*, to become his substitute in the Military Service, for a sufficient consideration paid and delivered to me, on the *30th* day of *November, 1864*, and having thus agreed with said *Albert B. Collins*, I do hereby acknowledge to have enlisted this *30th* day of *November, 1864*, to serve as a soldier of the Army of the United States of America, for the period of three years, unless sooner discharged by proper authority: I do also agree to accept such bounty, pay, rations, and clothing, as are, or may be, established by law for soldiers. And I do solemnly swear that I will bear true and faithful allegiance to the United States of America; that I will serve them honestly and faithfully against all their enemies or opposers whomsoever; and that I will observe and obey the orders of the President of the United States, and the orders of the Officers appointed over me, according to the Rules and Articles of War." [17]

This printed document had been filled in, in the proper spaces, which are here italicized, and was duly signed by

---

[17] From the compiled service records of Private Henry A. Mott, National Archives, Washington, D.C., as specifically identified in the reference section of this book.

Private Mott, the Justice of the Peace, the Provost Marshal, the Commissioner of the Board, and the Surgeon of the Board, Second District, Rhode Island.

According to records reposing in the files of the State of Rhode Island, Henry A. Mott had been mustered into Company I, Fifth Regiment, Rhode Island Heavy Artillery, on November 29, 1864,[18] at Providence, Rhode Island.

The bounty being paid in the State of Rhode Island in November, 1864, was three hundred dollars to each new or veteran recruit who joined either a Rhode Island regiment or a regiment of the Regular Army. One hundred dollars were paid the recruit at the time he was mustered into service of the United States and the remaining two hundred dollars were paid upon his reporting to the headquarters of the respective regiment in the field.[19]

Frederick Dyer tells us that the Fifth Regiment, Rhode Island Heavy Artillery, was attached to New Bern, North Carolina, on May 27, 1863. This regiment had been attached to the defences of New Bern, North Carolina, Department of Virginia and North Carolina, until January, 1865, and for the remainder of the hostilities the Fifth Regiment, Rhode Island Heavy Artillery, was assigned to the Sub-District of New Bern, Department of North Carolina.[20]

Private William H. E. Mott, alias Henry A. Mott, joined the Fifth Regiment from the depot at New Bern, North Carolina, on December 30, 1864. The January and February, 1865, company muster roll for Private Henry A.

---

[18] Adjutant General's Office. State of Rhode Island and Providence Plantations. *Index of AGORI 1861-1865 Report.* Providence, Rhode Island. p. 557.

[19] As set out in *General Order, No. 3,* Office of the Adjutant General of Rhode Island and Providence Plantations, dated March 30, 1864, and per correspondence from Chief Administrative Aide Joseph A. P. Lamothe, Office of the Adjutant General, Providence, Rhode Island, dated February 18, 1976.

[20] Dyer, Frederick H. *A Compendium of the War of the Rebellion.* Des Moines, Iowa: The Dyer Publishing Company, 1908. p. 1630.

Mott states that Private Mott was present, in confinement, with no explanation of his incarceration.

According to the March and April, 1865, muster roll for Private Henry A. Mott, it was discovered on March 21, 1864, that Private Mott had deserted from Fort Caston, New Bern, North Carolina, taking with him one haversack and canteen, one bayonet, scabbard, cap pouch and cone pick, gun sling, ball screw, screw driver and cone wrench, tompion and wiper.

On March 20, 1865, sometime during the day or night of that date, Private Mott had come into contact with Union authorities and had identified himself as a member of the Fourteenth Connecticut Infantry Volunteers and as an escaped prisoner. Who could deny any of that?

Providence, Rhode Island, was familiar territory to Private William Henry Edward Mott, and records indicate that someone up North owed Private Mott some money. It appears that Private Mott headed in that direction upon leaving the Rebels; the substitute pay that was due him may have been a strong incentive. More than that, bounty jumping and substitute work had become a lucrative business for those who eluded detection. Private Mott may have contemplated such potential as he whiled away the hours, days, and months at Andersonville, and other prisons in the South, at least one of which had been the Union Army Brig, Fort Caston, New Bern, North Carolina.

William Henry Edward Mott (alias Henry A. Mott) lived a long and colorful life, receiving a pension of considerable amount for the services he had rendered the United States.

Bounty jumping to Private Phelps, by this time, may have become a weary business; but that is not to say that all of Private Phelps' military affiliations have been discovered. Only those that are known have been discussed. It is not known how much is not known.

If the Confederacy did take Frederick M. Phelps under its stars and bars, it may have found his services not unlike those which he had rendered the Union Army under the stars and stripes. Private Phelps also lived a long life, never quite giving up the hope of obtaining a pension from the United States government.

* * *

Efforts on the part of Clinton Pettit father of Private Ira S. Pettit to contact Frederick M. Phelps were not effective until early autumn, 1865, at Cortlandville, New York. It was then and there that Clinton Pettit found Phelps, and from him learned that William Henry Edward Mott had Ira's diary, according to descendants of Clinton Pettit. What additional role Private Edmund Riedel may have played in assisting Mr. Pettit locate Frederick Phelps is not known. According to his descendants, Clinton Pettit ceased his search for William E. Mott when Mrs. Gregory informed him that Mott had departed for California.

The personal belongings of Ira S. Pettit which were not returned to his family may be among the artifacts of some Civil War history buff who knows not from where nor how they came.

* * *

The terrible sadness that Ira Pettit must have felt as evening came upon Camp Sumter that September 28, 1864, was probably mingled with a confident hope that he would live until his government liberated him.

* * *

The women and children, across the South, who were forced to feed their fowl (as thin as desert roadrunners) to the Western Army on its way to the Atlantic seashore, who stood by as their emaciated cattle and hogs were slaughtered to sate that army's insatiable appetite, and who watched as their homes were set ablaze, could well have been thankful that the soldiers of that army carried, instead of napalm, only bayonets, muskets, and matches.

311

Sherman's coming through the South had presaged terror, his passing had induced horror, and the path he had taken is still well-defined in the minds of those whose ancestors watched him go by.

Andersonville, Millen, and
Savannah in the State of Georgia

Henry Putney Beers provides some quite succinct information regarding Camp Sumter, Camp Lawton, and Savannah which gives some insight into the propagation of the military prison system of the Confederacy.

"Andersonville, Ga.

"Toward the end of 1863 when the need was greatest General Winder sent Capt. W. S. Winder to Georgia to select a site for a large prison. During the winter Capt. Richard B. Winder, an assistant quartermaster, superintended the construction of a stockade and prison buildings on a site chosen near Americus. The first prisoners were confined in Feb. 1864 and the total number of prisoners at Andersonville has been reliably set at 49,485. Of these, approximately 14,000 died.

"On the approach of General Sherman's army in Sept. and Oct. 1864 all except 5,000 unable because of sickness to be moved were transferred to Savannah and Charleston. Early in 1865 some of the remaining ones were able to be marched to Wilmington, N.C., for exchange and others were transferred to Charlotte. In April 1865 the last of the prisoners were taken to Florida and then paroled.

"Successive commandants of this prison: Col. Alexander W. Persons, Feb., 1864, Brig. Gen. John W. Winder, June 17, 1864.

"Camp Lawton, Ga.

"In Sept. 1864 a stockade was constructed near Millen, 80 miles north of Savannah, for prisoners of war from Andersonville and Savannah. In the enclosure of 44 acres the prisoners built huts from the timber felled in clearing the camp, and an inadequate hospital was also constructed. More than 10,000 prisoners were held at Camp Lawton in the fall of 1864, but as a result of General Sherman's operations they were removed in November 1864 to Blackshear and Thomasville, Ga.

"The Commandant of this prison was Capt. D. W. Vowles.

"No records of this prison have been found.

"*Savannah, Ga.*

"In July 1864, Federal prisoners arrived at Savannah from Macon and Cahaba. The prison was located on grounds adjoining the old U.S. marine hospital. By the end of the first week in September there were 1,500 prisoners at Savannah. Since there were not enough soldiers to guard the prisoners, they were moved to Charleston, Millen, and Blackshear, Ga., within a short time. Savannah was occupied by U. S. forces on Dec. 21, 1864.

"The commandant of this prison was Col. Richard A. Wayne.

"No records of this prison have been found."*

---

*Henry Putney Beers, *Guide to the Archives of the Government of the Confederate States of America* (Washington, D.C.: National Archives Publication No. 68-15, 1968), p. 250.

Et al

The temptation to peer into the lives of some of those whose paths crossed Private Ira S. Pettit's became irresistible. They are obscure to the historian, but each in his own way contributed to the web of history from which all stories about the Civil War emanate.

Private Elias A. Dunkelberg

Elias A. Dunkelberg was in a hurry to be a soldier. On September 28, 1861, almost three months before his eighteenth birthday, he enrolled in Battery M, First Regiment, New York Light Artillery, as an eighteen-year-old farmer. He was mustered into service on the 14th day of October, 1861, at Rochester, New York.

From Monroe County, New York, on October 18, 1861, Private Dunkelberg sent the following message to his parents:

"My dear Father. It is with Pleasure that I embrase the Present opertunity to let you know my whereabouts. We are yet at camp hillhouse under the care of our noble Captain. We are advancing very fast in military drill and we will soon be ready to advance towards the south, reddy for battle, and then we will let the rebbles know that we are brave and courageous, solddiers, We have nod got our uniform yet. But there are at Rochester and are reddy for our use. But the other companys are ahed of us and we must wait till they are uniformed and then we will have our turn, We may fetch them tomorrow and then we will be reddy till next Monday. Hurah for the artilera and the Lockport Boys. We have bully times here, it is the laziest work I ever got ahold of yet. We have nothing to do but to drill, wash dises stand guard and Play. We drill four hours a day when it is nice weather, and when it is nasty not at

315

all. I had to stand guard for the first time last night, from eleven till one and from five till seven, it rained the most of the time but I was under shelter. When I have nothing to do I sometimes wish I was at home and could help you along with your work and I would like to see you all again, I am not homesick yet and I want get as long as I get as mutch to eat as I do now. I have got a heartier apetite then I ever had before. I sometimes do not know when to give up eating. Therefore you can think that I have got jolly good times. If you have not send that money yet you will not ned to send it for I can get money here to conveigh me home, and then you can give me some. I have not forgot my God yet and when I red in bible this morning, I come to the words The Lord is my light and my salvation; whom shall I fear? the Lord is the strenth of my life; of whom shall I be afraid, and again, One thing have I desired of the Lord, that will I seek after; that I may dwell in the house all the days of my life to behold the beauty of the Lord and to _____* in his timple. Glory be to God for sutch a promis as that, But I will have to close up for this time. My best respects to all enquiring Friends. Direct your letters to Camp hill house West Brihhton Monroe Co. NY In care of Capt. Cothran artillery Co. Let me know who does your house work From your affectionate Son E. A. Dunkelberg."

But his first try at soldiering was cut short by orders from the Adjutant General to muster out all men in excess of those prescribed by law for Captain Cothran's Company M. Private Dunkelberg was honorably discharged on December 20, 1861, at Camp Barry, Washington, D.C.

More than nineteen years before, on the first day of January, 1842, John Dunkelberg(er) and Polly Fleisher had been married at Buffalo, New York. To them were born seven sons and one daughter. Elias was their eldest, having been born on December 26, 1844, in Lockport,

---

*Undeciphered cipher.

New York. (Their other children were S. F., born October 1, 1849, Samuel S., born November 25, 1851; Jeremiah D., born June 26, 1853; John C. F., born October 9, 1856; William T., born July 18, 1858; Saloma A., born October 22, 1860; and Moses C., born March 25, 1863.)

When Elias was almost three his parents bought a farm near Lockport, in Niagara County, Township 13, Range 6, bounded on one side by Mud Creek. It was there that Elias learned the life of a farmer.

If Private Dunkelberg rode the train to Canandiagua on the morning of the 20th of June with them, when the other recruits from Lockport were dispatched to that rendezvous, or if he arrived there ahead of them on June 19, 1862, is not known. In any event Captain Thomas Oliver Barri inducted this young lad into the Eleventh Regiment, United States Army, as a *first* time enlistee, on June 20, 1862, at Canandaigua. He was assigned to Company B, Second Battalion.

Private Dunkelberg's family always stated that his enlistment date was June 19, 1862. It is likely that he did join himself with that contingent of recruits in Lockport on that day, but was not officially sworn in until they arrived at Canandiagua on the 20th.

Private Dunkelberg was a blue-eyed, dark-haired lad with fair complexion, standing five feet and seven inches tall. He gave his age to Captain Barri as being twenty-one years. Since his days with Battery M he had aged six months and had grown one-half inch in height.

The following correspondence provides part of the poignant story of Private Elias A. Dunkelberg:

"Camp 11th U.S. Inft. New York Sept. 8th/63. My Dear Parants, It gives me pleasure to think that I am once more seated to write to you my dear parants the last letter that I wrote to you from Alexandria One for you and one for Solomon I have received no answer to them yet. I do not know whether you received them or not. at least I thought

317

I would let you know that I was well and enjoying good health. From Alexandria we took to sea and after rideing thirty hours we arrived safe in New York Harbor. we have got a very good place to encamp and we have got some large 'A' tents. we have plenty to eat, drink, & wear. they have isued new dres coats to us with scales and plug hats so we make quite a show. las sunday we had a dress parade in a large park. there were from ten to twelve hundred people preasant. they think it an awful sight to see a dres parade. I do not know how long we will stay here. I hope we will stay here all winter. we have got good times and very good quarters so we have nothing to complain—

"I have had the pleasure of being appointed Company Clerk of this Company. It is a good situation all I have to do is to write and attend dres parades and inspections. I have no guard duty to do nor do I have to drill go on fatigue or any thing of the kind. I hope these few lines will find you all well.

"Give my respects to all enquiring friends. Ever your dutiful Son Elias. A. Dunkelberg.

"P.S. Inclosed you will find a letter written to me from Cousin Daniel Sparash. I merely send it to show you the style of paper they have in the 'Southern Confederacy.' Direct Elias. A. Dunkelberg Co. 'F' 11th U.S. Inft Jones Wood, foot of 71st St. New York City."

War, history, and the postal service went on. The following letter was delivered to the Dunkelberg(er) farm home in November, 1864.

"Fort Hamilton New York Harbor Nov. 8th 1864. Sir I have the honor to inform you that your Son Elias was taken prisoner June 1st at Coal Harbor Va. He was when last heard of at Richmond in the Libby prison he was well and in good spirit. I take the liberty to remit to you his

318

letters which he left in my desk. I am Respectfully Augustus Lange 1st Sergt Co F 11th Infr."

On that same November 8, 1864, somewhere in the City of Richmond, Virginia, another letter was being written to Elias Dunkelberg's father:

"Richmond, Va., Nov., 8, 1864. Mr. Duncleburg—Dear Sir:—In our visits to the various hospitals, last Summer, we made several calls at one of the hospitals where the Federal wounded and convalescent were confined. There I saw your son. He had received a mortal wound in his thigh. His sufferings were great, though he bore them patiently. Not a murmur escaped his lips. The evening before his death he sent for me. I went to see him and found him in the agony of death. He repeatedly exclaimed, 'I cannot stand it—I shall go to Jesus.' We knelt in prayer around his bunk, after which he prayed as fervent a prayer as ever fell from the lips of man. We sung a hymn, 'Jesus I love thy charming name.' He sung it with us, and asked us to sing another which he also sung. It was the old familiar hymn, 'When I can read my title clear,' &c. He spoke of the good instruction, the good letters, and how kind his parents had been to him, and returned thanks to God that he had such parents. He died that night. Yours truly, J. T. Carpenter, Chaplain."

In an obvious effort to allay the fears of the Dunkelberg(er)s, and in seeming ignorance of what had transpired, another letter was written to Mr. Dunkelberg(er) on November 27, 1864:

"Lafeyette Barricks Baltimore M.D. November 27. Mr. Dunkleburger Sir Your Son Elias was taken Prisoner on the 2d of June at Cole Harbor. I was taken the same time but I made my escape about two months ago and I have joined here a few days ago. I was told by one of my Co that

319

he seen your Son in the Rebells hands and he thought he was wounded slightly when he seen your Son he was getting letters out of his knapsack and he did not have time to speak to your Son. I seen by the papers that they are exchanging Prisoners and I expect to see him soon. if he was wounded he was taken better care of then if he was not wounded. Perhaps he is in one of the Rebels Hospitals writing because they have no Clerks there all the men are in the army. Where I was in Prison there was a great many was sent there after there wounds was well and I watched every one that came in but he was not amongst them. And I made up my mind he was acting as Clerk in some Hospital.

"Indeed Sir I am sorry you have not heard from him but he cant send no letters out of the Confedersey. Sir I am sorry that he is not here I want him very bad here there is no Clerk in the Co since he was taken he was my best friend and Companion.

"Mr. Dunkleburger dont feel bad about him he will be back soon Yours Very Respectfulley Sergt Maurice Meade."

Crossed cross-communications would finally become untangled as more letters were written.

"Camp Parol Annapolis Md. Dec. 24/64. Miss Morton I have joined my company; I accertain that Mr. Dunkelberg has made inquires of his Son Elias. The letter was answered by a Sergeant of my company, but the truth was not told.

"I am sorry that I have to tell you, what I feard as soon I heard he had not written to you, start not Miss Morton He is among the happy ones in Heaven. He died between the 15th and twentieth of June in the second Alabama Hospital Richmond Va. the exat date is not known. There are men here that saw him dead, yes, even his nurse is here. Please pardon me for addressing you, his Father did not answer my letter and I fear he did not get my own I wrote to him from Fort Hamilton, N.Y.H. the same day I mailed your former correspondence with Elias, but I received no answer from you either. I was sick in bed that time, may be the orderly neglected to mail them. Please let me know did you get that parcel or not.

"I am V.R. Y.O.S. Augustus Lange 1st Sergt. Co. 'F' 11th Infantry direct to Washington, D.C. P.S. Inform his Father and give him my address."

"Mr. Dunkleberg I received this sad letter the other day and I thought that I could do no better than to send you the letter just as I received it. It was a sad blow to more than one. But especially do I mourn for you. He was stricken down in the morning of life but he died in a noble cause and God will reward him. Take this to heart as little as possible remembering that 'The Lord giveth and the Lord hath taken away blessed be the name of the Lord' He is now a shining angel in heaven as we have all reason to believe and therefore we should rejoice instead of mourn his loss. But I must close. from C. R. Morton."

According to Private Dunkelberg's prisoner-of-war record, he was captured at Gaines' Mill on June 1, and admitted to Hospital 21, Richmond, Virginia, on June 4, 1864. Regiment rolls reported him as 'missing in action,' on June 2, 1864. Sergeant Maurice Meade alleges that Private Dunkelberg was taken at the same time that he was on June 2. And it was on June 2, 1864, that the Eleventh Regiment lost forty-five of its men through capture by the Rebels.

Private Elias Dunkelberg had fudged a mite here and there about his age, but he had given in full measure of his courage.

(The files of Private Dunkelberg contain a variety of spellings of his last name, i.e., Dunkleberg, Dunkelberger, Dunkleberger, Damkleberger, Domkleberger, Duncleburg,

Dunkelburger, etc., but his own signature was consistently 'Dunkelberg.' His father identified himself as John Dunkelberger. Mrs. Polly Fleisher Dunkelberg(er) passed away at Raymond, Niagara County, New York, on April 20, 1889. The letters quoted herein are to be found in the files of Private Dunkelberg, and were submitted to the Pension Bureau in 1890 when John Dunkelberger made application for a father's pension based upon the military service of his son. File documentation identification is more specifically set out in the reference section.)

Note:

At Ladysbridge, County Cork, Ireland, on March 14, 1839, Maurice Joseph Meade was born the son of Jeremiah and Mary Lawless Meade.

On April 22, 1861, this auburn-haired, black-eyed lad, who stood five feet and five inches tall, was enrolled at Washington, D.C., in Company H, Sixth Regiment, Massachusetts Volunteer Militia, for three months. He was mustered out on August 2, 1861, at Boston, Massachusetts. On March 8, 1862, he enlisted in Company F, Eleventh Regiment, U.S. Regular Army.

Sergeant Meade was another of those of the Eleventh Regiment who was in action when captured near Gaines' Mill, Virginia, on June 2, 1864. The Confederates had taken Sergeant Meade to Richmond on June 3, and had sent him from there to Andersonville, Georgia, on June 8, 1864.

Maurice Joseph Meade successfully escaped from the Andersonville Stockade, and on November 11, 1864, he rejoined his regiment from missing in action. He was discharged the service on March 8, 1865, at City Point, Virginia, having served the U.S. Army for three years.

On May 7, 1865, at Woburn, Massachusetts, Catharine Creighton became Maurice Meade's bride. She had been born on May 12, 1841, in County Meath, Ireland, and had come to the United States when she was fifteen years old.

The Meades became the parents of a daughter Laura in 1867 and a son William Henry on November 2, 1871.

While living at 84 Main Street, Stoneham, Massachusetts, Mr. Meade, a retired shoemaker, died of apoplexy and arteriosclerosis, on November 11, 1916. He was survived by his wife and his son.

It is probable that he was the Sergeant Meade whom Ira mentioned in his letter dated June 21, 1864. As a *sergeant* of a squad in the stockade at Andersonville, Maurice Meade would have perhaps had better opportunity to make good an escape.

Private William H. Holmes

Private Holmes was another of those Wilson fellows who never made it big with the historians. Nevertheless, he must have been quite a swashbuckling adventurer.

On October 2, 1861, William Holmes enrolled at Lockport, New York, in Captain Ellsworth's Company, later known as Company G, New York Mounted Volunteers. This military organization was mustered in at Troy, New York, on November 6, and designated Second Regiment Cavalry by New York State authorities on November 18, 1861. The War Department subsequently called it the Seventh New York "Black Horse" Cavalry.

On November 23, 1861, the men of the Seventh New York Cavalry left the state for Washington, D.C., where they served in its defences until their muster out and honorable discharge from service on March 31, 1862.

According to Ira Pettit's diary, the Seventh Cavalry returned to the Wilson-Lockport area on Friday evening, April 11, 1862, but Private Holmes did not accompany this regiment home after discharge. Instead he set out to find Battery M, First Regiment, New York Light Artillery.

As Private Holmes searched for Captain George W. Cothran's Battery M it was moving from Winchester,

Virginia, through Strasburg, Woodstock, and Edenburg to the south fork of the Shenandoah and from there to McGaheysville.

His mode of travel and his method of locating Battery M is not known, but on April 28, 1862, Private William Holmes found the battery at New Market, Virginia, and then and there joined and was mustered into that battery of the First Regiment, New York Light Artillery.

By the time that Private Ira Pettit finished training and arrived at the front along the Rappahannock, Private Holmes was already a veteran in the business of war. He had summered in the Shenandoah Valley, run into an affray at Cedar Mountain and engaged in battles at Manassas and at Sharpsburg. Now he was on hand to join Ira on Burnside's 'Mud March' toward Fredericksburg, Virginia. The Rappahannock, the Rapidan and the plains along Bull Run were old stomping grounds to Private Holmes.

Before their lives went separate ways forever, Holmes and Pettit shared Chancellorsville and Gettysburg. They were often geographically close, and traveled somewhat similar routes to and from Adams County, Pennsylvania. They passed on June 27, after crossing the Potomac on the northbound chase. After leaving the Gettysburg Battlefield, they saw each other briefly just north of Burkittsville, Maryland, on July 16, 1863.

Following Gettysburg, Battery M was transferred from the Army of the Potomac to the Department of the Cumberland. That change guided Private Holmes' course into Tennessee, Alabama, and across Georgia by way of Atlanta and Savannah to the sea.

William H. Holmes had been born to Richard Holmes and Betsy Frost Holmes on October 22, 1840, and had grown into a hazel-eyed, sandy-haired, young man, standing five feet, five inches tall.

After his military discharge (which he always specified as having taken place at Jones Cross Roads, North

Carolina, April 27, 1865, but which the government recorded as having taken place at Raleigh, North Carolina, April 28, 1865,) he returned to his home at Wilson, New York.

On November 7, 1867, at Somerset, Niagara County, New York, this young veteran took Jennie Pettit as his bride. On August 5, 1877, Mrs. Jennie Pettit Holmes died.

In the early spring of 1881 (on March 24) William Holmes married Mary Elizabeth Tenbrook of Pendleton, Niagara County. (Mary Elizabeth Tenbrook was a native of Northumberland County, Pennsylvania, having been born there on December 18, 1843.) Of this marriage came two sons—Merle Howard Holmes and LeRoy Holmes.

Aside from his years in service William H. Holmes spent his life on a farm just east of Wilson, as a neighbor of 'Tip' Wright, Douglas Pease (Harvey Pease's brother), and Clinton Pettit (Ira Pettit's father).

As time went by the rigors of life and the exigencies of old age collected their toll. In his last years he served his community as a justice of the peace. William Holmes probably swapped many a story with other of the elderly citizens such as 'Tip' Wright, a surviving peer.

On May 11, 1914, he took leave of all these experiences. His tour of duty was ended, and he was interred in Greenwood Cemetery, Wilson, New York.

A well-defined path that passes by the grave of William Holmes is traveled by each succeeding generation of youngsters from Wilson, who with fishing poles in hand, somehow navigates the steep and wooded embankment to a creek that has carved a small canyon along a part of the cemetery's western boundary.

Many of these youngsters are descendants of comrades, friends and relatives of Niagara County Civil War soldiers interred there. Their subdued chatter is inaudible above the drone of the powered lawn mowers operated by other teen-agers as they manicure the grounds about their ancestors resting beneath the ancient evergreens that shade the graves from the summer's sun and softly sift for them a blanket of the winter's snow.

Private Harvey Usher Pease

Harvey Pease son of Enoch and Eliza Pease was born at Wilson, New York, on August 19, 1842. He enlisted in Captain George W. Cothran's Battery M, First Regiment, New York Light Artillery, on October 5, 1861, becoming number forty-two on the enlistment rolls of that battery. He was mustered in at Rochester, New York, on November 19, 1861.

Private Pease, one of the buglers of the battery, was five feet, four inches tall, with dark complexion, dark hair, and blue eyes. He had been a farmer at the time of his enlistment.

In mid-summer of 1862, after the battery's operations in the Shenandoah Valley, Private Pease became ill and was hospitalized near Alexandria, Virginia. On August 6, 1862, he was sent from Culpeper Court House, Virginia, to the hospital at St. David's Island, New York, and not until September of 1863 was he returned to duty.

Private Pease was among those thirty-seven thousand men who accompanied General Grant on his way to re-open the Tennessee River and rescue Major General Rosecrans at Chattanooga during the autumn of 1863. On February 5, 1864, Harvey U. Pease was discharged at Bridgeport, Alabama, by virtue of re-enlistment as a veteran volunteer. He was mustered into that same Battery M on February 12, 1864.

Harvey Pease found that his way back to Wilson, New York, was a long and circuitous route. He crossed Georgia and the Carolinas with General Sherman (and Willie Holmes), and from there he went on to Richmond, Virginia, and Washington, D.C. After the Grand Review in Washington, D.C., on May 24, 1865, he (along with all the members of Battery M) was mustered out at Rochester, New York, on June 23, 1865.

On September 30, 1866, Harvey Pease married Lucretia Mitchell, and to them were born two daughters— Katherine, on May 16, 1869, and Edna, on February 10, 1873. Mrs. Pease passed away shortly after the birth of their second child, and was interred in Greenwood Cemetery, Wilson, New York, in March 1873.

At Richmond, Indiana, on September 30, 1875, Mr. Pease and Margaret Rebecca Shover were united in marriage. They became the parents of four children— Charles R., born on September 7, 1876; Emma Bell, born on December 31, 1878; Nellie, born on April 3, 1880; and Lafayette Franklin, born on October 10, 1886.

Mr. Pease had taken his new bride back to Wilson, New York, where the family lived for a number of years, but in 1889 he went west again, this time to Missouri, where he homesteaded one hundred and sixty acres of land in the sparsely populated area near Willow Springs. For nine years this farm was home for the Pease family.

During 1898 the Pease family moved once more, this time to Indianapolis, Indiana, where schools were more accessible for their children and where many of Mrs. Pease's family lived. Mr. Pease owned and operated a dairy in Indianapolis until his retirement.

Mrs. Margaret Pease succumbed to cancer in 1902 at the age of fifty-two. And on October 14, 1914, Harvey Pease lost his daughter Emma Bell.

Sometime during 1860 while Harvey Pease was still a teen-ager, he had, as he chored about the family farm, run onto a hidden and rusty pitchfork which had punctured the instep of his left foot. Even though this injury had not prevented his serving in the military forces, as he grew older that foot and leg atrophied until it was considerably smaller than the other one. Rheumatism continued to plague him in later life also.

The patriotism which may have prompted Harvey Pease's enlistment in 1861 never flagged during the years. He yearly participated in the Memorial Day services honoring deceased veterans, and he was active in the G.A.R. In 1915 he attended the national encampment of veterans of the Grand Army of the Republic at Washington, D.C. All his correspondence to the government was cordially filled with pride for the country he had served.

One day in late May, 1917, as he was crossing a busy street in Indianapolis, Indiana, Mr. Pease was struck by a car. As he lay in his hospital bed suffering the mortal injuries of that accident, he agonized over who would blow 'taps' for the soon-to-be Memorial Day services in his stead.

On June 4, 1917, as spring and the promise of summer once again swept green the prairies of the Midwest, Private Harvey Usher Pease joined many of the comrades of his youth. He rests beside his wife in Crown Hill Cemetery, Indianapolis, Indiana.

Miss Nell Pease is the only surviving member of Harvey Pease's immediate family. After thirty-eight years of teaching in the Indianapolis School System, she presently lives in a retirement home at Greenwood, Indiana. Her charm, beauty, and mental acuity belie nearly half her years.

It was a great pleasure to provide Miss Pease a copy of this diary on the Eve of Christmas, 1972. As she read the few lines about Private Pease, Miss Pease exclaimed, "Oh, I had forgotten that Father limped." Suddenly there was a realization of the transience of physical frailties in the mind of humankind, and an awareness of the truly great compliment it was that she had just bestowed upon him. What Miss Pease did remember was that her father was always a very kind man, and after the death of her mother, a very lonely man.

Perhaps some of the influence of the culture and era of Harvey Usher Pease still abides in the countless students whose lives Miss Pease has touched.

Private Enoch Pettit

When the Civil War came along Enoch Pettit was on the edge of middle age.

Mr. Pettit had been born in Galway, New York, in 1820. At the age of twenty he had moved to Niagara County and become a farmer.

On August 26, 1862, Enoch Pettit enlisted in the One Hundred Fifty-first Regiment of the New York Infantry Volunteers and was mustered into Company C, as Chief Musician (fifer), at Lockport, New York, on October 22, 1862. Private Pettit stood five feet, eight and one-half inches tall, with brown hair, light complexion, and blue eyes.

The One Hundred Fifty-first was on duty at Baltimore until April 22, 1863. In the Gettysburg campaign it was at South Mountain before the battle, and afterwards pursued Lee (as had Ira's regiment and Battery M) to Manassas Gap, Virginia. Throughout the autumn and winter of 1863-64 Private Enoch Pettit's regiment was on the line of the Rappahannock and Rapidan.

When spring came once again, the One Hundred Fifty-first faced and fought the Rebels in the battles of the Wilderness.

After Private Enoch Pettit had marched with Private Ira S. Pettit to Port Royal, Virginia, his regiment moved into Maryland by way of Washington, D.C. From Georgetown Private Enoch Pettit's regiment marched for a day and a half, arriving at the Monocacy River just south of Frederick, Maryland, shortly after the bridge across it had been burned by some of General Jubal A. Early's troops.

With the bridge destroyed the Union soldiers were commanded to ford the Monocacy. Overcome by the heat of the July sun, the rapid march, and the comparatively cold water, Private Pettit and others of the regiment found themselves unable to move on. They were left to be taken to a hospital at Frederick, Maryland. The regiment was encamped near Martinsburg in the valley when Enoch

Pettit rejoined it, but recurrent bouts of rheumatism and diarrhea were to plague him for the rest of his life.

Enoch Pettit was in the fight at Cedar Creek on October 19, 1864, (when Sheridan made his famous ride), and he was in the battle near Winchester, Virginia, in which Private William H. Shearer had received his grievous wound.

Private Pettit had been called home in late December, 1864, because of the grave illness of his wife. Prior to this furlough he was transferred to Company F of the same regiment.

During May, 1865, Private Pettit was assigned duty at a military hospital, helping to care for sick and wounded soldiers. He was discharged, along with all of the members of his regiment, on June 26, 1865, near Washington, D.C.

Prior to his enlistment Enoch Pettit had dealt in cattle and farming and had owned considerable investments and holdings. When he returned to Wilson after the war, his farm had been considerably reduced. Relatives, it was said, had bought up the land because of unpaid taxes. His home and two and one-half remaining acres were located on East Youngstown Road just outside Wilson.*

Mr. Pettit's first wife Julyett Pratt Pettit (born April 14, 1827) had died in 1858, leaving an infant daughter Mary Evelyn. Although personal records concerning a second marriage are sparse, it appears that his second wife, whose name *may* have been Lois, and another daughter, whose name *may* have been Juliette, also preceded him in death.

Mary Evelyn Pettit married Alfred James Moody and became the mother of five children. However she too, preceded her father, succumbing to typhoid fever on April 25, 1894.

Private Pettit had been pensioned at $2.00 per month

*Information provided by Mrs. Mildred Moody Eakin, dated April 13, 1973.

from June 27, 1865, until September 28, 1881, for rheumatism and recurrent diarrhea, which he had suffered ever since the march to the Monocacy and the fording of it.

Mr. Pettit was almost sixty-two years old when this $2.00 per month pension was discontinued by the government, and for the next ten years there was a continuing debate between him and the government concerning his reinstatement as a pensioner.

The reason for the pension's discontinuance appears to have been that someone somewhere, during 1881, decided that Mr. Pettit had recovered from his war incurred disabilities or perhaps had not even been present when they occurred. The following is one of the many messages which was submitted to it during the ten years that that government considered restoration of Mr. Pettit's pension and his qualifications for it.

"Enoch Pettit being duly sworn says: That his post office address is Wilson Niagara Co N.Y.

"That he is the applicant in the above entitled claim.

"That in reply to departmental letter of Nov 2 1885 and which is returned herewith he says:

"That feeble health, poverty and the infirmities of body makes it impossible for him to travel around after comrades further—that he believes it is useless to do so, as he believes he has filed all the evidence in his application that it is possible to get as to the incurrence of his disabilities.

"His mind has lost its vigor and he had to rely upon others as to dates, and he verily believes there is still an error as to dates for the reason that your department says that Chauncey Wichterman & others were not present when I incurred any disability *when the fact is Wichterman was taken sick when I was, went in the same wagon at the same time I did & to the same hospital.* If Wichterman, Oliver, and the others wasnt there then I wasnt there and the date is wrong—

"Comrade O'Connor says the battle of Monocacy was fought the 9th day of July 1864—and that that's the time the bridge was burned, that must be about the date that I incurred my disabilities, for the bridge had just been burned across the Monocacy, I think only a day or so before and that was why we had to ford the Monocacy River and that is when I incurred my disabilities by getting chilled and wet after the terrible march under a scorching sun.

"Capt. W. W. Bush of Co B 28th N.Y. Vols War 1861 who says he was near by scouting, says that battle was fought and the bridge burned about July 9th, 1864.

"I relied as did others on Wichterman for dates as he is a young man with good memory, and very intelligent, but he must be mistaken when he thinks that the Monocacy battle was fought in September 1864.

"My disability was incurred the day of the Monocacy battle the same day or the day after the Monocacy bridge was burned.

"Under the circumstances deponent is reluctantly obliged to say he is unable to furnish other or additional evidence as to the incurrence of his disabilities."

Mr. Pettit had spent almost three years of his life in the Union Army; had seen active duty at Gettysburg, the Wilderness, Cedar Creek, Winchester, and Monocacy; had lost almost all of his property and fortune while serving in that army; had found himself considerably incapacitated from his war experiences; had spent ten years convincing that army's government that he had been at the Monocacy River in July, 1864, (and had been sent from there to a hospital, which he left to return to his regiment against the advise of the hospital doctor), and in seeking other witnesses who were at the Monocacy that hot July day in 1864; had implored that government to allow him to be examined by a board of surgeons of the Federal government; and at the age of almost seventy-two years, had finally convinced that government that the laws under which it operated justified his reinstatement for a veteran's pension.

In 1899 Private Enoch Pettit was interred in Greenwood Cemetery, Wilson, New York, among his family, friends, and comrades.

A German silver fife, a clarinet, a military identification button, and one bound volume of Harpers Weekly (volume V for the year 1861), all possessions of Private Enoch Pettit, were presented to the Gettysburg National Park Museum by Mr. Pettit's grandson Reverend Winfred Pettit Moody in 1968. Private Pettit's musician's sword was presented to the Wilson Historical Society in November, 1973, by the widow of Brigadier General Alfred Judson Force Moody, a great-grandson of Private Enoch Pettit and a casualty of Viet Nam.

Some of his great-great-great grandchildren presently live upon the land over which Private Enoch Pettit marched and fought in Maryland and Virginia during that war between states and among men.

Private Jason Lee Pettit

Except by the grace of fate Private Jason L. Pettit might have been one of those of the Second Mounted Rifles who were prison-mates of Private Ira S. Pettit at Camp Sumter.

Although the Second Regiment of New York Mounted Rifles was late in its organization (October 31, 1863, through February 13, 1864,), it was destined to participate in some of the most heated battles of the Civil War.

Jason Pettit was born at Wheatfield, in Saratoga County, New York, on April 19, 1839. He enlisted in the Second Mounted Rifles on January 15, 1864, and was mustered into Company C, at Norwich, New York, on January 16, that year. Mr. Pettit was a comparatively tall young man, standing five feet and nine and one-half inches tall, with blue eyes, brown hair, and dark complexion. He was a farmer.

The Second Mounted Rifles were in the thick of things during the battles in the Wilderness. They had been in battle (dismounted) in the same area at the same time that Private Ira S. Pettit was captured. They also participated in the siege of Petersburg, Virginia, from June 16, 1864, until April 2, 1865.

In front of Petersburg, Virginia, during August, 1864, Private Pettit contracted black jaundice and a disease of the gums which caused him to lose many of his teeth. He was hospitalized for about a month and then returned to duty.

The Second Mounted Rifles were present at Appomattox on April 9, 1865. Afterwards they were assigned provost duty in the Sub-District of Appomattox until August, 1865.

On August 10, 1865, Private Jason L. Pettit was honorably discharged from military service at Petersburg, Virginia.

Jason Pettit had lost his first wife prior to enlistment. On November 22, 1866, he married Mary Jane Olmsted at Ransomville, New York. To them were born two sons—Walter Sherwood, on October 1, 1873, and Elmer Everett, on November 11, 1879, (Elmer died sometime after his eighteenth birthday and before 1915, the exact date of which is not determined) and one daughter—Tressie Leah, on February 22, 1881.

The Jason Pettits made their home in Wilson, New York, until 1883. During that year they moved to Brockport in Monroe County, New York. In 1903 Mr. Pettit had had to have his left eye removed. By 1912 glaucoma had claimed the sight of his right eye.

The financial status of Jason Pettit, by the time that he became totally blind, was in such dire straits that it had become necessary for him to break up his home and sell all his personal belongings. By that time his wife was also totally physically disabled.

On August 27, 1912, from Congressman Henry Danforth, a letter was addressed to the Honorable James L. Davenport, Commissioner of Pensions, Washington, D.C., on behalf of Private Pettit:

"My dear Mr. Commissioner: Enclosed are two affidavits (one of the claimant and the other of a physician) in support of the claim for increase pension in behalf of Jason L. Pettit, late of Co. C, 2d New York Mounted Rifles, Inv. Cert. No. 1101351. In his affidavit the claimant makes a plea that the adjudication of his claim be made special, owing to the facts that he is blind, in necessitous circumstances, has no income except the present amount of his pension, and has dependent upon him a wife who owing to rheumatism is unable to assist him in making a living. The pitiful condition of these two folks, especially that of the soldier-claimant, appeals to me strongly, and I therefore earnestly urge, request and recommend that the adjudication of Pettit's claim be made special."

The above letter was answered with the following on September 11, 1912, addressed to Mr. Jason L. Pettit:

"Sir: Your above-entitled claim for pension under the Act of May 11, 1912, based on age and length of service, has been allowed at $21.50 per month, from date of filing claim, June 14, 1912.

"That part of your claim based on disability, is rejected on the ground of your manifest inability to furnish evidence of unfitness and incapacity for the performance of manual labor from causes directly due to your military service in line of duty. Very respectfully, L. Stillwell, Acting Commissioner."

The plea of the blind Private Jason Lee Pettit had fallen upon the deaf ears of the Pension Bureau. It literally took two years and an Act of Congress to procure any additional assistance for this helpless and destitute ex-soldier.

In the House of Representatives and the Senate of the United States of America, in Congress assembled, there was on July 1, 1914, enacted, "That the Secretary of the

335

Interior be, and he is hereby, authorized and directed to place on the pension roll, subject to the provisions and limitations of the pension laws—The name of Jason L. Pettit, late of Company C, Second Regiment New York Mounted Rifles, and pay him a pension at the rate of $50 per month in lieu of that he is now receiving."*

Although he could not see, Private Jason L. Pettit did not fail to recognize the 'angel of death' who visited him on January 14, 1916.

Second Lieutenant Marvin D. Pettit

Seth and Nancy Pettit made their home at North East, Pennsylvania, in that part of the state known as "The Triangle."

Their son Marvin had enrolled as a corporal in Company F of the One Hundred Eleventh Pennsylvania Infantry on October 22, 1861. He was mustered in at Camp Reed, Erie, Pennsylvania, on November 25, 1861.

During most of the year 1862 Corporal Pettit was on extra duty in Colonel Belger's office at Baltimore, Maryland. In November, 1862, he was transferred to Non-Com's Staff and promoted to sergeant major. At Aquia Creek, Virginia, his promotion was confirmed to date from November 1, 1862.

After the battles at Chancellorsville and Gettysburg, Sergeant Major Pettit was discharged by command of Major General Slocum in order that he might accept a commission of second lieutenant at Ellis Ford, Virginia, on September 3, 1863. He was again mustered in by Captain M. Veale, Company B.

In the latter part of September, 1863, the One Hundred Eleventh Pennsylvania Infantry was sent to Bridgeport, Alabama. On October 28th and 29th, 1863, the One Hundred Eleventh was on the battle line in the shadow of Lookout Mountain at Wauhatchie, Tennessee.

---

*Direct quote from pension file of Jason L. Pettit, more specifically identified in the reference section of this book.

The final moments of Second Lieutenant Marvin D. Pettit's life must have been spent in ominous excitement.

* * *

N. W. Lowell of Erie, Pennsylvania, received the following letter from an employee of the Cochranton Savings Bank, Crawford County, Pennsylvania, dated October 7, 1890.

"Dear Comrade, Yours of the 4th inst. at hand I note your request in behalf of the mother of Lieut. Marvin D. Pettit of Co. B. I know that he was killed in the night battle at Wauhatchie, Tenn. October 29, 1863. While on the line of battle during the severe struggle in which we were placed in front of our own artillery in order that we prevent its capture and owing to the position being so close we were compelled to lay down and keep in that position in order to allow the use of our artillery which were firing with very short fuse shell. My brother was killed by the premature explosion of one of the shells. But my recollection in the Pettit case is that he was on his feet at this time and the firing being done so low to the ground that his head was torn off by one of our shells in its course into the rebel line. He not being a member of my own company I am not clear in this feature of his being killed but know of his death, saw his body after the battle being laid with the other dead. And to that he with my brother was exhumed by the regt. and brought home with us on our veteran furlough to Pa. Please have them inform you if I am correct in detail and I will at once make the required statement. Also tender to Mrs. Pettit my kind regards to the Mother of the lamented dead soldier of the 111th Pa. Vols.

"I may be in Erie late this fall and most certainly shall visit you in the Home, Yours respectfully, Jesse Moore, Cashier."

At the age of twenty-three Marvin D. Pettit had been

brought home to rest in North East Cemetery, North East, Pennsylvania.

Had Second Lieutenant Marvin Pettit lived but one more month he probably would have participated in the Battle above the Clouds when Joseph Hooker's men took Lookout Mountain on November 24, 1863.

Private William Henry Harrison Salisbury

William Salisbury, who like Private W. H. H. Wright was known to his friends and family as 'Tip,' and whose last name was variously spelled Saulsbury and Salsbury in his military records, was also a young farm boy living on Slash Road, Wilson, New York.

Born August 28, 1840, William Salisbury enlisted on May 22, 1861, at Albany, New York, in the Twenty-eighth Regiment, New York Infantry Volunteers. He stood five feet, ten and one-half inches tall, with blue eyes, brown hair, and a fair complexion.

Leaving New York State in July, 1861, the men of the Twenty-eighth were sent to Martinsburg, Virginia, and were on an expedition to Point of Rocks, Maryland. From August, 1861, until February, 1862, they performed outpost duty on the upper reaches of the Potomac River. In March, 1862, the Twenty-eighth Regiment was sent to Winchester, Virginia, then to Manassas and back again to Winchester.

At the time that Private Salisbury probably received the letter which Ira Pettit had written to him on May 12, 1862, the Twenty-eighth Regiment (along with Battery M) was involved in the operations in the Shenandoah Valley, which would lead them to the Battle of Winchester on May 25.

During July, 1862, Private Salisbury became ill with malaria and diarrhea, necessitating his hospitalization for a time. The quality of army food and the extreme heat to those unused to a Southern climate brought much illness during that summer to the men of the Union Army.

338

The men of the Twenty-eighth Regiment saw action in the Battle of Winchester, the Battle of Cedar Mountain, the Battles of Groveton, Bull Run and Antietam before 1862 ended. Subsequently, they camped at Sandy Hook and Maryland Heights, Maryland, from September 22, until December 10, 1862. From there, they were sent to Fairfax, Virginia. Much of their movement paralleled that of Battery M. During January, 1863, these men were sent to Stafford Court House, Virginia, where they stayed until shortly before the Battle of Chancellorsville in which they participated.

On June 2, 1863, Private W. H. H. Salisbury, along with the rest of the survivors of the Twenty-eighth Regiment, New York Infantry Volunteers, was mustered out of the Union Army upon the expiration of his term of service.

At Clarendon, New York, on February 24, 1864, Mr. William Salisbury took as his bride Miss Permelia A. Harwick. The Salisburys became the parents of five daughters—Ella M. (Mrs. Richard Stockwell), Clara A. (Mrs. Joseph Overholt), Livia A. (Mrs. Lewis Brado), Winifred M. (Mrs. Reeve Harrison), and Myrtle L. (Mrs. Edwin Alvers); and three sons—Willie E., Frank E., and Leon L. Salisbury.

Mr. Salisbury continued to suffer the effects of the malaria and chronic diarrhea which he had contracted in the summer of 1862. At an age when many of those young veterans had begun to find a foothold in civilian life, Private Salisbury was terminally ill at the Soldiers' Home in Bath, New York.

Private W. H. H. Salisbury, who had survived the violence of many battles and skirmishes in the valleys, wildernesses, and across the hills of Virginia and Maryland, became a casualty of the subtle eventualities of war at the age of forty-four. He died at the Soldiers' Home, Bath, New York, on February 26, 1885, and is interred in that city.

The Privates Shearer

Azor was the older of the two brothers and had enlisted at Lockport, New York, on September 4, 1862, in the One Hundred Fifty-first Regiment, New York Volunteers, on its original organization. He was mustered into Company F on the 28th day of that same month.

Private Azor Shearer had been born in Canandaigua, New York, some thirty-one years before. He was five feet, seven inches tall, with blue eyes, a light complexion and light-colored hair. Before enlistment he had been a laborer.

When Private Ira Pettit was enroute to Virginia from Fort Independence in January, 1863, he had come into Baltimore via train and had been held over for a few hours. It was there that he had seen Azor and William H. Shearer, Lurin Wilson, and Enoch Pettit. They were stationed at Lafayette Park Barracks, Baltimore, Maryland, at that time.

Private Azor Shearer then had about eight more months to live. He contracted typhoid fever in later summer and, at the camp's regimental hospital near Bealeton Station, Virginia, he died on September 5, 1863.

By the time that Patience Snedeker Shearer reached the eighteenth year of her life she was a widowed mother of a handicapped son. At Newfane, New York, on September 13, 1860, she had become the bride of Azor Shearer. On July 16, 1862, she had given birth to their only child—a son whom they called George.

* * *

Private William H. Shearer was somewhat more fortunate than his brother Azor.

William Shearer was twenty-five years old when he joined Company F, One Hundred Fifty-first Regiment, New York Volunteers, at Lockport, New York, on the 27th day of August, 1862, a few days ahead of his brother. He, too, was a laborer. William Shearer stood five feet, six and one-half inches tall, and like his brother, he had light-colored hair, a light complexion, and eyes also blue

340

Shortly after his meeting with Private Pettit in Baltimore William Shearer was hospitalized with rheumatism for a time, but was returned to duty. He did not fall victim to typhoid fever. Instead, he ran almost head-on into a Rebel bullet on September 19, 1864, at the Battle of Opequan Creek near Winchester, Virginia.

The ball had entered just in front of his left ear, apparently lodging in the frontal bone over his left eye. It fractured the malar, frontal, and parietal bones. That eye was ever after sightless.

On June 13, 1865, Private William H. Shearer was discharged from the Satterlee U.S.A. General Hospital, West Philadelphia, Pennsylvania, and went home to Lockport, New York.

At Orangeport, New York, on August 6, 1859, Elizabeth F. Hudson had become the bride of William Shearer. Their daughter Maud was born in the autumn of 1866. Almost eleven years later, their son Frank arrived.

The Shearers spent the remainder of their lives in Lockport, New York. When he was able Mr. Shearer worked as a farm laborer.

By 1892 Mr. Shearer had become lame with rheumatism and walked with a very marked limp. The excruciating pain and physical damage from the bullet which he still carried in his head finally delivered him from its grip into a world of insanity. In the last year of his life he was confined to his room, completely helpless.

Mr. Shearer had been pensioned at $4.00 per month at the time of his discharge, but slowly over the years, with coaxings of affidavits, additional pension laws, and declarations, the government had raised his stipend, bit by bit, until he was finally drawing $16.00 per month.

In the early afternoon of February 21, 1905, at the age of sixty-eight years, Private William H. Shearer was mustered out of the prison of pain, which his body had become, to march the path of eternity.

The remains of his earthly existence were placed in Price Cemetery, Lockport, New York.

Private William Henry Harrison Wright

It would not be difficult to guess the political persuasion of the parents of William Henry Harrison (Tip) Wright who was born at Lockport, New York, on October 20, 1840. That was the year of 'Tippecanoe and Tyler, too.'

On October 7, 1861, just before his twenty-first birthday, Harrison Wright enrolled in George W. Cothran's Battery M, First Regiment, New York Light Artillery, as a bugler.

At the time of his enlistment 'Tip' Wright was a farmer, living on Slash Road just outside the Town of Wilson. He was five feet, eight inches tall, with blue eyes, light complexion, and sandy-colored hair.

While William Holmes searched for Battery M in April, 1862, an incident occurred to Private Wright which ultimately ended his military activities. In the Shenandoah Valley of Virginia at Berryville, sometime in early April, Private Wright's horse had become frightened as it was being watered, had run against a picket rope, and had thrown Wright, falling upon him. Private Wright, injured in his left chest area, was insensible for a time and apparently considered to be near death. His father was summoned (Ira's diary, April 12, 1862,) from Wilson to accompany his body home.

On May 2, 1862, First Lieutenant J. A. Peabody, Acting Captain of Battery M, sent to Major General Banks a request for a thirty-day furlough for Private Wright in order that he might return home with his father:

"Sir, I send you the following certificate in regard to Harrison H. Wright, 2nd Bugler. He has been very sick and I think if remaining in camp would be unfit for duty in two months. Could you grant him a furlough of thirty days I think he would recover at home by that time. His

342

Father and brother were telegraphed to take his body home as we hourly expected him to die. They now wish to accompany him back alive, with your permission."

Private Wright and his relatives returned to Wilson, New York, on May 11, 1862.

Private Wright's furlough expired June 1, 1862, but he did not return to camp until he was apprehended on September 10, 1862, at Wilson, by Lieutenant John Downer Woodbury. He was held for trial, charged with desertion.

Before his court martial in November, 1862, a letter was sent to Major General Banks on Wright's behalf from Newfane, Niagara County, New York, and follows:

"October 13, 1862. Dear Sir: The Bearer W. Wright, has a son sick near Harpers Ferry. He has been home on furlough some time. I got it extended for him, but at last he returned to the army, but was unfit to do so. He is down again, and I am satisfied that a permanent release from the service will be the only thing that will save him. I hope you will aid him. He is a very worthy young man and very desirous to serve his country and help finish up the war. He was unfit to return when he did, but was anxious to join his battery. He is an only son and the main dependence of his Father, and ought to be saved if possible. I am satisfied that he never will be fit for service again. What you do for him in this regard will be a great favor to his friends and bring me under obligations. Respectfully, ————————————,* M.C. 31st. Dist., N.Y."

Captain George W. Cothran, by that time Chief, Artillery, First Division, Twelfth Corps, was a witness for the prosecution at the trial of Private Wright. His testimony follows:

---

*Undecipherable signature.

"I know the prisoner he belongs to Battery 'M' 1st New York Artillery. He procured a furlough at Harrisonburg, Va. about the 2d of May for (30) thirty days. He did not return to the battery until about the 21st September he then returned with Lieut. Woodbury. When I was home about the 1st August I saw Wright at the Depot. He had been to Buffalo to see about getting his discharge. He had the proper discharge papers and he wanted me to sign them. I called his attention to the orders of the War Department with reference to absentees. I told him of the approaching muster and advised him to go to the Company or to Annapolis and be mustered and then get his discharge. We parted without his having come to any conclusion as to what he would do.

"This is the last that I saw of him until he returned to the Battery.

"He was mustered into the United States service October 14th in my presence and has received pay and clothing from the Government.

"There is pay now due him from the 1st of January.

"After the expiration of his first furlough he sent the proper papers to Lieut. Peabody for an extension of his furlough which Lieutenant Peabody neglected to get."

For his defence Private Wright introduced the furlough which Major General Banks granted, a letter from the commander of his company, a physician's certificate, and the letter from Newfane, New York, dated October 13, 1862. Private Wright stated to the court that he did not feel able to travel and therefore, had not returned to the battery or to Annapolis for muster.

Harrison Wright was acquitted of the charge of desertion. At the headquarters of the First Division, Twelfth Corps, near Sandy Hook, Maryland, on November 24, 1862, that acquittal was approved. Prisoner Private William Henry Harrison Wright was released and restored to duty.

On January 28, 1863, at Convalescent Camp, Alexandria, Virginia, Private W. H. H. Wright was given a certificate of disability for discharge, without having participated in *any* of the great battles in which Battery M so valiantly fought during the Civil War.

Less than two months after the convalescing Private Wright returned to his home in Wilson he was married to Catharine H. Starkey on March 24, 1863.

Harrison Wright farmed on Slash Road just outside Wilson until he was sixty years old. Retiring then, Mr. and Mrs. Wright moved into the Town of Wilson.

On February 24, 1915, at the age of seventy-four, William Henry Harrision Wright fell victim to uremic poisoning.

Private Wright had been pensioned from the time of his discharge in January, 1863, and Mrs. Catharine H. Wright, as his widow, was receiving a pension of $75.00 per month at the time of her death on October 3, 1918. Catharine H. Starkey Wright had been born in Greece, New York, on May 1, 1838.

The large tombstone which marks the graves of William Henry Harrison Wright, Catharine H. Wright, and J. Grant Wright (one of their five children) is but a few steps from that of William Holmes in the Greenwood Cemetery.

Captain John Downer Woodbury

Woodbury family legend holds that a few days after he apprehended Private W. H. H. Wright in their hometown of Wilson, New York, John Downer Woodbury's saddle was shot by a Rebel bullet, as Battery M, First Regiment, New York Light Artillery, confronted the Army of Northern Virginia on the rolling hills surrounding Sharpsburg, Maryland. That saddle was presented to the National Park Service in 1954 by Mr. Charles Woodbury, grandson of Captain John Downer Woodbury, and it is on display in the museum at the Antietam National Battlefield Site, Sharpsburg, Maryland.

345

John Downer Woodbury son of Jesse and Ester Downer Woodbury was born in Wilson, New York, in 1834. On August 21, 1856, he had married Susan A. Outwater, also of Wilson, and in 1857 they became the parents of a son named Chester.

A merchant before the war, Mr. Woodbury had enlisted in George Cothran's Battery M, October 1, 1861. After gaining promotions from private to captain, after becoming commander of the battery, and after serving in all the major campaigns of that battery until September, 1864, Captain Woodbury resigned the military service in Atlanta, Georgia, on September 26, 1864, because of poor and worsening health.

Captain Woodbury had suffered chronic diarrhea, catarrh of the lungs, and all the symptoms of ulcers since the Gettysburg campaign, receiving treatment intermittently in his quarters. At the time that many of the veterans of Battery M were re-enlisting the surgeon-in-charge considered Captain Woodbury unable to survive one more campaign. John Downer Woodbury had served his country for three years.

The Woodburys moved to Michigan after the war ended. They made their home in Portland, Ionia County, where Mr. Woodbury again became a merchant.

Mr. Woodbury passed away in Lansing, Michigan, on October 18, 1906, at the age of seventy-two years, one month and five days. He was returned to his home in Portland for burial there. At the time of his death Captain Woodbury had been receiving a veteran's pension of $17.00 per month. At the time of her death on June 11, 1913, Mrs. Susan A. Woodbury was receiving $12.00 per month, as the widow of this heroic Union officer.

* * *

No attempt is made here to explain the disparity of pensions among the various Union veterans and/or among the various Union veterans' widows. That must be left to those with expertise conversant with and equal to such rhetoric.

Despite his lofty claims and high ambitions, one is hard pressed to find any change in man and politics, in peace or war, in the last hundred years.

* * *

These are but a few of the men Private Ira S. Pettit knew and remarked upon during his military experience. Historians note them only statistically. But their lives, just as his and countless others, became the stones and mortar of the paths on which generals have marched to illustrious and lasting fame, and on which presidents and other assorted politicians have traveled ever since, some humbly, others outrageously, in an attempt to attain whatever it is that their egos seek.

* * *

Note:

The civil and military information and the quoted documents depicting the lives of *all* the soldiers discussed thus far, as well as those in the pages yet to be read, have been taken directly from the pension files, compiled service records, register of enlistments, and other military records found at the National Archives, Washington, D.C., and/or the respective states' civil, social, or military records, as specifically set out in the reference section of this book, unless otherwise footnoted. The activities of each individual's military regiment have been traced through Dyer's Compendium which is specifically identified in the bibliographical section. In some instances information has been obtained from direct descendants of an individual, and the people contributing such information are also listed in the reference section.

He Was One of Sherman's Men

Heinrich (Henry) Bockholt did a lot of traveling for a nineteenth century Midwestern farmer. He had been born in Prussia on June 13, 1823, and it is thought that it was as young adults that Mr. Bockholt and two of his sisters came to America. Mr. Bockholt settled upon the sparsely populated prairies of Bremer County, Iowa.

On March 23, 1857, four days before she celebrated her twentieth birthday, Johanna Friederike Bessmer became the bride of Heinrich Bockholt at Waverly, Iowa. Miss Bessmer, a native of Nabern, Germany, had come with her parents to America while still a youngster. Her family had settled in Waverly, Bremer County, Iowa.

On March 27, 1860, Henry Bockholt purchased (from Francis Jones) the first forty acres of what would become a one hundred and sixty acre farm. Before the Civil War would touch their lives, the Bockholts would become the parents of a daughter Antoinette (Mrs. William Kraft) and a son Henry John. Their third and last child Katharina Magdalena (Mrs. Frank Lucas) would not be born until after the Civil War.

Private Henry Bockholt would never hear of Private Ira S. Pettit, but he would join the man whom Ira had so hopefully awaited at the Andersonville Stockade in Sumter County, Georgia. And he would live the rest of his life as a not-too-distant county neighbor of Ira's sister Lucina on those prairies of the Midwest.

In October, 1864, as many of the farmers prepared to harvest their bountiful crops upon the Iowa plains, and as the native flowers of those plains withered under the warm October sun of Indian summer, Mr. Bockholt readied himself to become a part of General Sherman's

Western Army which would once again take him to the Atlantic seashore.

Leaving Mrs. Bockholt and their small daughter and son alone on their farm, Henry Bockholt journeyed to Dubuque, Iowa, where he was mustered into Company G, Fourth Regiment, Iowa Infantry, as a drafted recruit. At forty-one years of age, Private Bockholt stood five feet, eight and one-half inches tall, with brown hair and blue eyes. (Mr. Bockholt did not seek a substitute, nor did he buy himself free of the military obligations which his adopted homeland asked of him.)

From his draft rendezvous at Dubuque, Private Bockholt traveled southward where he joined his regiment at Vining, Georgia, on October 11, 1864. (Ira Pettit would live one more week.) Sherman had by now occupied Atlanta, and Hood had headed back toward Tennessee.

Private Bockholt was an educated man of quiet manner, whose letters, written in German, reflected a high degree of academic discipline in his native language, but he was not yet acquainted with the idiomatic construction of the English language.

On November 12, 1864, Private Bockholt wrote his family:

"Dear wife and children and brother-in-law, Will Haverkamp and wife and all my relatives,

"I am glad to be fresh and healthy and I wish I could hear from you.

"I will write a little from my trip. We went from Dubuque to Atlanta. It is still twelve miles from here in training. Our trip was dangerous. We had a lot of bad luck. I was lucky. I escaped. We did not think we would escape.

"Rizman carried the flag and was in our wagon and we all jumped out. I have not seen him since. Have heard he was hurt and he is in a hospital.

"Dear wife I have written you one letter and have received no answer. I will tell you what we think of war.

349

They tell us it is not dangerous, that the war should be over in three to six months.

"I have good hopes. I am satisfied here, that you are too. The time will pass. I can not write anything else. Writing is bad here.

"Best wishes, Heart loving wife and children. Do as good as you can, do what you think is best. Whatever you do is right."

Three days after Private Bockholt had written this letter General Sherman, in the company of the Fourteenth, Fifteenth, Seventeenth and Twentieth Corps, set out on a journey eastward. (Private Bockholt was a member of the Fifteenth Corps.) As the flames of Atlanta cast shadows beneath their footsteps, more than sixty thousand men started marching toward the beaches of the Atlantic Ocean two hundred and fifty miles away.

Near Milledgeville, Georgia, the Ninth Illinois Infantry, the Eighth Indiana Cavalry and the Thirty-first Ohio Infantry (of the Fourteenth Corps)* skirmished with Confederate Militia on the road to Savannah. Much to the despair of some of those Union soldiers, it was later learned as they viewed the scene of the battle, that their adversaries had been old men and young boys, unused to and unfit for the heavy responsibility of war.

"The army came up to Savannah on December 10. Sherman led it around to the right, striking for the Ogeechee River and Ossabaw Sound, where he could get in touch with the navy, receive supplies, and regain contact with Grant and with Washington. The XV Corps found itself making a night march along the bank of a canal; there was a moon, the evening was warm, and the swamp beside the canal looked strange, haunting, and mysterious, all silver and green and black, with dim vistas trailing off into shadowland. The men had been ordered to

---

*Dyer, Frederick H. *A Compendium of the War of the Rebellion*. Des Moines, Iowa: The Dyer Publishing Company, 1908. pp. 721, 1511.

march quietly, but suddenly they began to sing—'Swanee River,' 'Old Kentucky Home,' 'John Brown's Body,' and the like, moving on toward journey's end in an unreal light.'"* Private Bockholt had known this night.

Very soon after the year 1865 began, Sherman's men set out across South Carolina, and from somewhere in that state on January 31, 1865, Private Bockholt, deeply concerned about his wife and little ones, sent an answer to a letter from them:

"I have your letter. I am well and still going, and glad to hear from you but it makes my heart heavy . . .

"You write about grandma, maybe she could come and live with you. That would be alright with me . . .

"Dear wife, you write every thing is costing so much. That doesn't make any difference, I don't expect you to earn a living. Now I don't expect you to live as a hired girl, you are my wife, my loving wife and you will be that until God parts us.

"So believe me, dear wife, and do with everything you think is right. From me you will never hear a word in your life of disapproval. You are boss of everything we have. But don't work so hard. Then we won't be poor in one year, if you don't get the farm work done. Just make your garden and leave the land lay.

"You don't need it, to live on, as you have enough to live on for a year or more. You don't have to work yourself to the bone, dear wife. Don't think you have to watch over everything, the same as if I was there because it is impossible. Be satisfied, and after all this trouble there will be peace and happiness.

"Heart loving wife, I cannot send what you want, a picture. I don't know when I will have the chance and I would like a picture of you and the children. But am afraid if I saw it I would break down. Everyone thinks the war

---

*Catton, Bruce. *This Hollowed Ground*. Garden City, New York: Doubleday and Company, 1956. p. 361.

will soon be over. Our company has been ordered to watch, so long we are out of danger.* May be three or four months and my time is getting shorter.

"We are pushing all the people, also the red people. We burnt buildings and fields but took cattle and hogs with us. It is so hard to destroy crops and run over. I won't write any more as it will only make you sick.

"Received your letters January 27 and 30 and I am writing this the 31st. Heinrich Bockholt, Company G, 4th Iowa Infantry, 15th Army Corps."

Four days after Private Bockholt had written the above letter the entire First Division of the Fifteenth Army Corps skirmished at Buford's Bridge, South Carolina. Private Bockholt's regiment was in the Third Brigade of that division. On February 15, 1865, the Fourth Regiment skirmished at Congaree Creek, and on the 16th and 17th of February, that regiment skirmished around Columbia, South Carolina.

As this army moved into North Carolina, Private Bockholt found himself in the heat of battle at Bentonville on March 19, 20, and 21, 1865. Shortly after that battle ended Sherman's men headed for Goldsboro on their way to Raleigh. Despite the peace that had been declared on Palm Sunday, 1865, everything was not yet tranquil. Private Bockholt sent the following from Raleigh, North Carolina, on April 19, 1865:

"Beloved wife and children, I believe I am still fresh and healthy.

"I am thankful Grandma is with you, Sweetheart. I am glad she is happy there . . .

"I will write you about our march. We are since the 10th of April on the go. We marched from Goldsboro to Raleigh, where we the 12th of April came upon the rebels.

---

*Private Bockholt probably meant that his company had been assigned guard or picket duty during bivouac.

352

Chased them and they fled. We took their headquarters over. We went to Raleigh, and past, but then we had to pull back. We are now camping in Raleigh where we have good food and quarters.

".. . on the 16th of April we had to pull back and we are still laying on the same place and resting . . .

"Now I can't give you my full opinion about the farming. In reality it does not bring in over much money . . . Just be quiet, Dear Heart loving wife and children. I have good hopes we will see each other again in this life.

"Now if you can see the youngest Siggelkov, maybe he would cut some grass for hay.

"I received your postage stamps and five letters at Goldsboro and two letters I got in Raleigh. Lots of thanks for writing and hope that my letter will find you in good health.

"Best Wishes to you Heart Loving Wife and Children. Heinrich Bockholt.''*

The men of Sherman's army moved northward across the battlefields of Virginia, through Richmond and past the desolation of the Wilderness. Perhaps the spirits that had departed the yet unburied bodies of soldiers of the Army of the Potomac marched silently beside them as Sherman's men made their way across the hills and through the cedar thickets of northern Virginia to the banks of the Potomac.

On May 24, 1865, with its banners proclaiming the battles that it had survived, the Army of the Potomac, in dress parade, passed down Pennsylvania Avenue, Washington, D.C., and the next day the less formal army of William Tecumseh Sherman paraded in a similar manner, surprising even Sherman with its appearance and marching order.

*The letters and excerpts from the correspondence of Private Heinrich Bockholt, which have been quoted within, comprise a part of the estate of his granddaughter Mrs. Henry (Lena Bockholt) Albrecht, and have been translated from the German by Sophia Etgeton.

On May 31, 1865, at Crystal Spring, in Washington, D.C., Private Heinrich Bockholt was honorably mustered out of the United States Army. Mr. Bockholt returned to his farm and family near Fairbank, in Bremer County, Iowa.

Spring spread across the land that had recently been hidden for months beneath the frigid snows. As the oceans of snowdrifts trickled with ever-increasing speed toward the Gulf of Mexico, the fall-plowed sod turned black and then green with new-born plants. Henry Bockholt set about tilling his fields and tending his family's needs that had awaited his return. And as he cultivated those fields the red-winged blackbirds served notice of their territorial rights along the fence rows. Mr. Bockholt would tend his land for nineteen more summers.

On March 23, 1885, Mr. Heinrich Bockholt passed away at his farm home and was interred in the Fairbank Cemetery. Mrs. Johanna Bockholt remained a widow until her death at Oelwein, Iowa, on November 25, 1907. She rests beside Private Bockholt in Fairbank, Iowa.

Private Heinrich Bockholt did not make application to the United States government for a pension as a veteran of the Civil War, nor did his wife as the widow of a veteran, even though she would have been entitled to do so.

The farm where Mr. and Mrs. Heinrich Bockholt lived became the home of their son Henry John, who had married Miss Mary Spies of Black Hawk County, Iowa. Henry John and Mary Spies Bockholt were the parents of three children. Their daughter Martha became the bride of Fred Rewoldt. Mrs. Rewoldt passed away on January 6, 1970, leaving her husband and two sons. The Bockholts' daughter Lena became the bride of Henry Albrecht. Mrs. Albrecht is the mother of three daughters and one son, and at the age of eighty-three, Mrs. Albrecht actively participates in her community's affairs, and contributes her time and talents to the welfare of the ill and elderly in the surrounding area. The Bockholts' son Henry George passed away on November 25, 1961, leaving one daughter and two sons. Although Private Bockholt's descendants have settled throughout the United States many still make their homes in Bremer County, Iowa.

Private Heinrich Bockholt had participated in a segment of the Civil War that would be set to literature and history in countless volumes, and would be examined and re-examined by descendants of the opposing armies of that war for generations yet unborn.

. . . and although Henry Bockholt would never know Ira Pettit, one of his descendants would play a vital roll in the publication of Private Pettit's diary, and make time and distance seem irrelevant in the community of man.

In the quiet, sequestered places of the Midwest the compass plants, shooting stars, gayfeathers, orchids, lead plants, Turk's cap lilies, false indigo, and innumerable other wild flowers cannot help but explode into color as the mild Southern winds of springtime migrate across the prairies, unhampered by natural barriers. On the farm where Private Heinrich Bockholt had made his home in America one of his great-great grandsons goes about the business of tending that same land; not many miles distant the great-great nephew of Private Ira. S. Pettit also takes up the business of farming on the land of Lucina Pettit Shaw. Two peers with a common dream . . .

The Public Death of Private John McMann

On May 27, in the spring of 1862, at Pittsburgh, Pennsylvania, John McMann, a twenty-three-year-old laborer, was recruited by Lieutenant Irvin B. Wright for a period of three years in the U.S. Regular Army's Eleventh Regiment of Infantry. He was assigned to Company B of that regiment.

John McMann stood five feet and nine inches tall. He was a light-haired, hazel-eyed young man of dark complexion, who had been born in Scioto County, Ohio.

Whatever the circumstances of the life and times of Private John McMann before and while he soldiered for the United States Army, they, for the most part, elude determination. But it appears rather certain that on May 14, 1863, only nine days after the Eleventh Regiment had fled from the fields surrounding Chancellorsville, John McMann separated himself from that army.

On November 5, 1863, a General Court Martial was convened by virtue of Special Orders, No. 135, which had been issued on October 2, 1863:

"Camp 1st Brigade, 2d Division, 5th Corps. Camp Near 3 Mile Station Va. November 5th 1863.

"The Court met pursuant to the foregoing orders and to adjournment,

"Present

"1. Major L. B. Bruen	12th U.S.	Infty.
"2. Capt. A. J. Dallas	12th	do
"3. Capt. D. Krause	14th	do
"4. 1st Lieut. D. M. Brodhead	14th	do
"5. 1st Lieut. J. P. Pratt	11th	do

and Capt. Henry C. Morgan 12th Infantry Judge Advocate.

356

"Absent

"Capt. W. B. Pease   17th U.S. Infantry
excused on account of sickness,
"2d. Lieut. James Butler   2d U.S. Infantry.

"The Court proceeded with the trial of Private John McMann Co 'B' 11th U.S. Infantry who was called before the court and having heard the orders read appointing the court was asked if he had any objections to any members named in the orders, and replied that he had not.

"The court was then in the presence of the prisoner duly sworn by the Judge Advocate and the Judge Advocate was duly sworn by the President.

"The prisoner Private John McMann Co. 'B' 11th U.S. Infantry was arraigned on the following charge & specification.

"1. Charge   Desertion.

"1. Specification. In this that Private John McMann Co 'B' 11th U.S. Infantry did leave his company on a pass for a few hours, on or about the 14th day of May 1863 near Potomac Creek Va and did remain absent without permission until September 24th 1863 when he was brought to Co 'B' 1st Battalion 11th U.S. Infantry as a substitute for a conscript of the District of Columbia.

"To which charge and specification the prisoner pleaded as follows.

"To the Specification—Guilty.

"To the Charge—Guilty.

"The prosecution here closed, and the prisoner having no testimony to offer, made the following statement.

"I got a pass to go to Aquia Creek. I was under the influence of liquor or I would never have gone away. If I had not have been drugged, I never should have gone as a substitute if I had known what I was about. I was afraid to come back to my Regiment. I was in New York and Philadelphia from the time that I left Aquia Creek to the time that I found myself as a substitute in the City of

Washington. I have nothing more to say & leave myself at the mercy of the Court.

"The statement of the prisoner being thus in the possession of the court, the court was cleared for deliberation, and having maturely considered the evidence adduced find the prisoner Private John McMann Co 'B' 11th U.S. Infantry as follows:

"Of the Specification, Guilty.

"Of the Charge, Guilty.

and do therefore sentence him Private John McMann Co 'B' 11th U.S. Infantry to be shot to death by musketry at such time and place as the Commanding General may direct, two thirds of the court concurring therein."[1]

The signatures of Henry C. Morgan, Captain, Twelfth Infantry, Judge Advocate, and L. B. Bruen, Major, Twelfth Infantry, President, General Court Martial, appear at the bottom of this hand-written record of the trial of Private John McMann.

On November 19, 1863, at the Headquarters of the Second Division, Fifth Corps, Army of the Potomac, Brigadier General R. B. Ayres approved the finding of the court with the following statement: "Approved, And in accordance with the provisions of the Act of Congress, approved, December 24, 1861, respectfully transmitted for action of the Cmd'g. General of this Army." Signed, "R. B. Ayres BrigGenlComdg."[2]

And this document, subsequently submitted to General George Gordon Meade, is signed: "Approved. Geo. G. Meade, Maj. Genl. Cmd."[3]

On December 5, 1863, at the Headquarters of the Army of the Potomac, General Orders, No. 104, were issued, and read, in part:

"XIV. The proceedings of the General Courts Martial in

---

[1] From National Archives' Record Group No. 153, as specifically identified on page 414.
[2] Ibid.
[3] Ibid.

the foregoing cases having been transmitted to the Major General Commanding, the following are the orders therein:

". . . In the cases of . . . ; Private John McMann, 11th United States Infantry; . . . the proceedings, findings and sentences are approved. The sentences will be carried into effect in presence of so much of the Divisions to which the prisoners severally belong as the Division Commander can properly assemble, on Friday, the 18th instant, at such hour after 12, m., as the Division Commander may designate. By Command of Major General Meade. S. Williams Assistant Adjutant General."[4]

Thus, official dispositon of Private John McMann had been done.

The following letter, addressed to the Judge Advocate General and dated February 29, 1884, from the City of Washington, D.C., appears in the official files of Private John McMann:

"Sir. In the spring of 1862 I enlisted a man in Petersburg Penn named John McGraw or perhaps John McGrath. I sent him to Fort Independence, Boston Harbor, Mass—he was afterwards assigned to my Company, (Co. B ?d Batt 11 U S Inf) Just after the battle of Chancelloroville he deocrted and after nearly one year was returned. I preferred the charges against him myself he plead guilty and was sentenced to be shot and was shot near Bealton Station. I want to get his body and have him decently interred. For this purpose will you please give me the date when he was shot. As I always called him John only I don't know last name but it is either McGraw or McGrath.

"If you will please have a record made of his case you will very much oblige. Very Respectfully Irvin B. Wright."

By 1884 the distraught Lieutenant Wright had forgotten the technical minutia, i.e., John McMann's name or where he had recruited him, but he well remembered that it was

---

[4]See reference designation in reference section, page 414. Records of the Judge Advocate General (Army), Court Martial of Private John McMann.

he who had identified and brought the charge against McMann to the attention of the court.

The careful accuracy of Private Ira S. Pettit makes one wonder what it was that prompted him to describe Private John McMann as a 'tough case,' but it could have been nothing more than Pettit's own unswerving military indoctrination. The strict and quiet adherence to military discipline that embodied General George Gordon Meade would make one hesitate to hope that the general might disapprove or otherwise defer Private John McMann's sentence. And fate was unmindful of whether the bullet that was to end John McMann's life was that of a Rebel or a Yank.

If the Federal government found requited satisfaction in his execution, it could likewise be possible that John McMann found successful escape from war in the piece of earth that received him, wherever it may be.

There's almost enough Justice for nearly everybody

Private John Carrigan may have thought himself in rather precarious circumstances.

Before a General Court Martial, which had convened on December 5, 1861, at Alcatraces Island, Harbor of San Francisco, California, Private Carrigan had been charged with violation of the Ninth Article of War.

Specifically, this charge had read: "In this; that he, the said Private John Carrigan, of Company 'D,' 6th Regiment United States Infantry, being a prisoner in charge of the Guard, did offer violence to Sergeant Thomas R. Hall, of Company 'D,' 6th Regiment United States Infantry, by cutting and killing him with a knife—he, the said Sergeant Hall, being Sergeant of the Guard, and on the execution of his office. This in camp, at or near Mendocino City, in Mendocino County, State of California, on or about the 28th day of November, 1861."*

Although Private Carrigan's plea had been, "Not guilty," the court had found him so.

The sentence of the court had been that Private John Carrigan be hanged by the neck until he was dead, at a time and place to be chosen by the President of the United States. The needed approvals were obtained, and it was designated that the sentence be executed under the jurisdiction of the Commanding General of the Army of the Potomac.

On June 23, 1863, Private John Carrigan came into the custody of the guards of the Army of the Potomac, at least one of whom was a member of the Second Brigade, Eleventh Regiment, Company F, Fifth Corps. This seg-

---

*War Department, Adjutant General's Office. Washington, D.C. *General Orders, No. 126*, dated May 15, 1863.

ment of the Army of the Potomac was then encamped near Aldie, Virginia.

Special Orders, No. 168, by command of Major General Joseph Hooker, had directed that Private Carrigan's sentence be carried into effect on Friday, June 26, 1863, between the hours of 12 m and 4 p.m., in the presence of the Second Division and under the orders of its commander.

Two days short of that long rope for Private Carrigan, General Hooker issued Special Orders, No. 171, dated June 24, 1863, which postponed the execution of Carrigan's sentence until otherwise ordered.

A few days and many miles later Private Carrigan was sent to duty, while the soldiers who had recently been his guards made camp near Antietam Creek on their return from Gettysburg, Pennsylvania.

* * *

Alexander Chisholm, a native of Scotland, was a sandy-complexioned, grey-eyed, brown-haired young laborer who stood five feet, six and one-half inches tall. At the age of twenty-two he had pledged allegiance to the United States Army by enlisting at Watertown, New York, on the 27th day of June, 1862, for a period of three years.

At Fort Independence, Boston Harbor, Massachusetts, according to Ira's records, Private Chisholm was placed under arrest for striking a sergeant with the butt of a gun. But time must have healed the sergeant's wounds and satisfied Private Chisholm's superiors' sense of justice.

Having apparently regained the status of a trusted soldier, Private Chisholm was serving as a guard on post the night of Saturday, November 8, 1862, when he and three prisoners took a boat ride. The boat was found and returned the following week, says Ira. But, alas, not Private Chisholm!

On October 3, 1863, at Fort Independence, Boston Harbor, Massachusetts, Private Chisholm joined the United States Army once again, this time from desertion.

On May 19, 1866, (by virtue of the expiration of his term of service) Private Alexander Chisholm was discharged from the United States Army to pursue life in his own way as a living civilian.

The loom of fate had woven a different pattern for Private Chisholm than it had for Private John (ah, what's his name????, oh, yes!) McMann.

* * *

Motivated, as always in a Democracy, by a desire to assure equal justice under equitable law, the Thirty-seventh duly elected Congress of the United States of America, on July 17, 1862, during its second session, did enact some such laws, and here is excerpted from Chapter CCI, Second Session of the Thirty-seventh Congress, a section:

"*Sec. 5.* And be it further enacted, That the President shall appoint, by and with the advice and consent of the Senate, a judge advocate general, with the rank, pay, and emoluments of a colonel of cavalry, to whose office shall be returned, for revision, the records and proceedings of all courts-martial and military commissions, and where a record shall be kept of all proceedings had thereupon. And no sentence of death, or imprisonment in the penitentiary, shall be carried into execution until the same shall have been approved by the President."

On March 3, 1863, that same Thirty-seventh Congress (in its third session), further pursuing its interest in the matter of the military and its personnel, enacted some addenda to Chapter CCI of the second session.

From Chapter LXXV, Session III of the Thirty-seventh Congress, comes the following:

"*Sec. 21.* And be it further enacted, That so much of the fifth section of the act approved seventeenth July, eighteen hundred and sixty-two, entitled, 'An act to amend an act calling forth the militia to execute the laws of the Union,' and so forth, as requires the approval of the President to carry into execution the sentence of a court-martial, be, and the same is hereby, repealed, as far as relates to carrying into execution the sentence of any court-martial against any person convicted as a spy or deserter, or of mutiny or murder; and hereafter sentences in punishment of these offences may be carried into execution upon the approval of the commanding-general in the field."

"*Sec. 26.* And be it further enacted, That, immediately after the passage of this act, the President shall issue his proclamation declaring that all soldiers now absent from their regiments without leave may return within a time specified to such place or places as he may indicate in his proclamation, and be restored to their respective regiments without punishment, except the forfeiture of their pay and allowances during their absence; and all deserters who shall not return within the time so specified by the President shall, upon being arrested, be punished as the law provides."

And forthwith, the President did issue the following proclamation:

"Respecting Soldiers absent without leave. Executive Mansion, March 10, 1863.

"In pursuance of the twenty-sixth section of the act of Congress, entitled 'An act for enrolling and calling out the National Forces, and for other purposes,' approved on the third day of March, in the year one thousand eight hundred and sixty-three, I, ABRAHAM LINCOLN, President and Commander-in-Chief of the Army and Navy of the United States, do hereby order and command, that all soldiers enlisted or drafted in the service of the United States, now absent from their regiments without leave, shall forthwith return to their respective regiments.

"And I do hereby declare and proclaim, that all soldiers

364

now absent from their respective regiments without leave, who shall, on or before the first day of April 1863, report themselves at any rendezvous designated by the General Orders of the War Department number fifty-eight, hereto annexed, may be restored to their respective regiments without punishment, except the forfeiture of pay and allowances during their absence; and all who do not return within the time above specified shall be arrested as deserters, and punished as the law provides.

"And whereas evil-disposed and disloyal persons at sundry places have enticed and procured soldiers to desert and absent themselves from their regiments, thereby weakening the strength of the armies and prolonging the war, giving aid and comfort to the enemy, and cruelly exposing the gallant and faithful soldiers remaining in the ranks to increased hardships and danger, I do therefore call upon all patriotic and faithful citizens to oppose and resist the aforementioned dangerous and treasonable crimes, and to aid in restoring to their regiments all soldiers absent without leave, and to assist in the execution of the act of Congress 'for enrolling and calling out the National Forces, and for other purposes,' and to support the proper authorities in the prosecution and punishment of offenders against said act, and in suppressing the insurrection and rebellion.

"In testimony whereof, I have hereunto set my hand.

"Done at the city of Washington, this tenth day of March, in the year of our Lord one thousand eight hundred and sixty-three, and of the independence of the United States the eighty-seventh."

General Orders, No. 58, from the War Department, Adjutant General's office, also dated March 10, 1863, provided some thirty-six places at which soldiers might surrender themselves to join from desertion, and instructed commanding officers in the taking charge of said soldiers.

Very soon after the same court (comprised of the same six good men and true) had tried and passed its august judgment upon the errant John McMann, Private Osker M. Burns was brought before it to also answer to a charge of desertion.

More than a year before Osker M. Burns had been recruited by Lieutenant J. M. Ritner on August 22, 1862, at Madison, Indiana, for a period of three years in the Eleventh Regiment of the United States Regular Army.

"Camp 1st Brigade, 2d Division, 5th Corps, Camp Near 3 Mile Station Va November 5th 1863.

"The Court met pursuant to the foregoing orders and to adjournment.

"Present

"1. Major L. B. Bruen	12th U.S. Infty.	
"2. Capt. A. J. Dallas	12th	do
"3. Capt. D. Krause	14th	do
"4. 1st Lieut. D. M. Brodhead	14th	do
"5. 1st Lieut. J. P. Pratt	11th	do

and Capt. Henry C. Morgan 12th Infantry Judge Advocate.

"Absent

"Capt. W. B. Pease   17th U.S. Infantry
excused on account of sickness.

"2d Lieut. James Butler   2d U.S. Infantry.

"The Court then proceeded to the trial of Osker M. Burns, Co 'B' 1st Battl 11th U.S. Infantry, who was called before the Court, and having heard the orders read, appointing the Court, was asked if he had any objection to any member named in the orders, replied that he had not.

"The Court was then duly in the presence of the prisoner sworn by the Judge Advocate, and the Judge Advocate was duly sworn by the President.

"The prisoner Private Osker M. Burns, Co 'B' 1st Battalion 11th U.S. Infantry was then arraigned on the following Charge and Specification.

"1. Charge   Desertion

"1. Specification. In this the he (sic) Private Osker M. Burns, Co 'B' 1st Battl. 11th Infty did leave his company without permission on or about the thirtieth day of June 1863 near Frederick City, in the State of Maryland, the regiment at that time expecting daily to be engaged with the enemy, and did remain absent until the Twenty Seventh day of September 1863, at which time he was returned under guard.

"To which Charge and Specification the prisoner pleaded as follows.

"To the Specification
    "Guilty

"To the Charge
    "Guilty.

"The prosecution here closed.

"The Court then took a recess until 4 P.M.

"The Court reassembled and adjourned to 9. o'clock tomorrow Nov 6th 1863.

"Camp 1st Brigade 2d Division 5 Corps Near Three Mile Station Va November 6th 1863.

"The Court met pursuant to adjournment, and proceeded with the case of Private Osker M. Burns, Co 'B' 1st Battalion 11th U.S. Infantry.

"The prisoner having no witnesses to call for his defence, made the following statement to the Court. I left the Regiment at Frederick City Maryland. I afterwards hunted around to find the Corps. I could find nothing of the Regulars, and started off on my own hook. I was picked up on the Rail Road and taken to a Provost Marshal's and from there taken to General Meade's Head Quarters. I was kept there under guard, and asked what regiment I belonged to. I was then put in irons and kept that way for about three weeks, and from there I was sent to General Sykes Head Quarters, and from there to the Provost Guard of the Division. This is all I have to say.

"The Statement being thus in the possession of the Court, the Court was cleared, and after mature deliberation on the evidence adduced find the prisoner Private Osker M. Burns, Co 'B' 1st Battalion 11th U.S. Infantry as follows,

"Of the Specification   Guilty.

"Of the Charge   Guilty.

and do therfor (sic) sentence him Private Osker M. Burns, Co 'B' 1st Battalion 11th U.S. Infantry to be shot to death by musketry at such time and place as the Commanding General may direct, two thirds of the Court concurring therein." Signed by "Henry C. Morgan, Capt. 12th Infantry Judge Advocate," and by "L. B. Bruen Maj 12th U.S. Inf. Prest. Gen C. M."

"Headqtrs. 2d Division 5th Corps. A. P. Nov. 20, 1863. Disapproved. The neglect to state the names of the members present in the proceedings of the 6th inst! also whether or no the Judge Advocate and prisoner were present, is fatal. Private Burns is released from confinement and restored to duty." Signed "R. B. Ayres Brig Gen Comdg"*

At Richmond, Virginia, on November 22, 1865, Private Osker M. Burns was discharged from the Eleventh Regiment of the United States Regular Army by expiration of his three year term of service.

* * *

There are significant and immediately obvious differences in the cases of Private Osker M. Burns and Private John McMann. John McMann had deserted a few days *after* the Eleventh Regiment had successfully fled the Rebels at Chancellorsville. Private Burns had deserted

---

Record Group 153: Records of the Office of the Judge Advocate General (Army), No. LL-1042. Court Martial of Private Osker M. Burns, November 5, 1863. National Archives, Washington, D.C.

three days *before* the Eleventh Regiment met those Rebels again at Gettysburg. John McMann was absent from the regiment for about five months. Osker Burns was absent from the regiment for about three months. John McMann had returned to the Eleventh Regiment as a substitute for a conscript. Osker Burns had returned to the Eleventh Regiment as an apprehended deserter. The Court *did not* recess and adjourn until the following day during the trial of John McMann. The Court *did* recess and adjourn until the following day during the trial of Osker Burns.

For reasons unknown the Court reporter did not make note of who comprised the Court, or which members attended its session, on November 6 at 9 a.m.; nor did the reporter record whether Private Osker M. Burns was in attendance to hear the verdict of that present (or absent) Court that next day when that alleged Court re-convened.

The chances appear fair that a Court reporter and at least two of the Court's members were present on November 6 at 9 a.m. Henry C. Morgan, Captain, Twelfth Infantry, and Judge Advocate of that Court, and L. B. Bruen, Major, Twelfth Infantry, and President of that Court, signed the recorded proceedings of the trial, *which included the transpirations of November 6, 1863.*

Whether the failure of the Court reporter to identify each individual member of the Court, as well as the prisoner, by name, and to state either the presence or absence of each at the hearing on November 6, 1863, was a deliberate omission, or an error born of ignorance, cannot be determined on the basis of records known to be available.

General Romeyn Beck Ayres evidently felt it incumbent upon himself to pass a judgment upon a verdict which he apparently could not be completely certain had been reached by a duly appointed and present Court upon a prisoner whom Ayres could not be certain had received the verdict. It was his duty.

In truth, it would appear that the Court's reporter had

369

decided the verdict for the present or absent members of that Court, in the presence or absence of the present or absent prisoner, by virtue of not specifically identifying individually each member of said Court, or indicating the presence or absence of the Judge Advocate, which the presumed Court reporter alleged had met pursuant to adjournment on that morning of November 6, 1863, and by virtue of not specifically stating the presence or absence of the prisoner (whose alleged testimony was allegedly elicited by the alleged Court, or at least was recorded as having been given on that morning of November 6, 1863,), as that alleged present or absent Court, with a present or absent Judge Advocate, determined the fate of present or absent Prisoner Private Osker M. Burns.

Commanding General George Gordon Meade had been spared the confirmation, ceremony, red tape, and paperwork of another execution.

The awesome possibilities of courts martial and courts civil are infinite.

An Officer-of-the-Day

Irvin B. Wright was born in Logansport, Indiana, February 2, 1842. At the age of nineteen Mr. Wright stood five feet and ten inches tall. He had black hair and brown eyes.

Mr. Wright was a student at the time of his enrollment in the Twentieth Regiment, Ohio Infantry Volunteers, at Oxford, Ohio, on April 18, 1861, for a period of three months. He was discharged from this military organization at Columbus, Ohio, on June 1, 1861.

In December, 1861, at Indianapolis, Indiana, Mr. Wright enlisted in the Eleventh Regiment, United States Infantry, in which he remained unassigned until February 19, 1862. On that day President Lincoln appointed him second lieutenant in the Eleventh Regiment. He accepted this commission on March 20, and for the greater part of that year Lieutenant Wright was on recruiting service. He was promoted to first lieutenant on December 15, 1862.

Ira Pettit's diary tells us that First Lieutenant Wright was Officer-of-the-Day at Fort Independence, Boston Harbor, Massachusetts, on New Year's Eve, 1862, as he had been on other days during that month.

On July 2, 1863, First Lieutenant Wright was breveted captain at Gettysburg, Pennsylvania.

Just after the Mine Run campaign (November 26 to December 2, 1863,) in which the Eleventh Regiment took part, one of Lieutenant Wright's recruits was executed at Camp Near 3 Mile Station (near Bealeton Station), Virginia. Since the whole division was ordered to witness this ceremony, it is conceivable that Lieutenant Wright was among the spectators that late autumn afternoon, December 18, 1863.

Lieutenant Wright enjoyed the comparative safety of

routine duty as a member of the staff of General Patrick in Washington, D.C., from mid-winter until April, 1864. As that April burst into springtime across those cedared hills and plains of Virginia, others of the Eleventh Regiment were making portentous preparations to meet the Army of Northern Virginia once again.

Meanwhile, Lieutenant Wright became Provost Marshal of the Maryland Avenue Depot and 6th Street Wharf, Washington, D.C., where he remained until the following December. From there he was in the office of the Provost Marshal General, Army of the Potomac, until May, 1865.

As the soldiers of both the North and South, i.e., those who still lived, took stock of life after four years of fighting, Lieutenant Wright served as Provost Marshal General, Department of Virginia, until July, 1865. He then rejoined his regiment at Richmond, Virginia, until May 31, 1866.

Taking a six months' leave of absence on June 1, 1866, Lieutenant Wright returned to Washington, D.C., where he wedded Miss Minna Partridge on August 2, 1866. On October 2, 1866, he tendered his resignation as First Lieutenant, Eleventh Regiment, United States Infantry and brevet Captain, U.S. Army.

In civilian life Mr. Wright practiced law. In 1867 the Wrights became the parents of a daughter. Their son was born in 1870.

During the later years of his life Mr. Wright suffered from rheumatism, nervous prostration and heart disease, all of which he considered the result of his military service.[1] However, his military records furnished no evidence of disability.[2]

When he entered the Soldiers' and Sailors' Home at Sandusky, Ohio, on the day after Christmas, 1894, Mr.

---

[1] Sworn statement given by Irvin B. Wright in a declaration for invalid pension, dated November 22, 1894.
[2] Memo from George D. Ruggles, Adjutant General, to Commissioner of Pensions, dated January 18, 1895.

Wright was no longer able to provide for his existence through his own efforts.

A medical report concerning Mr. Wright, dated February 20, 1895, made these observations: "His tongue is slightly coated, teeth are mostly all missing, gums are soft and ulcerated, his skin is dry, applicant is weak and debilitated, has the appearance of a man in very poor health, his hands are tremulous, unable to stand with eyes closed. He suffers from rheumatism in the right shoulder joint, the joint is stiff, crepitant and impaired in motion, he is not able to bring his arm above a level with the shoulder joint. The action of his heart is irregular, no distinct murmurs the sounds are indistinct."

Another medical report concerning Mr. Wright, dated April 11, 1900, described the veteran in more and grave detail: "Claimant is in a very nervous state, muscles of arms, chest, neck and face constantly twitching, almost complete loss of power of voluntary motions of both arms, there is no other disturbance with the remainder of the muscular system. His gait is in every way normal, there is no evidence of injuries to cranial structures or contents, spinal column or peripheral nerves. In the absence of any other explanation of this condition, it is the opinion of this Board that claimant is suffering from severe nervous shock, owing to the fact that twenty-six of his relatives, including every member of his immediate family, died within a period of four years from 1884 to 1889, which was followed by a severe and protracted attack of La. Grippe.

"Claimant is unable to direct the actions of either arm to any degree of certainty. They constantly tremble and twitch. The trembling is equal to that of an aggravated paralysis agitans. The twitching amounts to a slight clonic spasm. It is impossible for this Board to determine definitely the cause of this condition of the arms as claimant's mental faculties seem to be unimpaired, except in point of strength. There is no vertigo, migrane or peripheral sensory disturbances . . ."

Lieutenant Wright who was fifty-eight years old at the time of this examination lived another five years. On August 7, 1905, less than five months after he had been discharged (March 24, 1905) from the Soldiers' and Sailors' Home, Irvin B. Wright again rejoined many of his regiment, some of whom he had personally recruited, in death.

Although the April 11, 1900, medical report stated that Mr. Wright had lost twenty-six of his relatives between the years 1884 and 1889 (including every member of his immediate family), it is assumed that this 'immediate family' did not include his wife, son (John Newton Wright), or daughter (Mrs. Delancy Gill), since he listed them as still living in a statement to the Pension Department in 1898. Information from the Soldiers' and Sailors' Home, Sandusky, Ohio, indicates that Lieutenant Wright was survived by a wife and daughter, but additional information held there concerning his family status is not now legible. There appears to be *no* pension file on behalf of a widow of Irvin B. Wright in the National Archives, Washington, D.C.

Efforts to determine Lieutenant Wright's burial location have been fruitless.

In February, 1884, Irvin B. Wright had written a letter to the Adjutant General of the United States inquiring about one of his recruits. There is no indication that the doctors who from time to time examined and treated Lieutenant Wright knew of his concern and anxiety over a young private he had enlisted in Pittsburgh, Pennsylvania, on May 27, 1862.

Captain Cothran of Battery M

Battery M, First Regiment, New York Light Artillery, was mustered into the army at Rochester, New York, on November 15, 1861. This battery was organized at Lockport, New York, under the auspices of George W. Cothran who became its first captain.

Captain Cothran, with more than a hundred other men from Niagara and Orleans Counties, left the Lockport area in mid-October, 1861, for battery muster and boot training at Camp Hill House, Monroe County, New York.

For various reasons Captain Cothran was unable to take part in Battery M's activities during most of the great battles in which that battery participated. George W. Cothran's military career was fraught with problems unrelated to enemy combat.

"Before a General Court Martial, of which Lieutenant Colonel Henry E. Turner, 1st New York Artillery, is President, which convened at Camp Barry, D.C., by virtue of Special Orders, No. 12, of February 20, 1862, from Office of Chief of Artillery, Army of the Potomac, was arraigned and tried Captain *George W. Cothran*, Company M, 1st New York Artillery, on the following charges and specifications, viz:

"Charge 1st.—'Neglect of duty.'

"Specification 1st—'That Captain *George W. Cothran*, commanding Company M, 1st New York Artillery, permitted Private Van Wagoner, of said Company, to lie sick in tent for more than one week without reporting him, as required by regulations, to the Surgeon; such neglect resulting in the dangerous illness and final discharge of said Van Wagoner. This at Camp Barry, Washington, D.C., between the 17th and 28th days of January, 1862.'

"Specification 2d—'That he *(Cothran)* failed to report the sickness of Private Shaw, of said Company, to the Surgeon; such neglect terminating after several days, in the death of said Shaw, without the benefit of proper medical attendance. This at Camp Barry, Washington, D.C., between the 17th and 28th days of January, 1862.'

"Specification 3d—'That he *(Cothran)* neglected generally, during the months of December, 1861, and January, 1862, to report the sick men of his Company, or to cause them to be reported, to the Surgeon, thereby depriving them of proper medical attendance. This at Camp Barry, Washington, D.C.'

"Charge 2d—'Disobedience of orders'

"Specification 1st—'That Captain *Cothran*, aforesaid, was informed by his commanding officer, Colonel G. D. Bailey, about the 1st of December, 1861, that only the authorized medical officers should have the care and treatment of the sick, and was prohibited by Colonel Bailey from employing a private in his Company as medical officer; that nevertheless, in defiance of such instructions and prohibition, the said *Cothran* used and employed one Private Thomas to doctor and practice upon the sick men of his Company. This, as a general practice, during the months of December, 1861, and January, 1862, at Camp Barry, Washington, D.C.'

"Specification 2d—'That the said Captain *Cothran*, having been ordered by Colonel G. D. Bailey, commanding 1st Regiment New York Artillery, not to remove the balls and chains from certain prisoners belonging to his Company, (said prisoners being under sentences of a General Court Martial,) and having been ordered to see that said sentences were duly executed, did wilfully disobey said order by removing the balls and chains from said prisoners, and permitting them to leave Camp without guard or impediment. This at Camp Barry, Washington, D.C., on or about February 12, 1862.'

376

"Charge 3d—'Conduct unbecoming an officer and a gentleman.'

"Specification 1st—'In this; that on or about February 12, 1862, the said Captain *George W. Cothran* falsely stated to Colonel G. D. Bailey that Private Thomas (mentioned in previous specification) has been doing all military duty in his Company, including regimental and stable guard duty, and all Company drills, with only one exception; whereas said Thomas had never drilled, and had served only one tour of guard duty since the arrival of his Company at Camp Barry, in November, 1861. This at Camp Barry, Washington, D.C.'

"Specification 2d—'That he *(Cothran)* falsely stated to a Board of Officers, officially assembled at Camp Barry, on or about January 28, 1862, that Private Thomas, aforesaid, had not been authorized to attend upon the sick men of his Company as medical officer or physician, and had not attended upon them with his *(Cothran's)* knowledge or consent; whereas he *(Cothran)* had encouraged said Thomas to practice upon the sick soldiers of said Company, had headed a subscription to place medicines in the hands of said Thomas, and had excused him from all military duty in consideration of his performing the duties of Surgeon for said Company. This at the place and time above stated.'

"Specification 3d—'That he, Captain *George W. Cothran*, in a written report to Major A. S. Webb, Assistant to the Chief of Artillery, dated at Frederick, Maryland, February 18, 1862, did falsely state, as a reason for removing the ball and chain from Leander E. Davis, a prisoner at Camp Barry, that it was *three* o'clock at the time of such removal, (claiming that the sentence against Davis required him to wear a ball and chain only from 10 to 11 a.m. and from 2 to 3 p.m.,) thus falsely justifying himself for removing said ball and chain in defiance of orders; the fact being that it was done at a time of day not later than *two* o'clock p.m.'

"Specification 4th—'That he, *(Cothran,)* in the aforesaid

written report to Major A. S. Webb, did falsely state that Robert Brown, a prisoner at Camp Barry, had no ball and chain on at the time he *(Cothran)* took him from the guard-house; and that he *(Cothran)* did not know by whose authority the ball and chain was removed from said Brown; the facts being that said Brown did wear a ball and chain at the time alluded to, and the same was removed by order or permission of said *Cothran*.

"Specification 5th—'That he, *(Cothran)* in the aforesaid written report to Major A. S. Webb, dated February 18, 1862, did falsely state that he never received any official copy of the sentence in the case of Robert Brown, and that he *(Cothran)* only knew what it was from what Brown told him; whereas, the order promulgating the sentence against said Brown had been published to the Company (paraded) of said *Cothran*, and an official copy thereof had been delivered at *Cothran's* tent, *he being present at the time*.

"Charge 4th—'Unofficerlike conduct.'

"Specification—'That he, the said Captain *George W. Cothran*, 1st New York Artillery, having neglected (upon the departure of his Company from Camp Barry) to furnish descriptive lists of certain enlisted men of said Company remaining behind, (comprising prisoners sick in hospital and sick outside of Camp,) as required by paragraph 1250, Army Regulations, and by General Orders, No. 8, Headquarters of the Army, dated December 16, 1861, and, having been instructed in an official communication from the Headquarters of the 1st New York Artillery, dated February 16, 1862, to furnish descriptive lists of the men above mentioned, did fail to furnish such descriptive lists, and, in lieu thereof, did write and forward to the Adjutant of said Regiment a communication of the following tenor and description, to wit:

"Headquarters, Cothran's 2d Battery, *Camp Keyes, Frederick City, Md., February 14, 1862*.

'W. Rumsey, *Acting Adjutant 1st N.Y. Artillery*: Sir: I am happy to inform you that I am now subject to the orders of Major General Banks, to whose Division my battery is attached. I am, sir, very respectfully, Your obedient servant, GEORGE W. COTHRAN, Captain and Garrison Commander of three Batteries.

"(The above being an exact copy.) This at the places and times above stated.

"Plea: 'Not Guilty.'

"The Court, having maturely considered the evidence adduced, does find the accused as follows:

"Of the 1st *Specification* of 1st Charge, 'Guilty.'

"Of the 2d *Specification* of 1st Charge, 'Guilty.'

"Of the 3d *Specification* of 1st Charge, 'Not Guilty.'

"Of the 1st Charge, 'Guilty.'

"Of the 1st *Specification* of 2d Charge, 'Guilty.'

"Of the 2d *Specification* of 2d charge, 'Guilty.'

"Of the 2d charge, 'Guilty.'

"Of the 1st *Specification* of 3rd Charge, 'Guilty.'

"Of the 2d *Specification* of 3rd Charge, 'Guilty.'

"Of the 3d *Specification* of 3d Charge, 'Not Guilty.'

"Of the 4th *Specification* of 3d Charge, 'Guilty.'

"Of the 5th *Specification* of 3d Charge, 'Guilty.'

"Of the 3d Charge, 'Guilty.'

"Of the *Specification* of 4th Charge, 'Not Guilty.'

"Of the 4th Charge, 'Not Guilty.'

"And the Court does therefore sentence the said Captain *George W. Cothran*, 1st New York Artillery, 'To be dismissed the service.'

"II . . . The proceedings of this Court Martial, having been transmitted to these Headquarters, in conformity with the act of Congress of 24th December, 1861, entitled 'An act relative to Courts Martial in the Army,' have been examined and are confirmed. Captain George W. Cothran, 1st New York Volunteer Artillery, ceases, from this date, to be an officer in the military service of the United States.

379

"By Command of Major General McClellan: S. WILLIAMS, *Assistant Adjutant General.*" [1]

Special Orders, No. 123, from the Adjutant General's office in Washington, D.C., dated June 2d, 1862, read, in part, as follows:

"6. The sentence of the General Court Martial in the case of Captain *Geo. W. Cothran*, 1st New York Artillery, promulgated in General Orders No. 94 of March 6, 1862, Headquarters Army of the Potomac, which dismissed him from the service, is by order of the President of the United States set aside, Captain Cothran is restored to the command of his company and will proceed without delay to join it.

"By order of the Secretary of War: (signed) L. Thomas, Adjutant General." [2]

On July 9, 1862, George W. Cothran was granted a thirty-day sick leave. In September and October, 1862, Captain Cothran was on detached service as Chief of Artillery, First Division, Twelfth Corps. He continued on detached service as Chief of Artillery, by order of Brigadier General Williams until December 24, 1862. On that day, by virtue of Special Orders, No. 147, Captain George W. Cothran was placed under arrest.

"Head Quarters, 1st Division 12th Corps, Fairfax Station, Va., Jany 3rd, 1863. General Order No. 1.

"Before a *General Court Martial* of which Lt. Col. *Jas. L. Selfridge*, 46th Reg't. Penna Vols. was appointed *President* in place of Major *G. L. Smith* by Gen. Order No. 30 of Date *Dec. 6th 1862* from these Head Quarters convened at *Fairfax C. H. Va.* was arraigned and tried:

"Captain *Geo. W. Cothran*, 1st N.Y. Artillery on the following charges and specifications.

"*Charge 1st.* Conduct unbecoming an officer and a gentleman.

---

[1] U.S. Adjutant General's Office. *Record Group 94*, more specifically identified in Reference Section of this book.
[2] Ibid.

"Specification 1st. In this, that he, Geo. W. Cothran, 1st N.Y. Artillery, did on or about November 1st 1862, cause to be passed for his benefit by various members of "M" Company 1st N.Y. Artillery of which he is Captain, in payment for goods bought of A. Remick, a citizen, by said members of "M" Company 1st N.Y. Artillery, about one hundred and four broken bank bills of the denomination of Five dollars each, on the Clinton Bank of Westernport, Md. which said bills he knew at the time to be worthless.

"This near Sandy Hook, Md.

"Specification 2d. In this, that he, Geo. A. Cothran 1st N.Y. Artillery did on or about Nov. 1st 1862, sell or cause to be sold, to various members of Company "M" 1st N.Y. Artillery about one hundred and four broken bank bills, of the denomination of Five dollars each, on the Clinton Bank of Westernport, Md. Knowing them at the time to be worthless, with the intent that said bills should be circulated, and which were passed by members of Co. "M" 1st N.Y. Artillery, on A. Remick, citizen, in exchange for goods bought of him with the knowledge and consent of said Capt. Geo. W. Cothran.

"This near Sandy Hook, Md.

"Specification 3d. In this that he Geo. W. Cothran, Captain, 1st N.Y. Artillery, when asked by said Remick in regard to the worthless money aforesaid, did deny all knowledge of the same, which denial was untrue.

"This near Sandy Hook, Md.

"Charge 2d. Conduct prejudicial to good order and military discipline.

"Specification. In this that he Geo. W. Cothran, 1st N.Y. Artillery did on or about Nov. 1st, 1862, sell or cause to be sold to various members of Company "M" 1st N.Y. Artillery about one hundred and four broken bank bills of the denomination of Five dollars each on the Clinton Bank of Westernport, Md. he knowing them at the time to be worthless.

"This near Sandy Hook, Md.

381

"*Plea—Not Guilty.*

"The Court after mature deliberation on the evidence adduced, do find the accused, Capt. Geo. W. Cothran, of Battery "M" 1st N.Y. Artillery as follows:

"*Of the 1st Specification, 1st Charge*	*Not Guilty*
"*Of the 2nd Specification, 1st Charge*	*Not Guilty*
"*Of the 3rd Specification, 1st Charge*	*Not Guilty*
"*Of the 1st Charge*	*Not Guilty*
"*Of the Specification, 2d Charge*	*Not Guilty*
"*Of the 2d Charge*	*Not Guilty*

"*And do therefore, most honorably acquit him.*

"The proceedings of the Court, in the case of *Capt. Geo. W. Cothran*, Co. "M" 1st N.Y. Artillery, having been laid before the General Commanding the Division, are by him approved—

"Capt. *Geo. W. Cothran*, 1st N.Y. Artillery will resume his sword and his duties.

"By Command of Brig. Gen. A. S. Williams, signed Wm. D. Wilkins, Capt. and Asst. A. Genl."[3]

Although there were certificates from doctors at various times in 1862 and 1863 which stated that Captain Cothran suffered from sciatica and requested leaves of absence because of this affliction, one such certificate drew the following response:

"This certificate is in due form as far as it goes, though it does not state how much the patient is disabled by it. A Sciatica, which allows a man to ride on horseback through rain and mud & make such a march as we have just accomplished, & then walk about in snow & mud, as I have seen the Capt. doing today, must have a severer grip upon the cerebrum than it has upon the Sciatic nerve, and as I have once before endorsed a similar paper I think it can be successfully treated in the field. A. Chapel, Surgeon U.S.A. & Med'l. Director, 1st Division, 12th Army Corps, Jany 30th, 1863."

---

[3]U.S. Adjutant General's Office. *Record Group 94*, more specifically identified in the reference section of this book.

On February 4, 1863, Dr. Chapel responded to yet another medical certificate concerning Captain Cothran's health:

"This certificate is the fourth one that has been presented in this case and is confessedly made from the statements of the officer, & not upon the judgments of the Surgeon, that a leave is deserved, or account of the disability stated. I have not the least objection to any man's obtaining a leave who is entitled to one, either for sickness, or otherwise, but I *do* object to such attempts to make tools of surgeons to that end for I know from this officer's own statement, that his case has not been subjected to an appropriate treatment here and further, that if he really had the disease he claims to have, he could neither walk nor ride about on horseback. A. Chapel, Surgeon U.S.A. & Med'l. Dir., 1st Division, 12th Army Corps, February 4, 1863."

On February 19, 1863, Captain Cothran went home to Lockport, New York, according to a special muster roll, dated February 28 to April 10, 1863. The surgeon's certificate which supported this absence follows:

"Capt. Geo. W. Cothran, of the 1st Regiment of N.Y. Artillery, Co. "M," having applied for a certificate on which to ground an application for leave of absence, I do hereby certify that I have carefully examined this officer, and find him suffering from Sciatica, since August 30th, 1862. Last did duty January 13th, 1863. Disease contracted in the line of his duty. And that, in consequence thereof, he is, in my opinion, unfit for duty. I further declare my belief that he will not be able to resume his duties in a less period than thirty days without risk of permanent disability. Dated at Washington, D.C., this twenty-fourth day of February, 1863. W. R. DeWitt, Jr., A.A. Surgeon, U.S.A."

On April 18, 1863, from Lockport, New York, Captain George W. Cothran sent the following message to Brigadier General L. Thomas:

"Brig. Gen. L. Thomas, Adjt. Gen. U.S. Army. General. On account of serious ill health, which has rendered me unfit for duty since about January 1st 1863, and, being informed by my attending physician that I will not be able to join my command in the field short of a year, and not wishing to draw pay from the Government when I am unable to perform service, I have the honor, (pursuant to instructions furnished from your office through Dr. Clymer) to tender my Resignation as *Captain of Battery "M," First Regiment New York Volunteer Artillery,* to take effect immediately. I have complied with your Instructions by transmitting the proper certificate of disability every 20 days. I Remain General Your Obt Servant George W. Cothran, Capt. Battery "M," 1st N.Y. Art, 1st Division 12th Army Corps."

"Headquarters Twelfth Corps, Army of the Potomac, Stafford C.H., Va. April 24th, 1863. Special Orders, No. 98. (Extract) II . . . The following named Officers having tendered their resignations are honorably discharged the military service of the United States: Captain G. W. Cothran, Battery "M," 1st New York Artillery. By command of Major General H. W. Slocum, (Sgd) H. C. Rodgers Assistant Adjutant General."[4]

On November 16, 1863, at Buffalo, New York, George W. Cothran was mustered into Company B, Seventy-fourth Regiment, New York National Guard, for thirty days with the rank of captain. His muster-out roll dated December 16, 1863, listed Captain Cothran as being, "Absent, sick."

So ended the military career of George W. Cothran. From the records it would appear that his administrative problems and his intermittant ailment of sciatica left little time for Captain Cothran to participate in the stratagem of war.

The Cothrans from whom George W. Cothran was

---

[4] From the compiled service records of Captain George W. Cothran, as set out in the reference section of this book.

descended had left Scotland in the middle of the 1700's because of political pressure and religious persuasion. They had gone first to France, then to Ireland, and finally to America. And in America the Cothrans found that the world was simply more of the same. There came a revolution and then a rebellion.

George Cothran was born in Royalton, New York, in 1834. He finished what would now be equivalent to high school in Lockport, New York, and subsequently studied law in Illinois, where he became counsellor for the Burlington, Quincy, and Northwestern Railroad.

When the Civil War started Mr. Cothran had returned to Lockport and set about organizing Battery M. After his tour of duty with that battery ended on April 24, 1863, Mr. Cothran made his home in Buffalo, New York. Family history holds that Mr. Cothran practiced law in the offices of Grover Cleveland in Buffalo, New York.[5]

While George W. Cothran was receiving his appointment as Commissioner of Deeds on March 28, 1865, in Buffalo, New York, the men of Battery M were involved in the post-battle operations in Bentonville, North Carolina. (Battery M had lost during service thirteen enlisted men killed and mortally wounded, and one officer and eleven enlisted men by disease, making a total of twenty-five men who did not survive and/or serve out their three year enlistment period.)[6]

Mr. Cothran's term as a judge of the Erie County Court began on January 2, 1877. In 1889 Banks and Brothers of Albany, New York, published two books authored by George W. Cothran, and entitled, "The Law of Supervisors as Embodied in the Statutes and Judicial Determinations of the Courts of the State of New York," and "Assessors and Collectors."

---

[5] Family history provided in letter to J. P. Ray from Ms. Catherine Cothran Simonds, dated February 15, 1976.

[6] Dyer, Frederick H. *A Compendium of the War of the Rebellion.* Des Moines, Iowa: The Dyer Publishing Company, 1908. p. 1392.

Mrs. Cothran, a victim of tuberculosis, preceded Mr. Cothran in death on September 13, 1892, at the age of fifty. (Mrs. Cothran was the former Jennie Mann.) Their adopted daughter Elsie also died of tuberculosis on March 19, 1898, at the age of twenty-three. Mr. Cothran survived his daughter by less than a year, dying of cancer on December 23, 1898, at the age of sixty-four.

Mr. Cothran, whose professional life was spent advocating and adjudicating the law, had had to, while in the army, extricate himself from its technicalities. And ironically, the deed, through which he had disposed of his assets, was set aside after his death, and his estate (a considerable fortune) was sold to satisfy his creditors.

The George W. Cothran family rests in Forest Lawn Cemetery, Buffalo, New York.

To Those Who Still Lived

At the Hodge Opera House, Lockport, New York, on October 11, 1881, George W. Cothran addressed the attending survivors of Battery M as they commemorated the Twenty-seventh Anniversary of that organization.

The text of that address, in its entirety, is made available through the courtesy of Mrs. Norman J. Thilk, Historian for the Town of Wilson, New York:

"COMRADES:

"Twenty-seven years ago today, a little band of patriots, from Orleans and Niagara Counties, less than 130 in number, quietly assembled in this city and, in the afternoon, departed on the railroad for the Military Camp at Rochester. There was no heralding of their coming, nor of their departure, as they were earnest men, actuated by pure and lofty motives, and, intent upon the accomplishment of a good object, they disappeared as quietly as they had assembled.

"Already the lofty vaporings of politicians and pseudo-statesmen, that the war was to be but a pic-nic and would be over in ninety days, had come to naught. Already the great and terrible disaster to our army, at Bull Run, had been written, in blood, upon the pages of the world's history. The two contending parties were gathering together all their strength, each intent on success. Our people had become aroused to the fact that a fierce and bloody war was to ensue. Men were called for, to serve for three years or during the war. It was under this call,—with no offer of bounties, but plenty of individual promises of support and protection of the helpless ones at home, were made, to be broken as soon as the occasion presented itself,—that that little band had departed.

"Those men were actuated by a single motive, to protect and defend the country that had defended and protected them. It was the patriot responding to the call of duty by his country. With the fire of patriotism burning intensely in their bosoms, they left behind them all they held near and dear on the face of the earth, and went forth to the picket line of the war. They went as brave men always go, without show or demonstration.

"They were all intelligent men, and represented nearly all the vocations of life. There were in that little band young men and old men; single men and married men; men with sweethearts and men without sweethearts; but they were brave and patriotic men. They were neither substitutes nor drafted men; but men who, hearing their country's call, and knowing her needs, dropped the tools and implements with which they supported themselves and their families, and *voluntarily* went to the front.

"No more sublime human spectacle can be imagined than to see such men leaving behind them everything but patriotism to give vitality and force to those patriotic words of General Jackson, "The Federal Union it must and shall be preserved!" Men actuated by such a high and noble purpose are invincible. Of these words it might well be said, "In hoc signo vinces!" And in furtherance of that purpose they went, they fought, and they conquered.

"That sturdy band of loyal citizens was the nucleus of Battery "M," First New York Light Artillery, and one of the most efficient batteries of the war.

"I stand here today to proclaim it, and I do so with all due respect for all the brave and noble men who fought under the stars and stripes, that no braver, more patriotic, or efficient men ever went to the war, or men who performed more faithful and efficient service, with the opportunities afforded them, than old Battery "M." It never lost a gun; it never surrendered; and it was never whipped. Foremost in pursuit of the enemy; it covered the rear of our retreating columns. Where hard fighting was to be done, where almost indefensible positions were to be held, there was sent that gallant battery; and it never disappointed the officer who gave the command. At Beverly Ford, on the Rappahannock, after one of our batteries had been practically demolished, its caissons exploded, and it driven from its position, Battery "M" was ordered by General Gordon to take and hold that Ford. On that hill, in that corn field, in that foggy August morning, was fought as gallant an artillery battle as ever was fought anywhere. Divine Providence seemed to aid our gunners and protect our men. We demolished three batteries, with but one man slightly wounded. Generals Gordon and Banks gave a glowing account of the engagement, speaking in the highest terms of praise of the achievements of the battery; but the reports still slumber amid the dust of the War Department.

"If you will turn to Part One, of Series One, of Volume Nineteen of the Records of the War, recently published by the Government, you will learn what General McClellan, General Williams, General Gordon, and other commanding officers thought of the services of the battery at Antietam. They give it credit for an achievement, such as was never accomplished by a field battery before, or since, of repelling repeated infantry charges, without the slightest support of any kind. By reading the official accounts of that stupendous struggle, you will learn what the brave men who witnessed what we did on that never-to-be-forgotten occasion, thought and said of us. Some of them (who did not belong to our corps) mention our achievements without mentioning the name of the battery, which was unknown to them.

"I do not intend to speak boastfully; I am merely calling attention to some things we did and what our superior officers thought of us. I desire that these fearless and valiant men who accomplished so much for their country, should receive the meed of praise that is their due. A brave man is always a modest man, and rarely gets credit for what he does, while the man who accomplishes but little and has more brass in his cheek than on his coat, is too frequently given precedence over his superiors. We found it so, too frequently, in the war.

"My old comrades! it does my very soul good to see so many of you alive and well, and here; and as I take you by the hand, my heart goes out to you, as in those days of danger when the messengers of death flew so thick and fast around us. It was there, on the field of battle, when none of us could foretell who would fall next, that we learned to know one another, and to appreciate each other's worth. It was then that brave men stood shoulder to shoulder with each other, and by their courageous example, nerved and encouraged the more timid, until all timidity disappeared, and all became veterans, in the true sense of the term.

"As we look back to the year 1861, when we entered the army, we perceive a vast country, about one-half of which was cursed with the foulest blot that ever dimmed the fair fame of a fair land. It was by the color of his skin that you were to determine whether a human being was a man or a chattel. The advocates of human bondage had concluded that the country could not endure much longer as a unit, that the opponents of their 'peculiar institution' were daily increasing in number, and that the number had already grown so great as to already stop the further extension of that 'institution,' and to seriously jeopardize it where it was, and for the purpose of severing the country on the line between the free and the slave states, so that they might maintain their system of human bondage uninterfered with, they precipitated upon the country that terrible war.

"The clash of arms came; and the thing which the South sought to give permanency to, was forced between the contending armies, and became pulverized into dust. The hand of God was in it, and He gave the victory to the cause that was just and merciful.

390

"Five years after that fratricidal war began, it terminated. As we cast our mental vision over the country again, we behold the flag of the Free floating, and the sun of Liberty brightly shining, everywhere, upon a land from which the 'primal eldest curse' had been forever removed. While we discover many poor and helpless people, we can discover no human chattel. That was one, and only one, of the beneficient results of the war.

"By means of that war, which brought gloom and sorrow into so many households, in the South as well as in the North, the people of those two sections of the country came to know and understand each other better, and a better state of feeling prevails between the two sections now, than at any former time; and should such a thing occur (but of which there is not the slightest possibility) as a war with Great Britain, you would find, in the same companies, Federal and Confederate soldiers, fighting side by side, in their country's cause.

"On these occasions, when we come together to renew the bonds of brotherly kindness and affection that bind us together, it is a source of congratulation that the results of the struggle in which you took so conspicuous a part, were and are so beneficient.

"We recognize the fact that the war has been over for more than twenty-three years. We are not here to fight over our battles, but to refer to some of the things we did to unite more firmly in the bonds of brotherly affection. We entertain no feeling of bitterness nor hatred towards those who fought against us; and we all rejoice that the Union stands upon a firmer and more enduring basis today than at any former period. God grant that it may endure forever.

"Looking to the future; the imagination in its wildest flight, cannot limit the greatness of this country. With its boundless resources; its mineral wealth; the productiveness of its soil; with a climate, better adapted to developing hale or hearty men than any other on the face of the earth; with a cosmopolitan population, combining many of the better elements of all nations, and skilled in all the useful and mechanic arts, we fear no competition, and may safely challenge the whole world. We certainly challenge the admiration, and we receive the respect, of the whole civilized world, now. The name, American Citizen, is a passport everywhere. We know, too, that if any nation disregards or interferes with the sanctity of that character, Uncle Sam's call for a million of men to avenge the insult, would be filled in thirty days.

"While I am rejoiced to see so many of our Comrades here today, I also perceive many of the wives, and sons, and daughters of veterans here, showing that the soldier, when he puts by the implements of warfare is no stranger to the arts of Love, and the conjugal duties of Life. Wives, sons and daughers, we greet you cordially, heartily, and with a soldier's welcome!

"We have, also, with us today, and as our honored guests, brave and intrepid soldiers who served our country in other organizations. We recognize their bravery, and take pride in their achievements. We extend to them our hands and brotherly affections, and bid them thrice welcome, and cordially invite them to participate in our proceedings. Veteran soldiers fraternize everywhere.

"It is a source of regret that there are several of our comrades absent on this occasion. Long distance has kept some of them away, while others were doubtless detained for reasons best known to themselves. Wherever they are, and 'though absent, they are to memory dear,' and while we recall and cherish the remembrance of their forms and features, and their soldierly qualities and conduct, we ask God's blessing upon them and theirs wherever they may be.

"There are still others who are absent, and who will never meet with us again this side of Eternity. They have discharged their duties; they have folded their tents and packed their knapsacks for the last time, and have been mustered out of service. With the proud consciousness that they have fearlessly obeyed the orders of their military commanders, and had rendered their country faithful service, they have obeyed the command of the Great Commander of the Universe, and have marched through the Valley of the Shadow of Death; and we trust they are now receiving their merited rewards.

"Fellow Comrades, it is my earnest hope to meet you all at these annual gatherings, many times, in the future. We are all growing older, and many of our most exquisite pleasures are remembrances of the past. The young live in the future; the old in the past. In the natural course of events, not many years will be vouchsafed to many of us in which we can meet. Our numbers are growing less, year by year. One by one the brave spirits depart upon that unknown march, and while we have health and strength let us come together as frequently as we can, and keep the embers of brotherly affection all aglow in our bosoms, until we hear that final 'tattoo,' to be followed too soon by 'taps,' at which the light of life is put out forever."

APPENDICES

ACKNOWLEDGEMENTS

Without the gracious generosity of time, talent, and knowledge shared by each person from whom I have sought assistance, this project would have long since been abandoned.

Special thanks are extended to the following people, each of them employees of the National Archives, Washington, D.C., who, with much patience and kindness, have helped me search out the answers to a myriad of questions: Mr. Albert U. Blair, Director, Research Room Branch; Mr. William E. Lind, Research Consultant; Mr. Dale Floyd, Archivist; Miss Camille Hannon, Research Room Librarian; Mr. LeRoy Jackson, Archives Technician; Mr. John Pontius, Archives Technician; Mr. William Stewart, Archives Technician; Miss Wilma Prudhum, Archives Assistant; Miss Dorinda Cartwright, Archives Assistant; and Mr. Burgess Powell, Archives Assistant.

I am most grateful to Dr. Donald F. Howard, Professor of History, University of Northern Iowa, whose opinions, guidance, and knowledge I have often sought and always found valid, and whose consultations launched me upon this work.

I am gratefully indebted to Mrs. George Burcker, who provided me information as well as moral support and encouragement from the outset of this undertaking; Mr. William H. Ray, who provided inestimable help in reading the original letters and diary, and who was entirely responsible for the maps; Mrs. Peter Crestodina, who kindly and patiently labored over the proofreading and my grammatical ineptitude for this present edition; and Lawrence H. Ray, who traveled with me many miles in quest of information, who shared my time and attention with this project, and who made many of the photographs included herein.

I wish also to express my gratitude to Mrs. Norman J. Thilk, Mrs. Paul Middleton, Mr. Lawrence D. Pease, and many other kind people in Wilson, New York, who assisted me in my every need and request regarding salient material while in that area; to Mr. Clarence O. Lewis and Mrs. Julia H. Winner, Lockport, New York, who provided me census background information concerning the Pettit family, as well as other pertinent data; to Mr. Charles H. Boyer, Curator, Niagara County Historical Society, who acquainted me with much of the history of Niagara County, New York; and to Mr. Harold P. Baecker, without whose assistance and extensive genealogical research I should not have been able to index or identify many of the members of Ira Pettit's family.

Thanks must also be extended to personnel at the University of Northern Iowa (Cedar Falls, Iowa,), the Waterloo Public Library (Waterloo, Iowa,), and the Waverly Library (Waverly, Iowa,), who have assisted me in obtaining reference works and have provided me prompt and efficient duplication of materials during the time spent working upon this book there.

To those countless people throughout this country and beyond, on whom I have imposed by phone, letter, and visit, offering nothing but questions to be answered, hopefully by them, I am able only to say thank you. Perhaps in my turn I may be given the opportunity to either pass on or return their many and considerate efforts to assist me.

Finally, I am unable to restrain myself from expressing an unrequited sadness for those young men who were the tools used in an attempted settlement of questions, ever basic, which Homo sapiens has not, even yet, learned to negotiate without recourse to violent means.

Background Information On Ira S. Pettit

Ira S. Pettit was a fifth-generation citizen, fourth-generation native of the United States. His great-great-grandfather had come to American in the early 1700's. Emigrant Pettit, whose first name is not known, was of French origin and his wife, Ira's great-great-grandmother, was German.

Being a sea captain Mr. Pettit never stayed long from the sea, and when he failed to return from a voyage he left upon these shores a widow with one son. It was presumed that Captain Pettit was lost at sea.

Seth, the only son of this seafaring Pettit, was the great-grandfather of Ira, and it is thought (though not confirmed) that the 'S' in Ira's name was the initial for Seth. Seth Pettit died on March 11, 1822, at Broadalbin, Montgomery County, New York.

The files of the Historian's office in Lockport, New York, hold the following census information relating to the family of Ira Pettit and various other Pettits located in Niagara County, Town of Wilson, New York, in 1865:

"The family of Clinton Pettit is located numerically at Number 72. Clinton Pettit: age 52; birthplace—Saratoga County (Galway); twice married; married now. Catharine Pettit: age 52; birthplace—Albany County; twice married; married now. Lucina H. Pettit: age 20; birthplace—Niagara County; child. George W. Pangborn: age 13; birthplace—Ohio; nephew. Clinton Pangborn: age 16; birthplace—Niagara County; nephew. Lucina Pangborn: age 12; birthplace—Michigan; niece."[1]

Other Pettits listed in this census information are: "No. 44—Jason L. Pettit: age 27, birthplace—Saratoga County;

---

[1]In correspondence received from Mr. Clarence O. Lewis and Mrs. Julia H. Winner, Lockport, New York, August, 1968.

widowered; sisters and brothers; now in the army, 2nd. Mtd. Rifles. No. 62—Thos. Pettit: age 57; birthplace—Saratoga County; wife and four children. No. 122—George Pettit: age 41; birthplace—Saratoga County; wife and two children. No. 126—Samuel H. Pettit: age 21; birthplace—Niagara County, wife. No. 127—Alexander Pettit: age 58; birthplace—Fulton; wife and two children; parents of six children. No. 128—William O. Pettit: age 44; birthplace—Fulton; wife, four children and mother. No. 129—Curtis Pettit: age 58; birthplace—Fulton; wife and niece and nephew whose last names are also Pettit. No. 132—Manerva Pettit: age 49; birthplace—Oneida; widowed; six children. No. 133—John Pettit: age 46; birthplace—Fulton; wife; one son, Levi, in service; two daughters.

Private Levi Gilman Pettit served in Company B, Eighth Regiment, New York Heavy Artillery and Company F, Tenth New York Infantry Volunteers. Private Pettit received a gunshot wound in his right arm at Cold Harbor, Virginia, on June 3, 1864, but was returned to duty on July 22, 1864. He was discharged at Bailey's Cross Roads, Virginia, on June 30, 1865, and returned to his home in Wilson, New York where he spent the remainder of his life. Private Pettit passed away on September 2, 1917, and is interred in Greenwood Cemetery, Wilson, New York. Mr. Pettit was the father of five daughters: Mrs. Gertrude A. Pratt, Mrs. Lena L. Bell, Mrs. Inez W. Baecker, Mrs. Helen M. Smith, and Mrs. Jennie E. Treichler.

No. 134—Enoch Pettit: age 45; birthplace—Saratoga County; twice married; now in the Army, 151st; wife, two children and brother-in-law.

"Listed as residing next door to Clinton Pettit, at No. 73, was S. V. K. Pangborn: age 49; birthplace—Albany County; and his family."[2]

---

[2]Information provided by Mr. C. O. Lewis and Mrs. Julia H. Winner, August, 1968.

The marriage of Samuel H. Pettit, age twenty, to Mary Elizabeth Case, age nineteen, on September 13, 1864, by a Presbyterian minister, was noted, as was the death of Ira S. Pettit, age twenty-three, at Andersonville Prison, in October, 1864.

Clinton Pettit (born August 11, 1813, died August 24, 1898,) and Clarissa Young Pettit (born September 22, 1813, died April 28, 1845,) were the parents of Mary Jane Pettit Whitman (born November 18, 1837,), a son who died in infancy in 1840, Ira S. Pettit (born May 12, 1841,), and Lucina H. Pettit Shaw (born May 4, 1844,). After the death of Clarissa, Mr. Pettit had married Mrs. Catharine Jane Pangborn Phillips.

Clinton and Catharine Phillips Pettit, aside from Mr. Pettit's own three living children, cared for six orphaned children during their lives together. Three of those orphaned children were Clinton, George, and Lucina (little Lucina) Pangborn, whom Ira wrote and referred to from time to time in his letters.

Clinton Pangborn (born August 26, 1849,) had made his home with the Pettits at an early age. He learned the carpenter trade from a Mr. Cooper (of Wilson), and worked with a Mr. Hutchings (also of Wilson) for sixteen years. In 1874 he married Mrs. Jane Pike of Albany, and it is thought that he had three daughters. Mr. Pangborn moved his family to Tonawanda in 1890, where he died on December 23, 1897.[3]

Lucina Pangborn became Mrs. Carswell, and the destiny of George Pangborn has not been researched.

Lucina H. Pettit became the bride of Newton Lawrence Shaw, a near neighbor on Slash Road, in 1871. Mr. Shaw had gone to Iowa in the late '60's, and purchased a farm in 1869. Mr. and Mrs. N. L. Shaw made their home on that farm, The Elms, near Waverly, Iowa, where Mr. Shaw

---

[3]From a news item in the local weekly newspaper, "The Wilson Star," Wilson, New York, December, 1897.

farmed and taught school. N. L. Shaw died at his beloved 'Elms' on December 29, 1915. Mrs. Lucina Shaw died in Waverly on September 21, 1939. Mrs. Shaw had survived their younger daughter by more than two years. Their other daughter passed away in 1955. The Shaws, their daughters and one grandson are interred in Harlington Cemetery, Waverly, Iowa.

Mary Jane Pettit Whitman wife of George H. Whitman died on October 27, 1919. The Whitmans had settled in Liberty, Kansas, and were the parents of three daughters and four sons.

Ira S. Pettit sleeps in Sumter County, Georgia.

Some General Orders

"War Department, Adjutant General's Office, Washington, March 22, 1862. General Orders, No. 28.

"I .. A military department to be called the Middle Department, and to consist of the States of New Jersey, Pennsylvania, and Delaware, the Eastern Shore of Maryland and Virginia, and the counties of Cecil, Harford, Baltimore and Ann Arundel, in Maryland, is hereby created. Major General Dix, United States Volunteers, is assigned to the command; headquarters at Baltimore.

"II .. No troops in the United States service will hereafter pass through the city of New York without reporting to the United States military authorities entrusted with the duty of providing subsistence and transportation in that city. Reports must be made and information obtained at the office, No. 79 White street.

"III .. His Excellency the Governor of New York has decided upon the following prices to be charged to the non-commissioned officers and privates of the several regiments from that State, now in the field, for articles of clothing heretofore furnished them by the State. The said prices have been fixed from the average cost of the several articles:

"For each infantry overcoat $8 63
    "   "   jacket 5 43
    "   "   trowsers 3 50
    "   fatigue cap 85
    "   pair of shoes, (pegged,) 1 20
    "   "   shoes, (sewed,) 1 98
    "   "   drawers 57
    "   "   socks 24
    "   shirt 88
    "   blanket 1 95

"By order of the Secretary of War:

"L. Thomas, Adjutant General. Official: E. D. Townsend, Assistant General.

"War Department, Adjutant General's Office, Washington, September 6, 1862. General Orders, No. 126.

"I . . The following is the organization of Regiments and Companies of the Volunteer Army of the United States:

"1. REGIMENT OF INFANTRY—*Ten Companies.*

"1 Colonel.
1 Lieutenant Colonel.
1 Major.
1 Adjutant (an extra Lieut.)
1 Quartermaster (an extra Lieut.)
1 Surgeon.
2 Assistant Surgeons.
1 Chaplain.
1 Sergeant Major.
1 Regimental Quarter Master Sergeant.
1 Regimental Commissary Sergeant.
1 Hospital Steward.

"*Company of Infantry.*

"1 Captain
First Lieutenant.
1 Second Lieutenant.
1 First Sergeant
4 Sergeants.
8 Corporals.
2 Musicians.
1 Wagoner.

"And (64 Privates—Minimum.
(82 Privates—maximum.

"2. REGIMENT OF CAVALRY—Twelve Companies or Troops.

"1 Colonel.
1 Lieutenant Colonel.
3 Majors.
1 Surgeon.
1 Assistant Surgeon.
1 Regimental Adjutant (an extra Lieut.)
1 Sergeant Major.
1 Regimental Quartermaster (an extra Lieut.)
. ʼgimental Commissary (an extra Lieut.)
1 Chaplain.
2 Hospital Stewards.

1 Quartermaster
   Sergeant.
1 Commissary
   Sergeant.

1 Saddler Sergeant.
1 Chief Farrier or
   Blacksmith.

"Company or Troop of Cavalry.

"1 Captain.
1 First Lieutenant.
1 Second Lieutenant.
1 First Sergeant.
1 Quartermaster
   Sergeant.
1 Commissary
   Sergeant.
5 Sergeants.

8 Corporals.
2 Teamsters.
2 Farriers or
   Blacksmiths.
1 Saddler.
1 Wagoner, and
78 Privates.

"There being no bands now allowed, the chief trumpeter authorized by law will not be mustered into service. If any have been so mustered, they will, upon receipt of this order, be mustered out.

"The law does not authorize *musicians for companies.* To remedy this defect, two musicians may be enlisted for each company. *They will be rated and paid as privates.*

"3. REGIMENT OF ARTILLERY—*Twelve Batteries.*

"1 Colonel.
1 Lieutenant Colonel
1 Major for every four
   batteries.
1 Adjutant (not an extra
   Lieutenant.)
1 Quartermaster (not an
   extra Lieutenant.)

1 Chaplain.
1 Sergeant Major.
1 Quartermaster
   Sergeant.
1 Commissary
   Sergeant.
1 Hospital Steward.

"Battery of Artillery

"1 Captain.
1 First Lieutenant.

1 Second Lieutenant.
1 First Sergeant.

1	Quartermaster Sergeant.	2	Musicians.
4	Sergeants.	2	Artificers.
8	Corporals.	1	Wagoner, and
		122	Privates.

"To the above organization of a battery, one First and one Second Lieutenant, two Sergeants and four Corporals may be added, at the President's discretion.

"The field officers, chaplain, and regimental staff—commissioned and non-commissioned—will not be mustered, or received, into service, without special authority from the War Department. As a general rule, Artillery will be called for, and received, by batteries, thus rendering the field and staff unnecessary.

"II . . Chaplains must meet the requirements of section 8 of the act of July 17, 1862, as follows:

'No person shall be appointed a chaplain in the United States Army who is not a regularly ordained minister of some religious denomination, and who does not present testimonials of his present good standing as such minister, with a recommendation for his appointment as an Army chaplain from some authorized ecclesiastical body, or not less than five accredited ministers belonging to said religious denomination.'

"After Chaplains are appointed, under section 9 of the act of July 22, 1861, they must be mustered into service by an officer of the regular Army, and thereafter borne on the field and staff roll of the regiment.

"Mustering officers, before mustering Chaplains into service, will require from them a copy of the proceedings on which the appointment is based. The said copy, if found conformable to the requirements of the law, will be endorsed by the mustering officer, and by him forwarded to the Adjutant General's office, for file with the muster-in roll.

"III . . The foregoing organization must be strictly adhered to by all concerned. Commanding Officers of

406

Departments, Armies, and Army Corps, will, without delay, direct an inspection to be made of their commands, to ascertain if the *regiments, and units thereof,* conform to this organization, and all deviation from it will be promptly corrected. Supernumerary officers, if any, will be mustered out of service from the date of receipt of this order. Reports of the inspection will be forwarded to the Adjutant General of the Army.

"No commissioned officer or enlisted man, of any grade, in excess of the legal organization, will be recognized. And any commander who may acknowledge, or receive, as in service, any such officer or enlisted man, will be brought to trial for neglect of duty and disobedience of orders. No person acting in the capacity of a supernumerary will under any circumstances, be permitted to receive pay and allowances from the government; and Paymasters, making payment to such supernumeraries, will be held individually accountable for amounts so paid.

"By order of the Secretary of War: L. Thomas, Adjutant General.

"Official: E. D. Townsend, Assistant Adjutant General." *

General Orders and Circulars—1862. U.S. Adjutant General's Office. National Archives, Washington, D.C.

REFERENCE SECTION

BIBLIOGRAPHY

Adams, James Truslow, Editor-in-chief and Coleman, R. V., Managing Editor. *Dictionary of American History*. Volume IV. Second Edition Revised. New York: Charles Scribner's Sons, 1951.

Adjutant General's Office. State of Ohio. *Certificate of Service of Private Irvin B. Wright, Twentieth Regiment, Ohio Infantry Volunteers—April 27, 1861 to June 1, 1861*. Columbus, Ohio.

Adjutant General's Office. Commonwealth of Massachusetts. *Certificate of Civil War Service of Private John A. Cain*. Boston, Massachusetts.

Adjutant General's Office. State of Rhode Island and Providence Plantations. *Index of AGORI 1861-1865 Report*. Providence, Rhode Island.

Army National Guard Records. *Report of the Adjutant General. State of New York*. Albany, New York.

Baecker, Harold P. *Genealogical Records—Pettit Family. Plates 1, 2, 3, 4, and 5*. Albuquerque, New Mexico.

Beers, Henry Putney. *Guide to the Archives of the Government of the Confederate States of America*. Washington, D.C., National Archives Publication No. 68-15, 1968.

Buffalo Enquirer, Newspaper. *Cothran Deed is Invalid*. Buffalo, New York, March 16, 1901.

Catton, Bruce. *Never Call Retreat*. The Centennial History of the Civil War. E. B. Long, Director of Research. Volume Three. New York: Pocket Cardinal, Pocket Books, a division of Simon & Schuster, Inc., 1969.

Catton, Bruce. *This Hallowed Ground*. The Story of the Union Side of the Civil War. Garden City, New York: Doubleday & Company, Inc., 1956.

Chipman, General N. P. *The Tragedy of Andersonville*. Trial of Captain Henry Wirz, the Prison Keeper Published by the Author, 1911.

Cothran, Captain George W. *Our 27th Anniversary, 1861-1888. An Address*. Property of the Town of Wilson Historian, Wilson, New York.

Dyer, Frederick H. *A Compendium of the War of the Rebellion*. Des Moines, Iowa: The Dyer Publishing Company, 1908.

Dyer, Frederick H. *A Compendium of the War of the Rebellion, Vol. II: Chronological Record of the Campaigns, Battles, Engagements, Actions, Combats, Sieges, Skirmishes, etc., in the United States, 1861 to 1865*. New York: Sagamore Press, Inc., Thomas Yoseloff, 1959.

408

Executive Documents. Printed by order of the House of Representatives during the Second Session of the Fortieth Congress, *Executive Document No. 23. Trial of Henry Wirz*. Washington, D.C., Government Printing Office, 1868.

Hoyt, William G. and Langbein, Walter B. *Floods*. Princeton, New Jersey: Princeton University Press, 1955.

Hunt, Irene. *Across Five Aprils*. New York: Grosset & Dunlap, Inc., Tempo Books Edition, by arrangement with Follett Publishing Company, 1965.

Intelligencer, The. Newspaper. *Trial of Claudius B. Lloyd*, June, 1862. Published in Lockport, New York, during Civil War years.

Lippincott's *Gazetteer*, 1901.

Lossing, Benson J., LL.D. *A History of the Civil War 1861-65 and the Causes that Led up to the Great Conflict*. A Chronological Summary and Record, compiled from the Official Records of the War Department. Illustrated with facsimile photographic reproductions of the official war photographs taken at the time by Mathew B. Brady. New York: The War Memorial Association, 1912.

McClellan, H. B. *I Rode with JEB Stuart, Life and Campaigns of Major-General J. E. B. Stuart*. Edited with an introduction by Burke Davis. Bloomington, Indiana: Indiana University Press, 1958.

McElroy, John. *Andersonville: A Story of Rebel Military Prisons*. Toledo, Ohio: Published by D. R. Locke, Blade Printing and Paper Co., Electrotypers, Printers and Binders, 1879.

McElroy, John. *This Was Andersonville*. Edited with an introduction by Roy Meredith. New York: Bonanza Books, 1957.

Michigan, State of. *Certified copy of Record of Death—Frederick M Phelps*. County of Oakland, Libr. 5, recorded March 30, 1920.

Miller, Francis Trevelyan, Editor-in-chief. *Prisons and Hospitals, The Photographic History of the Civil War*. Edition published by arrangement with A. S. Barnes & Co., Inc. Special contents of this edition by Thomas Yoseloff, Inc., New York: Castle Books, 1957.

Mitchell, Lt. Col. Joseph B. *Decisive Battles of the Civil War*. Greenwich, Connecticut: Premier Civil War Classics, First Premier printing, January 1962.

Nevins, Allan and Commager, Henry Steele. *History of the United States. The Story of a Free People*. U.S.A. Pocket Books, Inc., 1951.

O'Connor, Richard. *Company Q*. New York: Doubleday and Company, Inc., 1957.

Office of the Adjutant General. *Officers and Men of New Jersey in the War of the Rebellion*. Department of Defense, Trenton, New Jersey.

Oliver, John William. *History of the Civil War Military Pensions*,

1861-1885. A Thesis Submitted for the Degree of Doctor of Philosophy, University of Wisconsin, 1915. Bulletin of the University of Wisconsin, No. 844, History Series, Vol. 4, No. 1, Madison, Wisconsin, 1917.

Ontario County Journal. Newspaper. *Leonard Knapp Case.* Canandaigua, New York, July, 1862.

Pettit, Ira S. *Diary and letters, during the Civil War.* Presently held in the custody of the holder of copyright, comprising a part of holder's estate. Correspondence from Private Edmund Riedel and Mrs. John Gregory is also held under the same circumstances.

Phisterer, Frederick. *New York in the War of the Rebellion.* Albany, New York: F. B. Lyon Company, State Printers, 1912. p. 34.

Pratt, Fletcher. *A Short History of the Civil War (Ordeal by Fire).* United States: Cardinal edition, by Pocket Books, Inc., 1952.

President of the United States Abraham Lincoln. *A Proclamation. Respecting Soldiers absent without Leave.* Executive Mansion, Washington, D.C., March 10, 1863.

Report from the Office of the Adjutant General. State of Connecticut. Listing of men who served in Connecticut military units during the Civil War.

Revised United States Army Regulations of 1861. With an appendix containing the Changes and Laws affecting Army Regulations and Articles of War to June 25, 1863. Washington, D.C., Government Printing Office. 1867.

Swanson, Captain Albert A. *Chronological Listing of Events Concerning Fort Independence. 1630-1975.* Boston, Massachusetts.

U.S. Adjutant General's Office. *General Orders and Circulars— 1862.* National Archives, Washington, D.C.

Warner, Ezra J. *Generals in Blue. Lives of the Union Commanders.* Baton Rouge: Louisiana State University Press, 1964.

Wiley, Samuel T. and Garner, W. Scott, Editors. *Biographical and Portrait Cyclopedia of Niagara County, New York.* Philadelphia, Pennsylvania, Richmond, Indiana, Chicago, Illnois: Gresham Publishing Company, 1892.

Wilson Star. A local newspaper of Wilson, New York, in the 1800's.

SOURCE MATERIAL (Federal)

The bulk of the information contained in the epilogue of this compilation comes from the files of the Adjutant General's Office, National Archives, Washington, D.C., and without the existence of that agency such search for first-source material would have been tedious beyond accomplishment. However, this is not to say that other agencies of the Federal government have not made significant contributions; they have, and are also here listed:

U.S. Adjutant General's Office. *Record Group 15: Records of the Veterans Administration. Civil War Pension Application Files.* National Archives, Washington, D.C.:

File No. SO-90962 (Cert. No. SO-60221) based upon the service of Private John A. Cain in the Civil War, Company E, Second Regiment, Massachusetts Volunteer Cavalry.

File No. FO-425244 (Cert. No. FO-293266) based upon the service of Private Elias A. Dunkelberg in the Civil War, Companies B and F, Eleventh Regiment, U.S. Regular Infantry, and Battery M, First Regiment, New York Light Artillery.

File Nos. SO-1325862 and WO-1028282 (Cert. Nos. SO-1104042 and WO-785253) based upon the service of Private William H. Holmes in the Civil War, Company G, Seventh Regiment, New York Volunteer Cavalry, and Battery M, First Regiment, New York Light Artillery.

File Nos. (Cert. Nos. SO-333214 and WO-1090659) based upon the service of Private Maurice Joseph Meade in the Civil War, Company H, Sixth Regiment, Massachusetts Volunteer Militia, and Sergeant Maurice Joseph Meade in the Civl War, Company F, Eleventh Regiment, U.S. Regular Infantry.

File No. SO-977484 (Cert. No. SO-1040795) based upon the service of Private William E. Mott in the Civil War, Company F, Fourteenth Regiment, Connecticut Volunteer Infantry, and Company D, Second Regiment, Connecticut Heavy Artillery.

File No. SO-1043160 (Cert. No. SO-849918) based upon the service of Private Harvey U. Pease in the Civil War, Battery M, First Regiment, New York Light Artillery.

File No. SO-349818 (Cert. No. SO-246723) based upon the service of Private Enoch Pettit in the Civil War, Companies C and F, One Hundred Fifty-first Regiment, New York Volunteer Infantry.

File No. SO-1130056 (Cert. No. SO-1013510) based upon the service of Private Jason L. Pettit in the Civil War, Company C, Second Regiment, New York Mounted Rifles.

File No. SO-175571 (Cert. No. SO-821881) based upon the service of Private Levi Gilman Pettit in the Civil War, Company B, Eighth Regiment, New York Heavy Artillery, and Company F, Tenth New York Infantry Volunteers.

File No. MO-463503 (Cert. No. MO-336368) based upon the

service of Second Lieutenant Marvin D. Pettit in the Civil War, Companies B and F, One Hundred Eleventh Regiment, Pennsylvania Volunteer Infantry.

File No. SO-471562 (No certificate) based upon the service of Private Frederick M. Phelps in the Civil War, Companies A and D, Ninetieth Regiment, New York Infantry Volunteers and Companies F and/or E, Eleventh Regiment, Pennsylvania Volunteer Cavalry.

File No. SO-1844803 (Cert. No. SO-112587) based upon the service of Private Edmund Riedel in the Civil War, Companies H and F, Eleventh Regiment, U.S. Regular Infantry.

File No. SO-224995 (Cert. No. SO-426594) based upon the service of Private William H. H. Salisbury in the Civil War, Twenty-eighth Regiment, New York Infantry Volunteers.

File Nos. WO-70409 and MiO-128861 (Cert. Nos. WO-42673 and MiO-78852) based upon the service of Private Azor Shearer in the Civil War, Company F, One Hundred Fifty-first Regiment, New York Infantry Volunteers.

File Nos. SO-75376 and WO-901774 (Cert. Nos. SO-49645 and WO-601966) based upon the service of Private William H. Shearer in the Civil War, Company F, One Hundred Fifty-first Regiment, New York Infantry Volunteers.

File Nos. SO-308793 and WO-901774 (Cert. Nos. SO-238245 and WO-660835) based upon the service of Captain John Downer Woodbury in the Civil War, Battery M, First Regiment, New York Light Artillery.

File No. SO-1162316 (Cert. No. SO-890857) based upon the service of Private Irvin B. Wright in the Civil War, Company B, Twentieth Regiment, Ohio Volunteer Infantry and First Lieutenant Irvin B. Wright in the Civil War, Company B, Eleventh Regiment, U.S. Regular Infantry and Twentieth Regiment, U.S. Regular Infantry.

File Nos. SO-312218 and WO-1044009 (Cert. Nos. SO-213450 and WO-795329) based upon the service of Private William Henry Harrison Wright in the Civil War, Battery M, First Regiment, New York Light Artillery.

U.S. Adjutant General's Office. *Record Group 94: Compiled Service Records. Records of the Adjutant General's Office, 1780's—1917. Soldiers' Compiled Carded Military Service Records.* National Archives, Washington, D.C.

Private Heinrich (Henry) Bockholt, Company G, Fourth Regiment, Iowa Infantry, Civil War.

Private John A. Cain, Company E, Fourth Regiment, New Jersey Infantry Volunteers, Civil War.

Private John A. Cain, Company E, Second Regiment, Massachusetts Volunteer Cavalry, Civil War.

Captain George W. Cothran, Battery M, First Regiment, New York Light Artillery, Civil War.

Captain George W. Cothran, Company B, Seventy-fourth Regiment, New York National Guard, Civil War.

Private Elias A. Dunkelberg, Battery M, First Regiment, New York Light Artillery, Civil War.

Private Elias A. Dunkelberg, Companies B and F, Eleventh Regiment, U.S. Regular Infantry, Civil War.

Private William H. Holmes, Company G, Seventh (Black Horse) Regiment, New York Volunteer Cavalry, Civil War.

Private William H. Holmes, Battery M, First Regiment, New York Light Artillery, Civil War.

Private Henry A. Mott, Company I, Fifth Regiment, Rhode Island Heavy Artillery, Civil War.

Private William E. Mott, Company F, Fourteenth Regiment, Connecticut Volunteer Infantry, Civil War.

Private William E. Mott, Company D, Second Regiment, Connecticut Heavy Artillery, Civil War.

Private Harvey Usher Pease, Battery M, First Regiment, New York Light Artillery, Civil War.

Private Enoch Pettit, Companies C and F, One Hundred Fifty-first Regiment, New York Infantry Volunteers, Civil War.

Private Jason Lee Pettit, Company C, Second Regiment, New York Mounted Rifles, Civil War.

Second Lieutenant Marvin D. Pettit, Companies B and F, One Hundred Eleventh Regiment, Pennsylvania Infantry Volunteers, Civil War.

Private Frederick M. Phelps, Companies A and D, Ninetieth Regiment, New York Infantry Volunteers, Civil War.

Private Frederick M. Phelps, Company K, One Hundred Fifty-seventh Regiment, New York Infantry Volunteers, Civil War.

Private Frederick M. Phelps, Battery A, First Regiment, New York Light Artillery, Civil War.

Private Frederick M. Phelps, Companies F and/or E, Eleventh Regiment, Pennsylvania Cavalry, Civil War.

Private William Henry Harrison Salisbury, Twenty-eighth Regiment, New York Volunteers, Civil War.

Private Azor Shearer, Company F, One Hundred Fifty-first Regiment, New York Infantry Volunteers, Civil War.

Private William H. Shearer, Company F, One Hundred Fifty-first Regiment, New York Infantry Volunteers, Civil War.

Private William Henry Harrison Wright, Battery M, First Regiment, New York Light Artillery, Civil War.

U.S. Adjutant General's Office. Record Group 94

Private Ira S. Pettit, memorandum from Prisoner-of-War Records.

Private Ira S. Pettit, enlistment certificate.

Register of Enlistments, U.S. Army, 1798-1914, Vol. 54-55 (A-K) 1859-1863. M-233, No. 27, No. 504, *Alexander Chisholm*—Watertown, New York.

Register of Enlistments, U.S. Army, May 27, 1862, page 199. *Private John McMann*—Pittsburgh, Pennsylvania.

Register of Enlistments, U.S. Army, March 8, 1862. *Private (later Sergeant)* Maurice Meade, Boston, Massachusetts.

Register of Enlistments, U.S. Army, May 29, 1862, page 509. No. 197, *Ira S. Pettit*—Lockport, New York.

Register of Enlistments, U.S. Army, December 20, 1862, page 279, No. 840, *Irvin B. Wright*—Indianapolis, Indiana.

U.S. Adjutant General's Office, National Archives, Washington, D.C. Record Group 153:
Records of the Office of the Judge Advocate General (Army) No. LL-1042. Court Martial of *Private Osker M. Burns,* November 5, 1863.

Records of the Office of the Judge Advocate General (Army) Court Martial of *Private John McMann,* November 5, 1863.

U.S. Adjutant General's Office. National Archives, Washington, D.C. Record Group 391:
Records of United States Regular Army Mobile Units, 1821-1942. Miscellaneous Name File, 1861-66:
Private John Carrigan, Sixth Regiment, U.S. Regular Infantry.

Private Alexander Chisholm, Eleventh Regiment, U.S. Regular Infantry.

U.S. Adjutant General's Office. Compiled Service Records of Confederate Generals and Staff-Officers and Non-Regimental Enlisted Men. National Archives, Washington, D.C.:
Win—Wir, Micro-copy 331, Roll 271. Signature of Henry Wirz.

U.S. Adjutant General's Office. Miscellaneous Records of Federal Prisoners of War of the United States Army Who Escaped from Southern Prisons, Deserted to the Rebel Army, Illegally Paroled by the Rebel Authorities, and the Survivors and Perished of the Steamer Sultana, Sub-Titles—Records of Escaped Prisoners of War, U.S. Army and Record of Federal Soldiers Who Joined the Rebel Army. National Archives, Washington, D.C.
Compiled in the Adjutant General's Office from the original books now on file in the Division of Records of Prisoners of War: Vol. 1, pp. 36, 100, re William E. Mott.

U.S. Adjutant General's Office. National Archives, Washington, D.C.

General Order, No. 1, Headquarters, First Division, Twelfth Corps, Fairfax Station, Virginia, January 3, 1863, by command of Brigadier General Alpheus Starkey Williams. (Captain George W. Cothran)

General Orders, No. 28, Headquarters, First Division, Twelfth Corps, near Sandy Hook, Maryland, Army of the Potomac. November 24, 1862, by command of Brigadier General A. S. Williams. (Private W. H. H. Wright)

General Orders, No. 58, War Department, Adjutant General's Office, March 10, 1863, providing places of rendezvous for soldiers absent without leave.

General Orders, No. 94, Headquarters, Army of the Potomac, Washington, D.C., March 6, 1862, by command of Major General George Brinton McClellan. (Captain George W. Cothran)

General Orders, No. 104, Headquarters, Army of the Potomac, December 5, 1863, by command of Major General George Gordon Meade. (Private John McMann)

General Orders, No. 126, War Department, Adjutant General's Office, May 15, 1863, Washington, D.C., by E. D. Townsend, Assistant Adjutant General. (Private John Carrigan)

Special Orders, No. 10, Headquarters, Second Corps, Army of Virginia, near Annisville, Virginia, July 9, 1862, by command of Major General Nathaniel Prentiss Banks (Captain George W. Cothran)

Special Orders, No. 17, Headquarters, First Division, Fifth Army Corps, near Edenburg, Virginia, April 16, 1862, by command of Brigadier General Williams. (Captain George W. Cothran)

Special Orders, No. 91, War Department, Adjutant General's Office, Washington, D.C., February 25, 1863, by order of the Secretary of War; signed by L. Thomas, Adjutant General. (Captain George W. Cothran)

Special Orders, No. 98, Headquarters, Twelfth Corps, Army of the Potomac, Stafford Court House, Virginia, April 24, 1863, by command of Major General Henry Warner Slocum. (Captain George W. Cothran)

Special Orders, No. 123, War Department, Adjutant General's Office, Washington, D.C., June 2, 1862, by order of the Secretray of War; signed by L. Thomas, Adjutant General. (Captain George W. Cothran)

Special Orders, No. 135, Second Division, Fifth Corps, Camp near Culpeper Court House, Virginia, October 2, 1863, by command of Brigadier General Romeyn Beck Ayres. (Privates Osker M. Burns and John McMann)

Special Orders, No. 139, Headquarters, Second Division, Fifth Corps, Camp near Culpeper, Virginia, October 7, 1863, by command of Brigadier General Romeyn Beck Ayres. (Privates Osker M. Burns and John McMann)

Special Orders, No. 144, Headquarters, Second Division, Fifth Corps, Camp near Three Mile Station, Virginia, October 28, 1863, by command of Brigadier General Romeyn Beck Ayres. (Private John McMann)

Special Orders, No. 168, Headquarters, Army of the Potomac, June 24, 1863, by command of Major General Joseph Hooker. (Private John Carrigan)

Special Orders, No. 171, Headquarters, Army of the Potomac, June 24, 1863, by command of Major General Joseph Hooker. (Private John Carrigan)

Special Orders, No. 177, War Department, Adjutant General's Office, Washington, D.C., April 20, 1865, by E. D. Townsend, Assistant Adjutant General. (Private William E. Mott)

* * *

U.S. Department of the Army. Arlington National Cemetery, Arlington, Virginia. R. J. Costanzo, Superintendent.

U.S. Department of the Army. Office of the Secretary of the Army, Congressional Inquiry Division, Harold L. Brown II, Lieutenant Colonel, GS Deputy. Washington, D.C.

* * *

U S. Department of the Interior. National Park Service, Andersonville National Historic Site, Andersonville, Georgia. Mr. Paul R. Gordon, Park Historian (1972); Mr. John H. Flister, Superintendent (1975).

U.S. Department of the Interior. National Park Service, Antietam National Battlefield Site, Sharpsburg, Maryland. Mr. Ed Mazzer, Acting Superintendent (1975).

U.S. Department of the Interior. National Park Service, Division of Media Information, Office of Public Affairs. Ms. Sandra A. Alley (1975).

U.S. Department of the Interior. Geological Survey, Water Resources Division, Mr. G. A. Billingsley, Chief, Reports Section, Reston, Virginia (1975).

U.S. Department of the Interior. National Park Service, Gettysburg National Military Park, P. O. Box 70, Gettysburg, Pennsylvania. Mr. William A. Cole, Manager (1973); Mr. Lawrence H. Eckert, Jr., Museum Curator (1975).

U.S. Department of the Interior. National Park Service, Petersburg National Battlefield, P. O. Box 549, Petersburg, Virginia. Mr. Neil C. Mangum, Historian (1975).

* * *

United States Senate. Office of Honorable John C. Culver, Committee on Armed Services. Washington, D.C. (1975).

United States Senate. Office of Honorable Harold E. Hughes, Committee on Veterans' Affairs. Washington, D.C. (1972).

* * *

U.S. Veterans Administration. National Cemetery System, Cemetery Service, Bobbie R. Beller, Director. Washington, D.C. (1976).

* * *

The Library of Congress. Photoduplication Service, 10 First Street, S.E., Washington, D.C.

The Library of Congress. Geography and Map Division, Reference & Bibliography Section, Mr. Richard W. Stephenson, Head. Washington, D.C. (1975)

* * *

Smithsonian Institution. The National Museum of History and Technology, Department of Science and Technology, Ms. Mary J. Kofron. Washington, D.C., (1975).

* * *

(States and other)

The below listed agencies and organizations have been inordinately imposed upon for much information concerning the soldiers and events within:

California
    State of California, Office of the Commanding General, State Military Forces, Military Department, P. O. Box 214405, Sacramento, California, Kenneth S. Lloyd, CW2, Cal ARNG, Assistant Personnel Officer.

Connecticut
    Office of the Adjutant General, Department of Defense, State of Connecticut, Hartford, Connecticut.

Indiana
    Indiana State Library, Archives Division, Indianapolis, Indiana. Ms. Peg Sharpe.

Iowa
    Bremer County Office of the Clerk of Court, Waverly, Iowa. Mrs. Lois Slater, Clerk of Court.
    Bremer County Recorder, Waverly, Iowa. Miss Margaret Neubauer, Deputy Recorder.

Massachusetts
    Greater Boston Chamber of Commerce, 125 High Street, Communication Department, Boston, Massachusetts. Terry Sorenson.
    Commonwealth of Massachusetts, The Adjutant General's Office, War Records Section, 100 Cambridge Street, Boston. Vahan Vartanian, Mg. Mass. ARNG, The Adjutant General.
    Commonwealth of Massachusetts, Metropolitan District

Commission, 20 Somerset Street, Boston. Captain Albert A. Swanson, M.D.C. Historian.

Michigan

Michigan Department of Public Health, Vital Records Section, Lansing, Michigan.

Mr. Lynn D. Allen, Oakland County Clerk, 1200 N. Telegraph Road, Pontiac, Michigan.

Oakview Cemetery Association, Mr. Emerson C. Shaw, Assistant General Manager, Royal Oak, Michigan.

Register of Deeds, County of Oakland, State of Michigan. Mr. Lynn D. Allen, Ms. Ruth E. Lucas, Deputy Clerk.

New Jersey

Office of the Director, Riverview Cemetery, Trenton, New Jersey. Pat Guadagno.

Secretary, Chamber of Commerce, Trenton, New Jersey.

State of New Jersey, Department of Defense, Eggert Crossing Road, Box 979, Trenton, New Jersey. C. E. Hill, CW4, NJARNG, Assistant Adjutant General.

State of New Jersey, Department of Health, P. O. Box 1540, Trenton, New Jersey.

New York

City of Oneonta, Office of the City Clerk, Oneonta, New York. Grace E. Waite, Deputy City Clerk.

Clerk of Court, Erie County, Buffalo, New York.

Director, Forest Lawn Cemetery, Buffalo, New York.

Niagara County Historical Society, 215 Niagara Street, Lockport, New York. Mr. Charles H. Boyer, Curator.

Niagara County, Department of History, Lockport, New York. Mr. Clarence O. Lewis, Historian (1969), Mrs. Julia H. Winner, Deputy Historian (1969), Mr. I. Richard Reed, Historian (1975).

Ontario County Historical Society, Canandaigua, New York Mr. Clyde M. Maffin, County Historian.

Registrar, Towns of Cortlandville and McGraw, Cortland, New York. Ms. Christine Canestaro, Clerk.

State of New York, Department of Health, Executive Division, Bureau of Vital Records, Record Room Unit, Miss Jeanne Lohre, Supervisor. Albany, New York.

State of New York, Division of Military and Naval Affairs, Public Security Building, State Campus, Albany, New York. Captain Robert E. Larson (1973); James J. Kenney, LTC, SS, NYARNG, Chief, Bureau of War Records (1975).

Wilson Historical Society, Wilson, New York. Mrs. Norman D. Thilk, Historian.

North Carolina

University of North Carolina, Chapel Hill, North Carolina. Mr. Richard A. Shrader.

(From the Library's Manuscripts Department, Southern Historical Collection, General and Literary Manuscripts, University Archives, there was kindly provided a copy of a letter written by John H. Winder. General John H. Winder's letter is in no way copied or reproduced herein.

Censor marks on envelopes of letters written by Ira S. Pettit, while in Andersonville, bore marks, "Exd H.W.," but there appears to be no similarity between those initials and the signature of John H. Winder. Comparison was also made with the signature of Henry Wirz, a copy of which was obtained at the National Archives, Washington, D.C., but no similarity existed between Captain Wirz's signature and the initials on the censored envelopes.

Attempts to obtain information concerning the operations or habits of the postal service existing at Andersonville have been futile. Although it seems obvious that both Henry Wirz and John H. Winder would have been too occupied and preoccupied with other matters, the "H.W." coincidence deserved some little attention.)

Ohio

Erie County Probate Court, Sandusky, Ohio. Marcia L Rotsinger, Deputy Clerk.

Ohio Soldiers' and Sailors' Home, Sandusky, Ohio. Robert H Borders, Commandant, James L. Singler, Registrar.

State of Ohio, Adjutant General's Department, Division of Soldiers' Claims—Veterans' Affairs, Room 11, State House Annex, Columbus, Ohio. Mary Ellen Woodard, Chief, Records Section.

State of Ohio, Adjutant General's Office, Columbus, Ohio. James C. Clem, Adjutant General of Ohio.

Pennsylvania

Commonwealth of Pennsylvania, Pennsylvania Historical and Museum Commission, William Penn Memorial Museum and Archives Building, Division of Archives and Manuscripts, Box 1026, Harrisburg, Pennsylvania. Mr. Harry E. Whipkey, Chief, Division of Archives and Manuscripts; Mr. Harold G. Robison, Military Records Analyst.

Commonwealth of Pennsylvania, Department of Military Affairs, The Adjutant General, Annville, Pennsylvania. Donald K. Young, LTC (PA), GS, Military Personnel Officer.

North East Cemetery, North East, Pennsylvania. Office of the Cemetery.

Rhode Island

State of Rhode Island and Providence Plantations, Department of Corrections, Training Schools, 300 New London Avenue, Cranston, Rhode Island. Mr. Michael DiLorenzo, retired, and Mrs. Esther A. Reali, Assistant Superintendent.

State of Rhode Island and Providence Plantations, Office of the Adjutant General, Armory of Mounted Commands, 1051

North Main Street, Providence, Rhode Island. Col. Ralph L. Stermer, AGC, RIARNG, Assistant Adjutant General.

State of Rhode Island and Providence Plantations, Office of the Adjutant General. Providence, Rhode Island. *General Order, No. 3*, March 30, 1864.

Virginia

Virginia Historical Society, Post Office Box 7311, Richmond, Virginia. James Meehan, Assistant Librarian.

* * *

Nova Scotia, Canada

Office of the Registrar General, Ralston Building, Halifax, Nova Scotia. D. F. Arthur, Assistant Deputy Registrar.

Yarmouth Chamber of Commerce, 29 Porter Street, Yarmouth, Nova Scotia, Canada. Miss Charlotte Cain, Secretary.

Yarmouth County Historical Society, 22 Collins Street, Yarmouth, Nova Scotia. Mrs. Edith R. Topple, Librarian.

* * *

Correspondence and conferences with the following listed people have contributed substantially to the completion of this work:

Mrs. Lena Albrecht, Iowa; Mr. Harold P. Baecker, New Mexico; Mr. E. L. Brady II, New York; Mr. Raymond J. Cothran, New York; Mrs. Mildred Moody Eakin, Florida; Mrs. Norman J. Eick, Florida; Mrs. Emma Harrington, Michigan; Mrs. Vivian Hartzell, Pennsylvania; Mrs. Mildred Middleton, New York; Mr. Lawrence D. Pease, New York; Miss Nell H. Pease, Indiana; Mrs. Esther Reali, Rhode Island; Mr. Gene Reiter, Iowa; Mr. Henry Reiter, Iowa; Mr. Frederic Rewoldt, Iowa; Mrs. Peg Rose, Michigan; Mrs. Catherine Cothran Simonds, Illinois; Mrs. Alfred Streffling, Michigan and Florida; Mrs. Dorothy Thilk, New York.

Making a tangible reality out of this collection of data is the result of the technical and professional talents of Mr. John R. Hudson, Mr. William Crowder, Mr. Robert Yoke, and the many people who provided these men with their supportive expertise.

INDEX

421

428

429

Wichterman, Chauncey—331-32

Wilderness (Va.)—332, 334, 353

Wilkins, Captain William D.—382

Williams, Aceley—194

Williams, Brigadier General Alpheus Starkey—382

Williams, Fanny—78

Williams, Assistant Adjutant General Seth—359, 380

Williams, Warham—40-1

Wilmington (N.C.)—291, 313

Wilson, Ester—123

Wilson, George—123

Wilson, Captain Lurin—98, 340

Winchester (Va.)—323, 330, 332, 338, 341

Winder, Brigadier General John H.—241, 294, 313

Winder, Captain Richard B.—313

Winder, Captain W. S.—313

Wirz, Captain Henry—197, 236, 238-39, 243, 245, 261, 264, 266, 282, 293-94

Wood, a deserter—85

Woodbury, Charles—345

Woodbury, Chester—346

Woodbury, Jesse—346

Woodbury, Captain John Downer—343, 345

Woodstock (Va.)—324

Wren, Daniel—167

Wren, Eleanor—167

Wright, Lieutenant Irvin B.—85-6-7, 94, 342, 356, 359, 371

Wright, J. Grant—345

Wright, Jane—31

Wright, John Newton—374

Wright, Mr. W.—31, 343

Wright, Mrs.—29

Wright, Private William H. H.—17, 27, 31, 33, 42, 64, 78, 101, 111, 166, 325, 342

Yarmouth, Nova Scotia, Canada—243-44

York River—160

Young, Clarissa (mother of Ira Pettit, first wife of Clinton Pettit)—401

Young, John—78

Youst, a deserter—85

430

Private Ira S. Pettit

May 12, 1841—October 18, 1864

Blue eyes; blond hair; light complexion;
five feet, six and one-half inches tall.

Captured June 2, 1864, at Gaines' Mill,
near Mechanicsville, Virginia.

Died at Andersonville Stockade
of scorbutus.

Grave #11170 at Camp Sumter, Georgia.

Birthplace and home of Ira S. Pettit, Slash Road (now known as Maple
Road), Wilson, New York. This home was built circa 1835 for Mr.
Clinton Pettit. It is now the home of Mr. and Mrs. Norman Moore.

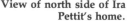
View of north side of Ira Pettit's home.

Corn crib, which Ira Pettit probably filled many seasons, and nearby a quince tree, which may be a descendant of those planted by him at his farm home.

Remaining orchard beside home of Ira S. Pettit.

Although the barn at the Pettit farm was lost in recent years by fire, the hog house is among several of the outbuildings which still stand.

One of the fields which Ira Pettit plowed with oxen.

Once the home of William H. Holmes, Wilson Burt Road, Wilson, New York. Now owned and resided in by Mr. and Mrs. Ronald Schearer.

Pinehurst Farms, Wilson, New York, home of Mr. and Mrs. Lawrence D. Pease. This residence, constructed of lumber and materials native to the farm, was built in 1880 by A. Douglas Pease, brother of Harvey U. Pease and grandfather of Lawrence Pease.

Home where William H. H. Wright lived in Wilson, New York, after retirement from his nearby farm.

Nearby Lake Ontario, where Ira fished and boated.

Canandaigua Courthouse, "as it looked in 1858, when it was erected as Ontario County's third courthouse. The edifice was completely remodeled in 1909 and the north and south wings were added. The statue of Justice was removed in 1954 because of deterioration, and was replaced in December, 1961." The Daily Messenger, March 1, 1962. (Etching to the paper and as here shown through the courtesy of Mr. Clyde M. Maffin, Ontario County, New York, Historian.)

The same beautiful courthouse in which Ira listened to the Knapp trial in 1862 still overlooks the wide main thoroughfare in this quiet and clean little city, which lies southeast of Rochester in the Finger Lakes region of New York State at the northern end of Canandaigua Lake. (Courtesy of Clyde M. Maffin.)

The jail which Ira Pettit visited at Canandaigua, New York, on June 24, 1862. Constructed in 1815 this building no longer stands, having been replaced in 1895. Today an even newer facility replaces the one built in 1895. (Courtesy of Clyde M. Maffin.)

FORT INDEPENDENCE,
BOSTON HARBOR, MASSACHUSETTS

Marker reads: *"Fort Independence dating from 1634, called Castle William in honor of King William III of England, prior to the Revolutionary War. Used as a garrison for British Troops until 1776. Rededicated by President John Adams in 1799 as 'Fort Independence.' The first home of the Boston Marine (now U.S. Public Health Service) hospital. (1799-1804) The fourth oldest hospital in the country which was established through the efforts of the Boston Marine Society, founded in 1742."* (Corner of Side No. 5 may be seen in background)

Side No. 1

Side No. 1, loopholes and sally port.

Side No. 2

Side No. 3

(All pictures on this page courtesy of Mrs. Kate Peterson.)

Abutment of Potomac Creek railroad bridge, north of Falmouth, Virginia, mentioned in letter to Lucina Pettit, dated March 7, 1863.

View of countryside between Ely's Ford and Kelly's Ford, Virginia.

Ely's Ford, where Private Ira S. Pettit waded the Rapidan by moonlight on April 29, 1863.

Home on the south side of United States Ford, used as hospital by Union Army; now the residence of Mr. and Mrs. John E. Pruit.

View of barn and terrain near the home of the John E. Pruits and United States Ford.

Gum Spring, Virginia, now known as Arcola.

Aldie, Virginia.

Looking westward across the Potomac River where Private Ira S. Pettit crossed at Edward's Ferry, June 26, 1863.

Marker at Edward's Ferry, Maryland shore.

C & O Canal bridge in background, and abandoned building on east bank at Edward's Ferry.

Jug-shaped structure which once stood at the end of the stone arch bridge over the Monocacy River, near Frederick, Maryland.

West abutment of stone arch bridge on which Private Ira S. Pettit crossed the Monocacy River, June 29, 1863.

Toll House at west end of Jug Bridge (the stone-arched bridge), east of Frederick, Maryland.

Libertytown, Maryland.

Little Round Top, Gettysburg Battlefield.

Plaque marking location of the arrival of the Fifth Corps, Army of the Potomac, the morning of July 2, 1863. Barnes' and Ayres' Divisions took possession of Little Round Top.

View of South Mountain from Braddock Heights, west of Frederick, Maryland.

Two examples of the beautiful homes in the area around Sharpsburg, Maryland, near Antietam Creek, whose residents must have heard the musketry and artillery at the Battle of Sharpsburg, and must have seen some members of the Army of the Potomac who camped along the creek after the Battle of Gettysburg.

Looking west from summit of Snicker's Gap, Virginia.

Looking east from summit of Manassas Gap, Virginia.

Post office at Orlean, Virginia.

Plaque which marks the site of the Marshall House, Alexandria, Virginia.

Holiday Inn—Old Town, 480 King Street, Alexandria, Virginia, which covers an entire city block, including the site where once stood the Marshall House.

Site of Beverly Ford on the Rappahannock.

Bridge now at Kelly's Ford, Virginia.

Looking south across the Rappahannock, Port Royal on far side.

Marker site at Gaines' Mill, Virginia.

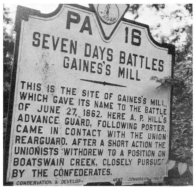

Plaque marking site near where Ira Pettit was captured on June 2, 1864.

New Cold Harbor, just east of Gaines' Mill, in vicinity where Private Dunkelberg received mortal gunshot wound, and where the Eleventh Regiment lost forty-five men through capture, June 2, 1864.

The main street of Mechanicsville, Virginia.

Site of Camp Parole, Maryland, near Annapolis, which is now a shopping center.

Church building at the end of Main Street, Saxonburg, Pennsylvania, in which Private Edmund Riedel and Emmaline Franke were wed, September 5, 1869.

Lucina Pettit Shaw

Newton Lawrence Shaw

Lucretia Mitchell Pease

Pvt. Harvey Usher Pease

Johanna Bessmer Bockholt

Pvt. Henry Bockholt

Lucina Pangborn Carswell

George Pangborn

Clinton Pangborn

Sara J. Pettit

Kate Pangborn

Grave marker for Captain Henry Wirz, C.S.A., Mt. Olivet Cemetery, Washington, D.C.

View of Mt. Olivet Cemetery. Captain Wirz's marker may be seen in the foreground.

Two close-ups of grave stones in Alexandria churchyard, described in letter to Lucina Pettit, dated September 22, 1863.

Church building in Alexandria, Virginia, where George Washington attended divine service.

Tombstone of Enoch Pettit, Greenwood Cemetery, Wilson, New York.

Memorial stone erected for Ira S. Pettit, Greenwood Cemetery, Wilson, New York.

Tombstone of Ira S. Pettit at Camp Sumter, Georgia. Courtesy of National Park Service, Andersonville National Historic Site.

Tombstone of William H. Holmes, Greenwood Cemetery, Wilson, New York.

Tombstone of William Henry Harrison Wright, Greenwood Cemetery, Wilson, New York.

Tombstone of the parents of Ira S. Pettit, Greenwood Cemetery, Wilson, New York.

Tombstone of Marvin D. Pettit, North East Cemetery, North East, Pennsylvania.

The Elms, home of Newton Lawrence Shaw and Lucina Pettit Shaw, near Waverly, Iowa.

Tombstone and markers of Newton Lawrence Shaw and Lucina Pettit Shaw, Harlington, Cemetery, Waverly, Iowa.

View of south side of The Elms.

"We slept, and forgot where we were."
Private John McElroy